Effective subject leadership

Kit Field, Phil Holden
and Hugh Lawlor

London and New York

First published 2000
by Routledge
11 New Fetter Lane, London EC4P 4EE

Simultaneously published in the USA and Canada
by Routledge
29 West 35th Street, New York, NY 10001

Routledge is an imprint of the Taylor & Francis Group

Typeset in Goudy by Taylor & Francis Books Ltd
Printed and bound in Great Britain by St Edmundsbury Press, Bury St
Edmunds, Suffolk

British Library Cataloguing in Publication Data
A catalogue record for this book is available from the British Library

Library of Congress Cataloging in Publication Data
Field, Kit
   Effective subject leadership / Kit Field & Phil Holden &
   Hugh Lawlor
   Includes bibliographical references and index.
   1. Teacher participation in curriculum planning–Great Britain.
   2. Educational leadership–Great Britain.   3. School improvement
   programs–Great Britain   I. Holden, Phil, 1950–   .   II. Lawlor,
   Hugh.   III. Title.
   LB2806.15.F54   2000   99–42580
   374'.001–dc21

ISBN 0-415-20303-1 (hbk)
ISBN 0-415-20295-7 (pbk)

Effective subject leadership

This book highlights issues which underpin the professional capabilities of existing and aspiring subject leaders. The content is designed to build on the skills, knowledge, understanding and attributes which serving heads of department and subject co-ordinators already possess.

Sections are provided on:

- essential knowledge and understanding for the role
- strategic planning and development
- monitoring and evaluating teaching and learning
- leading and managing staff to raise achievement

The emphasis throughout is on corresponding with the National Standards set by the Teacher Training Agency.

Through focused activities the book aims to set challenges in practical contexts and to help subject leaders to plan ahead and improve subject provision in order to raise standards.

Kit Field is Principal Lecturer in Education at Canterbury Christ Church University College and Programme Director for its established postgraduate Diploma/MA in Subject Leadership. **Phil Holden** is Director of the Centre for Education Leadership and School Improvement at Canterbury Christ Church University College and Centre Manager of South East NPQH Training and Development Centre. **Hugh Lawlor** is Visiting Professor of Education at Canterbury Christ Church University College and a consultant with the Teacher Training Agency.

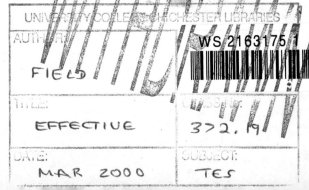

Contents

Figures

Activities

The authors

Kit Field is a Principal Lecturer in Education at Canterbury Christ Church University College. He is Programme Director for a postgraduate Diploma/MA in Subject Leadership. Kit has worked as a PGCE tutor for Modern Foreign Languages and has written extensively on that subject. He has also published articles and chapters on mentoring and OfSTED inspections.

Phil Holden is Director of the Centre for Education Leadership and School Improvement at Canterbury Christ Church University College and is the Centre Manager for South East NPQH Training and Development Centre. Phil has previously led and managed teams in schools, Local Authority Advisory Services, Initial Teacher Training and the Teacher Training Agency. He also lectures on all aspects of leadership, team-building and enhancing creativity.

Hugh Lawlor is a Visiting Professor of Education at Canterbury Christ Church University College and is a consultant with the Teacher Training Agency. Until recently, he was the Director of Continuing Professional Development and Research at the TTA and was closely involved in developing national standards for teachers and head teachers. Prior to joining the TTA, Hugh was a Senior Inspector with the Kent LEA. He is also a Registered Inspector with OfSTED.

Acknowledgements

Our approach to subject leadership has been influenced by a wide range of people: colleagues in schools, educators, advisory staff and teachers following award-bearing CPD courses in leadership and management. It is impossible to thank them all individually, but we want to take this opportunity to acknowledge their influence on our thoughts and writing. Particular thanks go to secretarial staff, including Alun Davies and Angela Barker of the Centre for Education Leadership and School Improvement, and Brenda Didman with her colleagues in the Central Secretariat at Canterbury Christ Church University College. Nina Stibbe, Jude Bowen and colleagues at Routledge have provided important support and forbearance for which we are grateful.

Introduction
Effective subject leadership

Quote this

The key to regular and systematic school improvement rests with the expertise and commitment of teachers and headteachers. The close correlation between good teaching and pupils' achievement is recognised by all, not least by the pupils (OfSTED 1998). Leadership, whether of the school or subject or area of experience has a measurable, though usually indirect, effect on pupil achievement (Hallinger and Heck 1998).

The importance of effective leadership in our schools and the need for relevant and high-quality professional preparation for leaders was recognised by the Conservative Government in 1995 with the announcement of the development and introduction of the National Professional Qualification for Headship (NPQH) as a means of preparing aspiring headteachers. The Teacher Training Agency (TTA) was tasked with piloting and introducing the qualification by September 1997. The current government has supported this initiative and by November 1998 4,900 aspiring headteachers had registered for the qualification in England and Wales. Indeed the Green Paper *Teachers: Meeting the challenge of change*, issued in December 1998, proposes making the qualification mandatory for new headships in maintained schools by 2002 (DfEE 1998a). The same Green Paper heralds a new national college for school leadership, which could become the policy and planning unit, as well as the central resource for training and development in school leadership. Much attention has been focused on institutional leadership, either on the NPQH as preparation for headship or the more recent Leadership Programme for Serving Headteachers (LPSH) also developed by the Teacher Training Agency and introduced in November 1998. This book recognises the equally crucial role of effective subject leadership in improving the quality of teaching and raising pupil achievement. As yet there is no professional qualification for subject leadership, but this book is informed by and follows the TTA's national standards for subject leaders (TTA 1998a), which could form the basis for such a professional qualification in the future.

The purpose of this book is to promote a greater understanding and application of leadership and management concepts and practices for those teachers with faculty or departmental responsibilities in secondary schools, subject responsibilities in primary and special schools, and for those staff who are required to exercise leadership and management responsibilities for specific reas of work in the school (e.g. Special Educational Needs, assessment, careers education). It is also designed to develop the professional skills and knowledge of subject leaders within their own schools. Generic leadership and management skills are identified, and different ways of implementing these skills and knowledge are discussed, including ways of establishing and sustaining effective working climates.

Leadership and management are often seen as inseparable concepts and it is true that effective managers have to lead as well as have operational responsibility for ensuring objectives and targets are met and tasks completed. If management is generally concerned with meeting objectives and targets through effective planning, organisation, supervision and the deployment of human and other resources, leadership is essentially about inspiring and galvanising the talents, energies and commitment of others. This involves developing and sustaining a shared vision and set of values, providing clear direction, motivating those around you and releasing their energies, ideas and skills. Leadership is a relatively new concept in relation to school contexts and in particular in relation to primary schools where resources for leadership and management are limited. This is not the case outside education where several writers have looked at leadership in a range of organisations (e.g. Adair 1983, Handy 1993). Although the focus in this book is on effective leadership, in practice it is not possible or desirable to separate leadership and management, and indeed it is the successful integration of both that will often distinguish the effective leaders from the merely competent.

Effectiveness will be defined by the perceptions of the various stakeholders inside and outside the school. MacBeath notes that 'effective leadership may depend on from where it is viewed or what social and psychological set of preconceptions one brings to it' (MacBeath 1998, p.13). Nothing is neutral in education and pupils, parents, teachers, headteachers and external agencies (including government) will have some common criteria for effective leadership, but there will also be specific differences and emphases. Pupils tend to focus on the quality of relationships in the school and on the leaders' role in providing a safe and secure environment (see research by Kathryn Riley, cited in MacBeath 1998), whereas the government through the TTA's national standards for headteachers and subject leaders places prime importance on securing high-quality teaching and improving standards of learning and achievement for all pupils (TTA 1998a). The different perceptions of effectiveness and the need to consider leadership in relation to specific situations and contexts illustrate the immensely complex nature of the concept.

In order to promote the systematic professional development of subject leaders the TTA has developed generic leadership and management national standards (TTA 1998a). These are part of a wider development of a framework of national standards for the award of Qualified Teacher Status (QTS) for subject leaders, for Special Educational Needs Co-ordinators (SENCos) and for headteachers. The standards have been developed by teachers, headteachers, governors, advisers, lecturers and representatives of business and industry in response to the growing demand from teachers for a framework that would provide personal and professional development in a structured and cohesive way. From 1998, newly qualified teachers will begin their professional lives and development using a career entry profile which enables them to set targets for their personal and professional development and progression (TTA 1998a).

The main aims of the national standards as stated by the TTA are to:

1 set out clear expectations for teachers at key points in the profession;
2 help teachers plan and monitor their development, training and performance, and to set clear and relevant targets for improvement;
3 focus on improving the achievement of pupils and the quality of their education;
4 recognise professional expertise and achievements;
5 ensure training and development is relevant and well targeted.

(TTA 1998a, p.1)

Each set of national standards defines the professional knowledge, understanding, outcomes, skills and attributes required to carry out effectively the key tasks of that role. The standards have been formulated to reinforce national priorities, in particular the government's key educational targets in relation to literacy, numeracy, information and communication technology, target-setting and as part of the overall strategy for school improvement and raising pupils' achievement. The standards are also designed to provide a more structured basis for appraisal, to help teachers and headteachers set relevant targets for school improvement, to form part of evaluation plans, to help identify further priorities and, not least, to celebrate success. The standards do not prescribe curriculum-content or school cultures or values, but rather provide the language and professional development targets for pedagogic leadership and management.

NATIONAL STANDARDS FOR SUBJECT LEADERS

The standards focus on generic leadership and management knowledge, understanding, skills and attributes related to the key areas of subject leadership. The core purpose of the subject (or area-of-work) leader is:

to provide professional leadership and management for a subject (or area of work) to secure high quality teaching, effective use of resources and improved standards of learning and achievement for all pupils.

(TTA 1998a, p.4)

In the light of the above core purpose, it is worth looking briefly at certain aspects of subject leadership:

1   Effective team leaders have a commitment to and contribute to whole-school policies, as well as being responsible for a particular subject or area of work.

Subject leaders may belong to several teams, one of which will be the school team. Contributions to that team will be at an individual professional level; but subject leaders also ensure that policies and practices in their own subject or area of work relate to overall school aims, objectives and targets. 'Lone ranger' subject leaders have no place in today's school, not least because of their disservice to the pupils. Chapters 4, 5 and 6 look in detail at these aspects of the subject leader's work.

2   Subject leaders are responsible for meeting the needs of all pupils in their area of work through planning that emphasises individual needs; through teaching that recognises the importance of clear learning objectives and high expectations for all pupils; through assessment that informs planning and learning; through close collaboration with other staff in devising and implementing individual education plans, and through the deployment of staff and resources as determined by pupils' needs. This places a particular responsibility on subject leaders to develop and agree systems and procedures with members of the team.

3   Effective leaders motivate and support all those involved in teaching and learning in their subject or area of work. This will include recognising and acknowledging the contributions of others, building and maintaining a team with clear aims, direction and targets, and helping others and self to set and meet appropriate professional development targets. Part of Chapter 10 looks at motivating pupils, Chapter 13 at team-building, and Chapters 9 and 14 at different aspects of professional development.

4   Leaders will have responsibility for monitoring and evaluating the effectiveness of teaching and learning in their subject or area of work, in particular to help set targets for pupil and staff performance, and determine any priorities in relation to the subject or area of work. The extent to which a subject leader exercises responsibility for monitoring and evaluating depends to a large extent on the size of the school and in many smaller primary schools the headteacher may retain a major responsibility for monitoring and evaluating both pupil and staff performance. The subject leader will still want to use evidence of pupils' achievement to set targets and plan for improvement. Chapter 7 looks at key strategic issues relating to establishing monitoring, evaluation and review systems.

LEADERSHIP SKILLS AND ATTRIBUTES

These skills and attributes do not exist in isolation, but will be applied in various combinations according to the tasks or challenges confronting the subject leader. The key areas of subject leadership as defined in the TTA's national standards will be considered in detail later, but at this stage it is helpful to identify the four key areas:

- Strategic direction and development of the subject or area of work (Chapters 4–7)
- Teaching and learning (Chapters 8–10)
- Leading and managing staff (Chapters 12–13)
- Efficient and effective deployment of staff and resources (Chapter 11)

Subject leaders will need to be confident about and have expertise in their subject or area of work – in terms both of knowledge and understanding and of pedagogy. Chapters 1, 2 and 3 look in detail at the essential knowledge and understanding for subject leadership – statutory requirements, Special Educational Needs and the Code of Practice, and the value and place of cross- and extra-curricular activities.

The following skills and attributes will be applied in the above key areas of subject leadership according to specific contexts and circumstances.

Leading and managing people

It is helpful to look at what distinguishes the subject leader from other teaching or support staff in a subject. For this it is necessary to return to an earlier defini-tion of leadership – it is about inspiring and galvanising the talents, energies and commitment of others. The subject leader will:

1   work with others to ensure there is a clear aim and direction for the subject or area of work;
2   be able to plan, set targets, organise and review in order to meet the aims and objectives for the subject, as defined by the National Curriculum;
3   build, sustain and work as part of a team;
4   recognise and utilise the talents and expertise of others;
5   monitor and evaluate pupil and staff performance against the aims and objectives;
6   be an exemplar teacher of the subject and have credibility through raising pupils' achievements in the subject;
7   use research and inspection findings in the subject to raise staff perfor-mance and improve practices;
8   ensure that development planning in the subject is guided by and contributes to whole-school priorities and targets.

Communicate effectively

1   Subject leaders will be able to write clearly, accurately and concisely for a variety of audiences – senior managers, other teachers, support staff, pupils, parents, governors and external agencies.

2   They will have well-developed information and communication tech-nology skills – in terms of knowledge, understanding, application, access to data and networking. They will be expected to promote and encourage the use of ICT in meeting the aims and objectives of the subject.

3   Subject teachers will also be required to have oral skills that are effective in small as well as large groups.

4   Other communication skills will include chairing meetings effectively, negotiating and consulting appropriately, and establishing and maintaining efficient communication channels for those working in the subject as well as between other areas of work in the school. Most, if not all, of these communication skills are needed for effective teaching. Subject leaders will build on these skills and will have to apply the most appropriate skills according to specific tasks and contexts. Chapter 12 looks in detail at this area of communication.

Managing time and setting targets

1   It is self-evident that subject leaders require the ability to manage their own time and priorities, in particular between teaching, leading and managing the subject, and involvement in school developments.

2   They must also set challenging targets for themselves and others if the subject is to develop and pupils' achievements are to be raised. Subject leaders will have to establish systems for setting targets, monitoring progress and evaluating outcomes.

3   Subject leaders will not only take responsibility for their own professional and career development, but will be committed to the continuing profes-sional development of teaching and support staff in the subject or area of work.

Making decisions

1   A key characteristic of effective subject leaders will be the ability to think creatively, to anticipate and forecast changes in the subject (internally or externally driven), and to help others prepare for and take maximum advantage of any changes.

2   Subject leaders will know when to consult, when to defer to senior manage-ment and, critically, when to take decisions themselves.

3   Decision-making will be informed by knowledge and use of relevant research and inspection findings, as well as by the accurate interpretation of information and data.

4   Subject leaders will promote appropriate extra-curricular activities and, as required, contribute to cross-curricular activities and projects.

5   Subject leaders will need to balance being innovative in the subject with the maintenance of effective policies and practices. The national standards are not designed to constrain subject leaders, but rather to provide a frame-

work in which knowledge, understanding, skills and leadership approaches can be combined and integrated in the most appropriate way according to the specific situation or context.

Attributes

Many of these will have been identified in the above skills, but some justify repetition:

1 willingness and enjoyment from looking forward – anticipating changes and planning ahead;
2 ability to motivate others – in part by recognising the skills and energies of others, but also by trusting others to take responsibility for aspects of the subject or area of work – in effect promoting genuine teamwork;
3 self-confident subject leaders are more likely to inspire and galvanise others;
4 a strong and passionate commitment to the subject or area of work, and to maximising achievements for all pupils;
5 inspired leadership is not mechanistic or atomistic, and effectiveness requires creative and intellectual ability to handle several issues and to integrate the range of skills, knowledge and understanding according to specific contexts and situations. It raises the question whether effective leaders are born effective. Inheritance may well be a factor, but so will experiences, environment and emotional intelligence (non-cognitive features such as knowing and controlling one's emotions, motivating and handling relationships, etc. – see Goleman 1995) and perhaps most crucially relevant training, development and support.

OUTCOMES OF SUBJECT LEADERSHIP

The national standards define the outcomes for effective subject leadership for key stakeholders from pupils to parents. Some of the outcomes are measurable (e.g. pupils' achievement in the subject) whereas others are more affective (e.g. pupils' attitudes to the subject). In achieving these outcomes the subject leader will have to adopt the most appropriate leadership style. Several typologies of leadership styles have been developed (Likert 1961, Nias 1980), with that developed by Tannenbaum and Schmidt being particularly helpful. Their model defines leadership and management styles and decision-making using four categories: **telling** (leader gives instruction and has a strong control instinct); **selling** (leader has clear views and values and attempts to convince others); **consulting** (leader presents ideas, invites comments and suggestions, and decision is reached by consensus), and **sharing** (leader develops other staff and delegates' actions and decisions within clearly defined limits) (Tannenbaum and Schmidt 1973). Most effective subject leaders will operate using a hybrid of styles depending upon the particular incident, task or situation. A wide repertoire of styles allows the leader to make quick decisions when necessary, to consult as appropriate and generally to act according to the situation and conditions at the time.

For pupils

It is expected that effective subject leadership will result in systematic and sustained achievement in the subject by the pupils – in terms of subject knowledge, understanding and skills. Progress in the subject or area of work will be assessed against prior attainment and will focus on meeting the needs of all pupils. Pupils will be efficiently and effectively prepared for any tests or examinations in the subject or area of work. They will be more competent learners – in the sense of seeking information about the subject, looking for patterns or sequences in the work, posing questions, enjoying solving problems, applying what has been learnt to unfamiliar situations and evaluating their work on a regular basis.

An additional outcome will be the attitude of pupils to the subject or area of work – the extent to which they are motivated and challenged, their enthusiasm and interest in the subject, their co-operation with other pupils and staff, and their willingness to collaborate to meet specific learning outcomes.

For teachers and support staff

Effective subject leadership will result in a team of teachers (including non-specialists) and support staff who are committed to the aims and overall direction for the subject or area of work, and who believe that working together to achieve aims and objectives is the most efficient and effective approach. All will feel involved in formulating policies, in planning to meet objectives and in evaluating outcomes. Teachers and support staff will be committed to raising achievement in the subject for all pupils by setting challenging targets. They will be highly motivated and will set high expectations of themselves and the pupils. All will be committed to improving their own subject knowledge and pedagogy as part of their continuing professional development. They will take account of relevant research and inspection findings to improve their own performance and practices. In addition, teachers and support staff will liaise and co-operate with other staff and agencies to raise pupils' achievements (e.g. Special Educational Needs, pastoral cross-curricular activities, senior managers, welfare officers, etc.). The relevance, manageability and quality of documentation for a subject or area of work will be one measure of leadership effectiveness. Policies and schemes of work need to be accessible working papers that guide new as well as experienced staff and cater for pupils of all abilities.

For parents

Parents will be well informed about their child's achievements in the subject and will be aware how they can contribute to their child's progress, and will have realistic expectations of their child's achievements in the subject. Parents will be encouraged to have regular and open contact in order to accurately assess their child's progress in the subject.

For governors

Governors are fully informed about the aims and objectives of the subject and how they relate to the school's vision, priorities for development, policies and practices. Governors will be familiar with the pupils' and staff achievements and targets for improvement. They will know the total resources devoted to the subject and how they are deployed. In addition, governors will know how they can support the subject and be aware of any planned changes.

For headteachers and other senior managers

Senior leaders and managers in the school will be familiar with the aims and objectives, and be aware of current issues and development in the subject. They will be fully informed of pupils' and staff achievement in the subject and of any targets for improvement. They will know how resources are deployed in the subject and whether these are being used efficiently and effectively. Senior leaders and managers will be able to relate priorities and developments in the subject to the school's aims and development plan.

KEY AREAS OF SUBJECT LEADERSHIP

Subject leaders are expected to apply professional knowledge, understanding, skills, attributes and the most appropriate leadership style to the tasks within the key areas below. However, leadership is not about the application of sepa-rate or specific knowledge, skills or attributes to a task, but rather about the integration of the most appropriate knowledge, skills and attributes to a task or set of tasks in a given context or situation. In this complex process the tasks of subject leadership are not the same in each school and there will be variations according to size, type and phase. The key areas of subject leadership taken from the TTA's national standards (TTA 1998a) are divided into:

Strategic leadership and improvement of the school: The contribution of the subject and the subject teacher

Subject leaders will be responsible for formulating and implementing a policy for the subject or area of work; for devising short-, medium- and long-term plans; for setting challenging targets; for promoting effective practice; and for reviewing progress. These activities will involve all the staff who contribute to the subject or area of work and will relate directly to the school's vision, policies, priorities and targets.

Managing teaching and learning in the subject or area of work

Subject leaders will be responsible for ensuring that teaching in the subject or area of work is effective; that teaching is regularly and systematically monitored and evaluated; that pupils' achievements in the subject are regularly and systematically monitored and evaluated; that targets for improvement are set and reviewed; that appropriate resources are available, and that resources are used efficiently, effectively and safely.

Leading and managing staff to raise achievement

Subject leaders will be responsible for creating an effective communication system for all those involved with the subject or area of work; for building, developing and sustaining a team; for motivating, supporting and challenging all those involved with the subject or area of work, and for promoting good practices and remedying under-performance.

CONCLUSION

Subject leaders cannot work in isolation and must liaise closely with the headteacher, senior managers and other middle managers. Subject aims and objectives will be guided and defined by the school's vision and strategic direction, which themselves will have been formulated with contributions from subject leaders and members of their team. Cohesive and complementary development serve the interests of pupils and usually stem from a collaborative and team culture in a school. For this reason subject leaders will also work closely with staff who have responsibility for whole-school areas of work, such as Special Educational Needs, assessment and pastoral care.

The book is arranged so that in each section theoretical perspectives are summarised, recent issues and developments are outlined, and activities are provided for the teacher to pursue or reinforce professional and practical applications. By organising the book into key areas of subject leadership, readers can focus on those aspects of the role which are of immediate concern or which are the most relevant for them. Activities are designed to support the continuing personal and professional development of the subject leader and are contained within a training and development framework which will cater for individual needs. Readers can move from section to section according to their specific individual and school needs, or focus on one particular section or chapter. The activities throughout the book are designed to be used by individual subject leaders and subject teams and could form part of a team meeting or staff-development day. The book should help teachers build on their own good leadership and management practices by raising current issues of leadership and management and by basing practices and policies on a firm theoretical foundation. It should also make subject leaders more confident and better equipped to respond to external pressures and changes. The authors believe that the development of leadership and management skills and knowledge at middle and senior levels will equip schools to interpret external influences and help them make the necessary internal changes.

Part I
Essential knowledge and understanding for subject leadership

INTRODUCTION

OfSTED inspection evidence and Section 3 of the *National Standards for Subject Leaders* (TTA 1998a) demonstrate a clear need for knowledge and understanding in order to fulfil the role of a subject leader. The body of knowledge required varies according to many factors: the school, the personnel and the particular subject for which a leader is responsible. The common job-specification provided by most schools for heads of department and subject co-ordinators does assume a common knowledge-base. This link between knowledge and understanding and the role of a middle manager lies at the heart of this new concept of subject leadership.

The role of a subject leader is relatively new in primary schools. Up until the early 1980s, the headteacher was seen to be the key leader in a school. DES (1982) stated clearly that

> in all cases the head's leadership is of paramount importance

and this assertion was fully supported by HMI:

> leadership of the headteacher determines the quality of education throughout the school.
>
> (HMI 1984)

Waters (1979) went one step further in claiming that the head occupies the best position to initiate change, development and improvement. Such a level of responsibility has since become impossible to maintain.

However, the introduction of the National Curriculum, following the Education Reform Act (1988), placed huge demands on headteachers, forcing them to turn to teaching colleagues for support. Full coverage of all curriculum subjects requires an understanding of all subjects and their contribution to the wider curriculum: too great a task for the holder of a single post in any school. There has been a need to provide advice and documentation in order to interrelate the constituent elements, and resources have been co-ordinated to ensure that teaching provision covers statutory requirements (OfSTED 1994).

The breadth and depth of knowledge required has led to Paisey's definition of a one-dimensional 'congenital approach' (Paisey 1984, p.35) to leadership being challenged. Until this point in time, much of the literature viewed leadership qualities as being innate personality gifts, leading to a 'natural authority'. Adair (1988), on the other hand, sees authority being achieved through a combination of position, personality and knowledge.

Headteachers have been compelled to devolve responsibility and the subject structure of the National Curriculum has meant that the usual secondary model of creating subject leaders has been adopted in the primary sector too. In both phases, subject leaders co-ordinate teams, and rely on respect and trust to inspire commitment from that team. Adair sees knowledge as the basis for this respect:

> Like courage for the soldier, such knowledge does not make you into a leader, but you cannot be without it.
>
> (Adair 1988, p.17)

Other commentators (e.g. Dennison and Shenton 1987, Gray 1988) also see knowledge to be at the core of effective leadership, whatever the profession. The acquisition and use of knowledge to solve problems are key factors. Gray lists the objectives of any curriculum leader, which include the acquisition of information and skills, improved understanding of roles and relationships, and an awareness of team members' strengths and weaknesses. With such knowledge, subject leaders can begin to develop the skills to put this to good use.

The TTA's *National Standards for Subject Leaders* identify, in Section 3, the bodies of knowledge essential for subject leaders. What the *Standards* do not do is define the 'types of knowledge' required. Sackman (1992) and Ribbins *et al.* (1991) categorise types of knowledge required to fulfil the role of an educational leader. An awareness of the culture of an institution is of paramount importance. This extends beyond being aware of 'levers' (Ribbins *et al.* 1991, p.174) which inform a leader who should be approached with an idea; but also how colleagues interrelate and respond to different leadership and management styles. This combination of 'recipe' and 'axiomatic' knowledge (Sackman 1992) demands a sensitivity and empathy born from experiential learning. Sackman also presents the need for 'dictionary knowledge', or what has to be done to meet statutory requirements. In combination with a 'directory knowledge', the leader can determine not only what changes should be made to existing practice, but also how the changes can be made. Ribbins *et al.* (1991) label this combination as 'decision knowledge', which requires an understanding of a theoretical perspective as well as practical requirements.

'Knowing how' is also essential. Leaders are accountable for performance within their particular subject area. Monitoring and evaluation generate an ongoing, ever changing form of knowledge. It is the product of reflection and the relating of hard facts to theory and a collective vision that produces useful information for the subject leader. Such an approach is particularly relevant when a subject leader attempts to explain how assessment data relate to teaching methodologies employed; a necessary part of realistic target-setting.

Bennet *et al.* (1994) conclude that successful organisational leaders require greater specialist knowledge and a broader range of related interests than other team members if they are to gain the respect necessary to lead. The knowledge, in all its forms and types, is insufficient to form leaders, but is an essential part of leadership. The knowledge allows for a vision to be articulated and spread throughout the team and the school. The *Standards* define the body of knowledge, but what follows is a demonstration of how such knowledge can be classified under different types: institutional knowledge, decision knowledge and reflective knowledge.

INSTITUTIONAL KNOWLEDGE

Schooling has undergone huge changes in the last two decades, changes which have led to a shift in terms of the organisational culture of schools. Rarely do schools fit a traditional/classic model (Bennet *et al.* 1994) as power and authority has been devolved from headteachers to teachers. Bennet *et al.* (1994) argue that the shift has not been so extreme that heads and governors have adopted a 'human resources model', as groups and teams of staff are not able to influence change in a fully democratic way. 'Systems models' are more common: managers and leaders have had to come to terms with imposed change and to develop policies and procedures in order to interpret the 1988 Education Reform Act (ERA) in an appropriate way. Subject leaders therefore need to appreciate the organisational structure and culture of their schools as a whole. The subject is, of course, one part of the whole curriculum and must therefore contribute to the 'direction of change' (Bennet *et al.* 1994). Day *et al.* (1993) note also that, as well as being adaptive and responsive to external influences, the subject leader must be an enthusiastic model of the values espoused by the school as a whole. This is more than understanding the organisational structure and hierarchy of the school, but is also an appreciation of the intricacies of professional interrelationships.

Subject leaders need to be able to recognise and articulate school values, shared norms and the impact of teaching and learning of their subject on the school as a whole (West 1995). Such a knowledge is, of course, active. As Schein (1985) makes clear, the culture of a school is created by leaders' actions, and is also embedded and strengthened by them.

Such knowledge underpins the leadership style of subject leaders. They should lead in a way which not only reflects the characteristics of the leadership style prevalent in the school, but also serves the needs and meets the expectations of colleagues in a team. A new subject leader, therefore, has to find out staff preferences, existing curricular objectives, links with other subject areas and the resources available (see Dennison and Shenton 1987), which is a confirmation of the need for information explained by Mintzberg (1973).

A head of department in a secondary school is not the only potential subject leader and will draw on the leadership qualities of colleagues within the team. In primary schools, it is not uncommon to be a co-ordinator for more than one subject (see West 1995). Sensible co-ordination and management is also to draw and learn from colleagues' subject expertise. It is for this reason that any subject leader must have a certain maturity. Subject knowledge must integrate with organisational values. The subject leader is responsible for this process of institutionalising subject knowledge. Day *et al.* (1993) stress the need to be aware of the relationship between colleagues' own needs and those of the institution. A subject leader will defend the subject specialist's viewpoint in whole school discussions, but at the same time will present core values when in discussion with subject specialist colleagues (Harrison 1995a). This obviously extends the repertoire beyond subject knowledge to application and pedagogy. As Day *et al.* (1993) explain, *how* a subject is taught transmits values and messages to learners, probably as forcefully as *what* is taught. It is certainly part of what distinguishes one school from another.

A knowledge of the organisational structure of the school assists in 'getting things done'. Ribbins *et al.* (1991) speak of management 'levers' (p.163) which facilitate the setting of targets, the selection of personnel, the allocation and use of resources and the monitoring and evaluation of performance. A good institutional knowledge enables the subject leader to undertake core tasks in what Bennet *et al.* (1994) refer to as 'task behaviour'. Knowledge leads to respect for the leader, who consequently is able to initiate, elaborate, co-ordinate, support, encourage or, in short, act as a 'gate keeper' for the subject (Bennet *et al.* 1994, p.24).

The value of institutional knowledge is immeasurable. How to acquire it is more easily expressed. An adaptation of Harrison's (1995b) proposals serves as a useful guide. Subject leaders should:

- read the staff handbook
- examine displays
- read inspection reports and relevant statutory guidance
- keep a record of leadership actions taken and responses to them
- talk to the head about particular subject provision and its recent history
- analyse the budget, how it has been spent and in what proportions

A formalised and structured process designed to help the subject leader to acquire institutional knowledge will accelerate the acquisition of essential knowledge and even provide a greater degree of objectivity. Relying purely on experiential learning, or learning by osmosis, will not guarantee equal levels of validity, reliability and objectivity.

DECISION KNOWLEDGE

Packwood's (1984) case study of introducing staff responsibility for subject development in a junior school throws up an interesting disagreement between teachers and headteachers. Teachers concluded that subject leaders did not require specialist knowledge of the subject, but do need to consider how knowledge is applied. Headteachers, on the other hand, feared that a lack of specialist knowledge could lead to unimaginative, mechanical teaching. More contemporary thought supports the view of headteachers. A sound subject-knowledge 'will inform their executive decisions and actions' (Ribbins *et al.* 1991, p.173). Guthrie argues that a broader knowledge than merely a subject-specific understanding is necessary to support decision-making: that of 'instructional and learning theories ... the components of curriculum construction and the fundamental importance of subject matter integrity' (Guthrie 1984, p.162). These arguments are supported by research findings. Hargreaves (1992) concluded that expertise in a National Curriculum foundation subject leads to team members regarding the subject leader as an expert and a resource.

Too great a focus on specialist knowledge when formulating policy and procedures can, Bennet (1995) argues, lead to teachers becoming over directive. Nevertheless, subject leaders in both primary and secondary phases do occupy a position of authority and, as Everard and Morris (1990) claim, subordinates do expect to be told what to do and how to do it (high task behaviour) at moments of uncertainty or when they lack confidence. Good subject and pedagogical knowledge does enable the level of discussion to be elevated above what Hargreaves (1992) recognises to be common amongst teachers: an anti-intellectual mistrust of talking seriously about education. Curriculum leaders need, therefore, to be able to justify their actions and decisions, and to be able to model them in the classroom to demonstrate the application of knowledge (Day *et al.* 1993).

Subject and pedagogical knowledge is, for teachers, technical knowledge. It includes an understanding of the content of syllabuses and of the subject curriculum in order that these can be translated into a practical and meaningful programme of study. These technical procedures of curriculum design and the organisation of teaching, Bower (1983) argues, must be complemented by political 'know-how'. Of course subject leaders need to appreciate the implications of statutory requirements, but they must also, in the context of their own school, be able to predict the outcomes in relation to input (Dennison and Shenton 1987).

Knowledge is clearly essential in the processes of planning and target-setting. Many writers (e.g. Adair 1986, Everard and Morris 1990, Bennet *et al.* 1994) list what is necessary to plan effectively. To make the plans and to monitor their impact, the subject leader must know how to articulate the targets, measure progress, set realistic attainable goals, recognise cost implications and appreciate the effort and expertise required to realise the targets set.

Decision knowledge is closely related to the subject and the application of subject knowledge in the classroom. Everard and Morris (1990) recognise the close links with the purchase and use of teaching resources. Basic knowledge, such as the cost and availability of equipment, is essential. The decision to purchase or not must be founded on knowledge – the leader needs to distinguish between the useful and the gimmick, the potential effectiveness and efficiency and, of course, how to use the equipment. The optimal use of resources is, therefore, the responsibility of the subject leader. This will inevitably relate to existing staff expertise and, as a resource to all team members, the subject leader must consider the need for and implications of staff training.

In most subject areas in the secondary sector, subject knowledge is assumed. However in some curriculum areas (e.g. science and modern foreign languages) a full breadth of knowledge cannot be taken for granted. West points out that primary schools often do not have a range of staff to cover the wider curriculum terms of specialist knowledge

> many teachers … have been willing to take up the shortfall on the basis of an interest in the subject. Many such teachers have taken advantage of 'top up' courses designed to assist them in their endeavours.
>
> (West 1995, p.10)

Reading and the observation of others assist in developing a pedagogical knowledge. An examination of how other subjects are taught can inspire ideas, which need to be recorded and discussed by all team members. The political 'know-how' required to develop subject provision is usually gained through experience. Once again this process can be accelerated though recording and reflecting on all professional actions and contacts with colleagues.

REFLECTIVE KNOWLEDGE

It is very clear in the TTA's *National Standards for Subject Leaders* (TTA 1998a) that subject leaders should be able to monitor and evaluate the subject provision in their school. Monitoring and evaluation are more than mere measurement, they include a knowledge of how to improve performance given institutional considerations and constraints. That is not to say that the use of comparative data, inspection evidence and local and national standards of achievement do not serve a purpose in providing useful benchmarks. Leaders should be continuously striving for improvement and development. Survival and the maintenance of standards through a climate of stability is, Leigh (1994) points out, stifling. Day *et al.* (1993) explain that, in the face of imposed change, a climate of certainty and predictability can lead to a siege-victim mentality, when teachers feel de-skilled, long-held beliefs and practices are challenged and morale suffers.

Effective leaders should lead a process of change and development. Pedler *et al.* (1978) concluded from their research that it is a combination of knowing the organisation, being able to analyse data and information, and creating a capacity for creativity which allows development to take place. Subject leaders must, therefore, 'understand the various behavioural processes which may be at work, and use our knowledge to influence or "lead" individuals or groups' (Everard and Morris 1990, p.15).

Subject leaders are part of subject teams and, therefore, exert a major influence in the process of change. Leigh argues that in this privileged position, subject leaders must develop an adaptable management style of their own, around an amalgam of 'personal values, hunches, attitudes, beliefs and perceptions' (Leigh 1994, p.12). Hodgkinson's (1983) credo of 'knowing yourself' stands firm. Through reflecting on one's own inner beliefs and on the impact of one's actions, the leader can begin to understand what they really stand for. It is important to note Leigh's assertion that leaders should develop an *adaptable* model of management, one which can be altered to suit particular circumstances. It is through professional knowledge emanating from what Handy (1984) would call a 'task culture' that values commonly held amongst the team members emerge. The leader needs to assert authority in a way which suits the character of the team.

Bennet states that a subject leader requires a 'recipe knowledge' and an 'axiomatic knowledge' (Bennet 1995, p.103) in order to maintain an orderly working climate. The leader has to understand what needs to be done and how the changes can best be achieved. West accepts intervention by the leader provided it 'relates to their [colleagues'] learning contexts' (West 1995, p.6). Teams working towards a common goal within agreed procedures need not be hierarchical. Handy's (1984) 'task culture' does not require interference but, as a subject leader with vested authority, it would be naïve to remain passive. Nias (1980) argues against a detachment characterised by a 'bourbon leader', who asserts discipline from afar. A 'positive leader' is more able to set high standards from within, through an understanding of the issues and the team.

A 'supportive approach' (Dennison and Shenton 1987, p.37) demands a high level of knowledge. Reflection on events and interchanges is a key method of building this type of knowledge. It requires time and effort, as well as openness. Action research and illuminative evaluation techniques lend themselves well to the collection of qualitative data. What is certain is that reflective knowledge is ever changing, reflecting the relationships of team members. Reflective knowledge, is not, therefore a body of knowledge that a subject leader can bring to the job, but one which is constantly accrued and amended. The acquisition of such knowledge is part of the role of a leader, it contributes to and assures development. Reflective knowledge supports a dynamic approach to leadership, as opposed to a knowledge which supports stability and stagnation.

CONCLUSION

It is clear that the *National Standards for Subject Leaders* (TTA 1998a) were informed by existing good practice; itself (at least in part) articulated in the OfSTED (1994) publication *Primary Matters: A discussion of teaching and learning in primary schools.* The examples of effective practice resemble what Bennet *et al.* (1994) call 'strategic leadership', in that good subject-leaders need to define how the organisation of the subject in school works. Evidently effective leaders also require 'operational leadership skills' in that it is they who have to respond to day-to-day events. Sayer (1988) comments how teachers' own professional development has been enhanced by an involvement in curriculum development, and thus the emergence of the subject-leader role is to be viewed as part and parcel of the drive to improve standards in schools.

By drawing on good practice, there is an assumption underpinning the TTA's (1998a) *Standards* that the knowledge required by a subject leader is not purely content-based. It would not be possible for a subject leader to possess all the necessary knowledge from the outset. Institutional, decision and reflective knowledge are all a combination of received wisdom and experiential learning. The knowledge base is dynamic and not static. Different models of leadership exist, as Goulding *et al.* (1984) explain. Some leaders opt to consult, investigate and develop a subject-framework collaboratively. Others impose a structure. At either extreme, part of the subject leader's role is to effect 'policy, values and philosophy through collective organisational action' (Dennison and Shenton 1987, p.51). Knowing the subject, the team and the school are all therefore essential components.

Knowledge is not the only prerequisite for successful leadership. Dennison and Shenton explain

> the ability to convert knowledge into skills appropriate to the situation is a necessary adjunct to any knowledge.
>
> (Dennison and Shenton 1987, p.122)

Without knowledge, however, skills are defunct. If the acquisition of knowledge is continuous, subject leaders need to know *how* to learn 'on the job'. Kolb (1983) presents models of experiential learning which include concrete experience, reflective observation, abstract conceptualisation and active experimentation. Subject leaders are not simply the recipients of knowledge, but must also be actively involved in generating it.

1 Statutory requirements

Curriculum and assessment

INTRODUCTION

Knowledge and understanding of the National Curriculum statutory guidance and assessment procedures are an essential for subject leaders. In order to make necessary decisions regarding the teaching and learning of the subject, it is crucial to plan, to develop policies, to implement good practice and to monitor provision and understanding of the framework within which schools are compelled to operate. This knowledge and understanding obviously extend beyond the content of centrally produced documentation. In order to exercise the competencies of subject leaders in knowing the subject, planning and evaluating, determining an effective approach and methodology, and transmitting whole-school values to staff and learners, the subject leader must draw on institutional knowledge (O'Neill and Kitson 1996). West-Burnham (1997) also points out that it is the subject leader who must ensure that values and principles, agreed by all team members, underpin the teaching and learning process. It is only through a thorough understanding of what must be taught and how it can be taught that the whole-school aims and vision can be integrated into the process. Attitudes and practice with regard to Special Educational Needs, Health Education and Equal Opportunities need to be compatible with approaches and policies in other subject areas. By reflecting on the interface between whole-school aims, policies, subject requirements and actual practice, subject leaders build their reflective knowledge.

Activity 1.1   Contributing to whole-school aims

Read through the school's mission statement and overall aims. These should be available in the school brochure.

1   List ways in which you feel your subject specialism contributes to these. Ask colleagues in the same subject area to do the same thing.
2   Draw up a list of the ways your subject has an impact on pupils' development of learning strategies (e.g. memory, problem solving, literacy, numeracy etc.).

Understanding of the place of a subject in the whole curriculum is dependent upon a government view in a centralised education system. For this reason it is worth scrutinising literature surrounding the implementation of the National Curriculum. In this way subject leaders are able to learn 'why' as well as 'what'.

The purpose of this chapter is, then, to demonstrate the types and forms of knowledge required to understand: first, what has to be done in terms of subject provision and, second, why. In appreciating this knowledge underpinning the role of a subject leader, the chapter also provides an insight into how a subject leader must be aware of institutional factors including staff expertise and whole-school policies. By relating external and internal influences through a process of reflection, subject leaders acquire the reflective knowledge necessary to monitor, evaluate and develop further the teaching and learning of the subject for which they are responsible.

DECISION KNOWLEDGE

Webb (1994) sees subject co-ordinators' key role to be becoming familiar with subject orders and to disseminate the order's contents to colleagues. Indeed, the provision of documentation by a range of government bodies has provided teachers with a meta-language for the different subjects and for the construction of a curriculum as a whole. The need to demonstrate an understanding of documentation issued by (most recently) the Qualifications and Curriculum Authority (QCA) is all the more necessary as schools need to present policies, guidance and schemes of work in preparation for OfSTED inspections. The plethora of guidance is seen by some (e.g. Beattie 1990) as evidence of a mistrust of teachers' professional judgement. However, Webb (1994) acknowledges class teachers' need for support and guidance in the interpretation of and planning for implementation of statutory orders.

Activity 1.2   Professional bodies

1   What do the acronyms QCA and TTA stand for?
2   In what ways have these bodies such as the QCA and TTA affected what you teach in your given subject area and how has your approach been affected both as a teacher and as a subject leader?
3   Are there any other subject-specific support groups?

It is the co-ordinators and subject leaders who take responsibility for the preparation of internal documentation, who inform colleagues about National Curriculum requirements and often who engage in the monitoring of colleagues' work:

Responsibility for revising or producing policy documents was an important aspect of the co-ordinator's role, especially in relation to preparing their school for an OfSTED inspection.

(Webb 1994, p.61)

In particular the National Curriculum documentation supports the development of policies and schemes, and more and more, Webb (1994) points out, teachers turn to the OfSTED manual to assist in the monitoring of subject provision.

National Curriculum documentation, in conjunction with examination board syllabuses, defines (at least broadly) the content of subject curricula. The traditional subject-based curriculum reflects the fact that:

Our world is organised in terms of logically distinct forms of knowledge.

(Woodhead 1993, p.27)

Secondary currricula are structured in a way that reflects this view and the primary curriculum has had to move in this direction in order to meet statutory requirements.

An understanding of the content of such documentation, therefore, does assist in the justification and location of the subject in the National Curriculum. Winkley (1990) claims that all subjects have their own internal logic and it is for the subject leader to represent this logic in the precise selection of content and of teaching and learning processes.

Teaching a particular subject does involve the transmission of knowledge. Hirst (1993) argues that knowledge is fundamental to judgement, values, attitudes and beliefs, and must therefore form the basis of the curriculum. Subject leaders must therefore know and understand the content of the curriculum before even giving consideration to the application of the knowledge.

Activity 1.3   Knowledge and application

Look through a unit of work in your subject and isolate the content (i.e. the knowledge to be transmitted to pupils).

1   How could pupils apply this knowledge outside the classroom?
2   Do core activities in the scheme of work reflect the possible real applications of this knowledge?

An example is given below for Modern Foreign Languages.

Unit: Around town

Knowledge	Real application	Classroom application
Vocabulary related to places in town	Describing their home town	Producing brochures of a town
Prepositions (next to, in front of, on the left/right of, of a town opposite)	Understanding town plans Understanding descriptions	Using authentic materials Locating places on a town plan by listening and reading
Asking simple questions	Asking and giving directions	Learning a song containing directions off by heart
Imperative forms of verbs		Blind Man's Buff
Telling the time	Asking for and telling opening and closing times of local attraction	Completing a 'tourist survey'
	Finding out about a town in France	Role play in a Tourist Information Centre

The post-Dearing National Curriculum is less prescriptive than the original. The re-issuing of documentation involved the replacement of much of the technical jargon. Nevertheless, the paperwork does contain a phraseology which needs to be understood (Ashcroft and Palacio 1995). As West (1995) intimates, subject leaders need to provide a framework for a 'task group' to undertake the formulation of guidelines, policy and schemes of work. West distinguishes clearly between the guidelines, policy and schemes of work, but for each to be developed certain 'new' concepts must be understood.

An external examination body issues a *syllabus*. The syllabus is a 'sketch of the terrain' (Duffy 1990), which contains information concerning what should be learnt and demonstrated by learners by the end of *a programme of study*. A programme of study, within National Curriculum guidelines, is a non-exhaustive list of learning experiences which should be made available to learners over a period of time. *Attainment Targets* assist curriculum planners with sequencing learning experiences. Section 2 of the Education Reform Act defines Attainment Targets as:

> the knowledge, skills and understanding of different abilities and maturities [which] are expected ... by the end of each key stage.
>
> (DES 1988b)

In planning a course, subject leaders are able to set feasible aims, draw from and include a set of relevant activities in order to cover a defined body of knowledge.

The introduction of the National Curriculum was accompanied by the requirement that all learners should be assessed regularly against agreed criteria. Post-Dearing terminology includes *Level Descriptions* which are to be used to describe how a learner's performance best fits into a programme and continuous scale representing attainment.

The understanding of such terminology and the subsequent development of policy without a deeper appreciation of issues can lead to a situation in which policies do not clarify or support, but become what Bailey (1986) would call 'a source of mystification' and a symbol of the remoteness of managers.

Developing policy, guidance and schemes of work within a National Curriculum framework is time-consuming and exhausting. Subject leaders need to understand the structure of a curriculum. The curriculum is the teaching and learning of all subjects in amalgamation. As West (1995) points out, a teaching and learning policy should be common to the whole school and not a collection of nine or ten separate subject policies. Consequently, all subject leaders have a responsibility in the development of such a policy, incorporating the needs and requirements of their own subject areas. Indeed, West (1995) warns against the over-production of documentation and foresees the risk of elevating the importance of producing paperwork above the importance of that paperwork's actual purpose in facilitating teaching and learning.

The curriculum is, however, subject based and SCAA's (1995) recommendation is that courses are divided into units of work. Units may be 'continuous' or 'blocked' (West 1995). Subject leaders need to decide if discrete lessons over a period of time, or the identification of subject-relevant material within an integrated topic-based approach, provide best coverage of subject content within a unit. The *scheme of work* is the key planning instrument. It must, according to West (1995), contain the content of a unit of work, means of ensuring continuity, time-scales, links with other areas of the curriculum and an element of flexibility to enable colleagues to interpret the scheme. Clear objectives assure the completion of relevant tasks and activities. Such a structure provides staff with the opportunities to answer questions such as 'what do I teach?', 'how do I sequence learning?' or 'how free am I to adopt my own approach?'. The curriculum is of course more than the knowledge to be transmitted. Kelly (1986) points out that it is the engagement with knowledge which is at the heart of a curriculum, a view supported by Fowler who distinguishes between 'knowing that' and 'knowing how' (Fowler 1990, p.77). Subject leaders need to be aware that the objectives for the National Curriculum should be broad, balanced, relevant and differentiated (Emerson and Goddard 1989). It is therefore through the engagement with content that teaching should help the development of information handling, organisation of work, communication skills, collaborative skills and personal qualities (DES 1989c).

This interface between the subject curriculum and the broader curriculum provides a purpose and justification for the subject. Subject leaders also need, in planning, to bear in mind the contribution of the subject to cross-curricular themes and dimensions, determined by the NCC: economic and industrial awareness, health education, environmental understanding and citizenship. Emerson and Goddard (1989) would add to this list: consumer affairs, information technology and media studies.

Planning the subject curriculum requires extensive knowledge and understanding. Similarly, assessing pupils' progress demands a high level of conceptual understanding. Following the ERA (DES 1988b), teachers bear considerable responsibility for the preparation of pupils for external examinations and testing, as well as ongoing continuous assessment. Tasks need to be devised to demonstrate performance against nationally agreed criteria and to assist pupils in their progression through the provision of useful information. Judgements, according to the TGAT Report (DES 1988a) have to be moderated, ensuring a degree of objectivity. Annual reports must articulate pupil's progress and attainment against the National Curriculum Attainment Targets with each subject. Not only do subject leaders need to be aware of these requirements, but they also need to know how to design assessment tasks and the means of recording and reporting, taking into account the four key aspects of assessment: formative, diagnostic, summative and evaluative. Taking these four aspects into account means that assessment procedures must generate data which helps to inform pupils' future progress (formative), identify particular learners' needs (diagnostic), provide an indication of all that has been attained (summative) and assist the teacher in ascertaining how effective the teaching methods have been (evaluative). Merttens and Vaas (1991) warn also that teachers must take care to devise methods which record what has been learnt as opposed to what has been taught.

In applying the statutory requirements laid out by the ERA (DES 1988b), decision knowledge is crucial to subject leaders. They need to know the content of documentation through an understanding of the language contained within. By developing a framework for planning and policy-writing, teaching and learning of the subject can be enhanced. Monitoring and evaluation, too, require an understanding of the centralised requirement, documentation for which (OfSTED 1993a) is readily available.

INSTITUTIONAL KNOWLEDGE

Decision knowledge enables subject leaders to plan a subject curriculum at a distance. Institutional knowledge is necessary to inject an element of realism into the process. Brighouse and Moon (1990) point out that Osborn's assertion that 'Individual schools ... and determined teachers in the privacy of their own classrooms manage to violate numerous regulations and traditions' (Osborn 1972, p.14) still stands true. In order to assure a quality provision, subject leaders need to have an overview of curriculum management which includes an awareness of whole-school planning demands and also of colleagues' strengths and weaknesses contained within their own 'teacher repertoire' (West 1995).

Activity 1.4 Teaching and learning

1 You should issue the following to all subject team members:

How often do you employ the following teaching and learning methods in the delivery of the specialist subject? You may add to the list if you or any colleagues wish.

Investigation	5	4	3	2	1	Example
Problem-solving	5	4	3	2	1	Example
Hypothesising	5	4	3	2	1	Example
Trialling	5	4	3	2	1	Example
Testing	5	4	3	2	1	Example
Explaining	5	4	3	2	1	Example
Exploring	5	4	3	2	1	Example
Communicating	5	4	3	2	1	Example
Memorising	5	4	3	2	1	Example
Repetition	5	4	3	2	1	Example
Drilling	5	4	3	2	1	Example
Improvising	5	4	3	2	1	Example
Inventing	5	4	3	2	1	Example
Designing	5	4	3	2	1	Example
Brainstorming	5	4	3	2	1	Example
Role playing	5	4	3	2	1	Example
Evaluating	5	4	3	2	1	Example

Note: 5 indicates 'very often' and 1 means 'never'.

2 What are the collective strengths and weaknesses in your team in terms of teacher repertoire?
3 Does this information help you, as a subject leader, to identify how the teaching of your subject may contribute to the fulfilment of the aims of a whole-school policy on teaching and learning?

It is accepted that teaching and learning processes can have as forceful an impact on learners as the actual content (see Introduction), and consequently subject leaders in planning and implementing do need to take into account the range of teaching and learning activities with which colleagues are comfortable. Duffy (1990) notes that teachers do take a pride in their own particular strengths, which may or may not be reflected in their salary structure. This, Duffy argues, locks the planning of subject delivery into a traditional subject curriculum structure. Leaders ignore colleagues' contributions, therefore, at their peril. The flip side of this belief is, of course, that teachers can hide their own problems and difficulties by adapting their own teaching styles and classroom management techniques. HMI (1991) are very clear that teachers' responsibilities extend beyond the transmission of subject knowledge. In their report of the implementation of the National Curriculum in its first year, they stress that due emphasis should be placed on particular aims and objectives which fall outside the scope of the core and other foundation subjects.

This demand raises several key questions. Notably, it is for individual schools to determine the values which underpin the curriculum. Duffy notes a '*Polo* syndrome' (Duffy 1990, p.86), in that the National Curriculum does not require schools to place any particular values at the heart of its documentation. The ERA, however, stresses the 'whole curriculum' (DES 1988b, Section 1) and provides a legislative framework to ensure that this is broad and balanced, contains opportunities for spiritual, moral, cultural, social and physical development, and is, in short, a suitable preparation for adult life (Hall 1992).

This concern was answered by requiring schools to deliver cross-curricular themes and dimensions, most commonly through (rather than in addition to) subject delivery. Subject leaders are required to contribute through careful planning to a broader education, which includes health education, multi-cultural understanding, economic and industrial awareness, environmental education, citizenship and a European dimension. All this is encompassed within an equal opportunities framework.

Activity 1.5   Cross-curricular themes and dimensions

1   Read your subject schemes of work. Highlight aspects which you feel contribute to:

- economic and industrial understanding
- health education
- environmental education
- citizenship
- careers education

2   Cross-relate your findings with those of a leader of another subject in your school.
3   Now read the NCC Curriculum Guidance booklets. Could you do more in your subject to assure continuity and progression in the teaching and learning of cross-curricular themes?

For both primary and secondary schools, this requirement is not altogether new. Verma notes that these beliefs and values have long underpinned primary school pedagogy (Verma and Pumfrey 1994) and Duffy (1990) feels that the influence of TVEI in the 1980s in secondary schools was that the cross-curricular skills, themes and dimensions issued by the NCC have now become part and parcel of teachers' understanding of the learning process.

The complication for subject leaders is, though, the approach to planning units of work. Winkley asks 'how do we deliver a linear curriculum, without undermining the cyclical nature of the learning experience?' (Winkley 1990, p.100). A subject-based curriculum, Coulby (1996) argues, undermines innovations in teaching and learning, such as the focus on life-skills, and political, economic and social awareness. The simple lack of time causes frustration in the delivery of equal opportunities and multi-culturalism.

Answers lie in the co-ordination of the whole curriculum. Subject leaders have a responsibility to represent their own subject, but also, of course, to appreciate the contribution of other subjects to learners' overall development. This, through an agreement on the processes of learning in the school as a whole, often articulated in the form of overarching policies, is how the necessary breadth and balance of a curriculum are provided.

West's (1995) recommended process for policy development demonstrates the need for institutional knowledge. The first stage is descriptive analysis. Leaders need to know what colleagues do, and what they can and cannot do. Research of such information will inform future planning. It also allows subject leaders to identify how much variation in classroom practice is permissible if the criteria of a policy are to remain meaningful. Types of learning activities (e.g. investigation, problem-solving, hypothesising, trialling, testing, exploring, communicating and memorising) can be identified, repetition avoided and gaps in provision discovered.

Successful completion of this first stage allows for the leaders, in collaboration, to embark upon the second – identifying what *should* be done. This involves going beyond current practice and leaders do need to consult with all staff to ensure progress. Colleagues must feel confident expressing concerns and identifying training needs as part of the policy itself. In knowing colleagues' needs and preferences, a subject leader can devise in-service training appropriately. Webb criticises the common 'cascading' (Webb 1994, p.63) methods of in-service training. Teachers state a lack of time to feedback and too great an emphasis on intensive training methods. It is through a good institutional knowledge that subject leaders can direct teacher development.

The third stage of West's (1995) process of policy-writing is to present a draft document for discussion. All teachers should be able to confer and share concerns. Participation in the first stage, through what Webb calls 'whole-school brainstorming' (Webb 1994, p.61) ensures that all are aware of their strengths and developmental needs. The public clarification of this form of institutional knowledge facilitates a realistic approach to the implementation of statutory curriculum requirements.

Institutional knowledge extends beyond an understanding of school values and staff preferences. Emerson and Goddard claim that following the ERA:

> teachers will be expected to know what levels of attainment pupils are generally likely to meet at particular ages and to set pupils objectives which reflect these.
>
> (Emerson and Goddard 1989, p.25)

Assessment must inform learning and not dictate it. Subject leaders in setting targets must therefore be aware of pupils' potential and needs. This view is supported by the original TGAT Report, which did not regard the concepts of objectivity and pupil attitudes as mutually exclusive (Fowler 1990). Subject leaders need to understand the purposes of assessment and to relate these to their own schools and subjects. An assessment policy should, Emerson and Goddard (1989) feel, be based on a range of methods, which are fully integrated into day-to-day teaching.

It is acceptable that these ongoing assessment techniques are not sharply focused, as the key stage tests for core subjects and optional tests for foundation subjects periodically add the necessary objective edge.

Activity 1.6   Assessment

1   Look through a unit of work and list all the ways pupils are assessed (e.g. spelling tests, reading to the teacher, completing a worksheet, answering questions orally, completing written exercises, etc.).
2   Which assessment activity generates information that is:
   • formative?
   • summative?
   • diagnostic?
   • evaluative?
   One activity, may of course, serve several different purposes.
3   Can the assessment evidence be related to National Curriculum Performance Descriptions in a range of Attainment Targets?

The National Curriculum documentation provides guidance for assessment. The language does need interpreting, however. Shorrocks *et al.* (1993) recommend that schools, through internal discussion, determine precise meanings for 'performance verbs'. The difference between, for example, 'understand, interpret, identify, find, sort, demonstrate and select' (Shorrocks *et al.* 1993, p.39) cannot depend on a definition imposed by the subject leader. In interpreting such a language, institutional knowledge is in fact generated.

The process of defining levels to fit National Curriculum Performance Descriptions, will inevitably involve the scrutiny and analysis of pupils' work. In moderating pupils' contributions by a process of 'levelling' and agreeing standards of actual pupils' work, once again teachers will create a high level of understanding in terms of their own pupils' performance. It is for the subject leader to crystallise and articulate the outcomes of meetings with colleagues, if this new knowledge is to be accessible to all. This level of understanding, lastly, permits an accurate and informative method of reporting attainment and progress. Winkley's (1990, p.111) recommendations for reporting demand considerable institutional knowledge. He insists that a profile of performance should contain:

- reference to broad achievements across Attainment Targets
- descriptions of emotional and personal development
- descriptions of ability
- contributions from pupils and parents
- samples of pupils' work as examples of progress
- the avoidance of tick lists
- reference to long-term performance
- useful information
- a celebration of success

Effective assessment, recording and reporting is more than teachers doing as they are told. It requires an awareness of overall performance, the identification of needs, recognition of progress, an acknowledgement of success on an individual basis and it should inform future planning. All of this is institutional knowledge and, to develop and manage an effective process, the subject leader must create an environment which allows for the generation of institutional knowledge.

Activity 1.7   Reporting assessment outcomes

1   Do your reports/profiles contain:

- records of success?
- examples of pupils' work?
- information on how to improve?
- identification of weaknesses and their causes?
- links with the whole-school curriculum?
- attainment in relation to the National Curriculum?
- details of progress made?

2   Where can evidence of the above be found?

Institutional knowledge is necessary for successful policy-writing. Subject leaders need to collaborate to generate whole school policies. They also need to know and understand their own team members. It is only through collaboration and effective enquiry strategies that subject leaders can avoid what West (1995, p.39) calls 'Parkinson's Law' (work expands to fill the time available). It is by gathering useful institutional knowledge that key decisions regarding curriculum and assessment planning can be implemented.

REFLECTIVE KNOWLEDGE

Relating decision knowledge and institutional knowledge is, in fact, reflective knowledge. National Curriculum documentation is intended to be guidance, determining the knowledge to be transmitted to pupils and the skills to be acquired. It does not determine, within subject, how this is to be achieved:

> The National Curriculum is not a straitjacket. It provides for greater clarity and precision about what should be taught while enabling schools to retain flexibility about how to organise their teaching.
>
> (NCC 1989c, para. 1.2)

No subsequent documentation from official sources has since contradicted this assertion.

The ERA does not, therefore, prescribe methodology, which Day *et al.* see as 'the birthright of the teaching profession' (Day *et al.* 1993, p.106). Reflective knowledge is necessary if, in developing a corporate approach, subject leaders can incorporate their local knowledge when interpreting statutory requirements. Reflective knowledge is experiential and to articulate it as it develops is to promote a climate of reflection and learning. Goddard and Leask (1992) lament the fact that mathematics and science subject leaders who held back from developing policies and schemes of work in the early 1990s, gained the most as the NCC revised the framework continuously. We argue that in learning how to implement national guidelines it was they who *learnt* most!

The knowledge contained within the curriculum documentation, is of little value unless pupils use it productively to develop intellectual and cognitive abilities. Teachers need, therefore, to plan for pupils' application and interaction with knowledge.

It is in thinking how the content of a unit of work can be presented in an interesting, relevant and stimulating way that teachers draw on experience and intuition. Through the sharing of ideas, the formulation of schemes of work and regular ongoing evaluation, teachers engage in systematic reflection – in fact theorise about teaching and learning, and simultaneously learn to theorise. Fowler points out that:

> A vital omission in the Government's case for a National Curriculum was the lack of any underlying theory upon which a curriculum structure could be based.
>
> (Fowler 1990, p.76)

Teachers can and will justify the place of their specialist subject in the curriculum. Subject leaders cannot impose such values and attitudes, but (through processes of discussion and sharing) leaders and teams can develop a collective vision and mission. In relation to statutory guidance, Fowler (1990) recommends that the subject is justified in terms of its relationship to nine 'areas of experience' common to LEA's curriculum statements since 1944. These are represented by nine categories:

- aesthetic and creature
- human and social
- linguistic and literary
- mathematical
- physical
- scientific
- technological
- moral
- spiritual

These categories differ from Woodhead's distinct bodies of knowledge (see earlier in this chapter) in that they represent ways of thinking and processes of learning, rather than serving as a means of defining content. The identity of a subject team is, then, in no small way discernible through its collective view on why and how the subject is taught.

Activity 1.8   Justifying the subject within the whole curriculum

1   Ask team members to analyse to what extent your subject contributes to the whole curriculum and how this contribution is made.
    The table below provides a model for collecting relevant information:

Curriculum elements	Syllabus content	Teaching and learning methods
Aesthetic and creative		
Human and social		
Linguistic and literary		
Mathematical		
Physical		
Scientific		
Technological		
Moral		
Spiritual		

2   Do all team members agree?
3   If there are gaps, can these be filled without detracting from the teaching and learning experience within the subject?
4   Do teachers need guidance?

The subject leader requires the skills and knowledge to identify and articulate these descriptors in relation to an agreed and established framework.

To a large degree reflective knowledge is the product of collaboration. In discussing pupils' work as part of the assessment process, subject leaders are facilitating such a process. The production of a portfolio of pupils' work to exemplify standards, recommended by Shorrocks *et al.* (1993), gives discussions a purpose and direction. The final outcome is useful and valuable. The subject leader needs also to note and make public the key contributions, as it is essentially these which inform collective assessment decisions.

Activity 1.9   Moderation and levelling

1   Select samples of pupils' work in a range of tasks, covering all the Attainment Targets. Read the work and allocate marks to it which represent attainment in relation to National Curriculum Performance Descriptions. Ask colleagues to do the same, with the same samples of work.
2   Have you allocated similar grades? Can you both justify your decisions? Can you identify features which represent discernible levels of performance?

The outcomes of such a task can serve as the basis for a departmental assessment portfolio.

This procedure is in the spirit of the TGAT Report in that moderation is taking place and a degree of objectivity is injected into the teachers' judgement. Subject leaders need also to ensure that teachers prepare pupils for SATs. By reflecting on the outcomes of teachers' ratings of pupil performance and SATs, subject leaders are able to use assessment evidence for evaluative purposes.

Part of evaluation and monitoring is to ascertain if statutory requirements are being met. A constant focus on improvement of provision inevitably leads to the identification of weaknesses and developmental needs. Staff development and in-service training are, in part, a responsibility of subject leaders. They are a resource and a facilitator. Relating staff needs to provision is reflective knowledge. Different development methods suit different staff members and different needs. Webb (1994) quotes research which suggests that subject leaders are uncomfortable with instructing colleagues, that the 'cascade' methods of training are not effective and that simple discussions with colleagues are not particularly successful. O'Neill and Kitson (1996) draw similar conclusions and recommend collaborative teaching as an effective tool for teacher development. The idea is not new. Alexander *et al.* (1993) suggested that a generalist teacher in primary schools should work collaboratively with subject leaders. Joint planning, delivery and evaluation should be recorded to provide a (reflective) knowledge-base. Statutory requirements provide a framework for such reflection. Webb (1994) comments that such an approach leads to improved subject-knowledge and application within the subject.

Inevitably the subject leader is not always the best 'partner' for collaborative teaching. Time constraints determine the opportunity to observe and teach with colleagues. The subject leader, therefore, needs to develop user-friendly means of researching and reporting on collaborative work for the benefit of the whole team. Reflective knowledge serves a purpose only if it is accessible and renewable.

Reflective knowledge is relevant if the focus of attention is the quality of learning. Reference to statutory requirements encourages a more quantitative approach. The subject leader needs to consider the means by which colleagues can contribute meaningfully to the planning, implementation, assessment and evaluation of the curriculum. Consequently, the subject leader is compelled to draw on qualitative data and to relate aspects of classroom practice to the hard quantitative data.

CONCLUSION

Despite the prescriptive nature of the National Curriculum and therefore an apparent mistrust of teachers' professional judgement, good teaching is not achieved by following a manual. Certain edicts must be respected, however, and teachers must know how to apply statutory requirements. Subject leaders are in a privileged position of being able to interpret and guide practice. Knowledge of curriculum and assessment procedures is necessary, yet it is also important that in applying such knowledge due account is given to institutional features and characteristics. The dynamic relationship between teachers and learners requires an ongoing evaluation and reflection on classroom activities. Statutory requirements provide a framework which offers a sharp focus and an emphasis on precision and clarity. Decision, institutional and reflective knowledge all play a key role in a subject leader's responsibility to apply the National Curriculum.

2 Special Educational Needs and the Code of Practice

INTRODUCTION

Since the Warnock Report (Warnock 1978) the trend in Special Educational Needs (SEN) provision has centred around the concept of integration. This has led to a sharp rise in the numbers of SEN pupils in mainstream primary and secondary schools. Not only has the number of statemented children risen in total from a projected 2 per cent of school-age children to 3 per cent in 1997, but the number in mainstream schools has doubled (to 134,000) since 1991 (DfEE 1997a). The Warnock Report also predicted that 20 per cent of all school children would have a Special Educational Need at some time during their school career.

The move towards inclusion is based, at least in part, on educational grounds:

> Teachers have been concerned with the entitlement of young people to broaden their experiences and to offer them greater equality of opportunity, which includes access to everything that is happening alongside their peers.
> (Wyllyams 1993, p.99)

This view, that *all* pupils have an entitlement to *all* curriculum opportunities (Wolfendale 1992), is not simply a case of positive discrimination. Farrell (1997) argues strongly that, if our ultimate goal is to contribute to a more compassionate and caring society, integration benefits all mainstream pupils and teachers.

This educational and philosophical stance is supported by the government position:

> Modification and disapplication of subjects and assessments should therefore be needed only in exceptional cases.
> (DfEE 1997a, p.19, para. 1.24)

The integration of SEN pupils has major implications. The Code of Practice (COP) (DFE 1994) implies that the labelling of pupils as in need of additional support must be supported by detailed evidence (Hornby *et al*. 1995). The identification of an individual pupil's needs must be documented in order that appropriate provision can be made, and also so that progress can be monitored and recorded. This simplistic presentation of a process is an obvious extension of research findings (e.g. Mortimore *et al*. 1988) that there is a clear link between pupils' needs on entry into schooling and the final outcomes on exit.

All schools must appoint a Special Educational Needs Co-ordinator (SENCo). The identification, provision and assessment of all SEN pupils, when such pupils are entitled to equal access to all areas of the curriculum, is far too great a task for one single person (DfEE 1997a, p.61, para. 6.2). Integration means that all teachers have a responsibility and the SENCo's role is one of co-ordination (DFE 1994, Hull 1994).

The first task is the collation of evidence through focused assessment at all stages. Wyllyams (1993) argues that ordinary class- and subject-teachers have a professional duty to generate information for reviews of pupils' progress which must be undertaken regularly. Stakes and Hornby (1997) define the curriculum as all the opportunities for learning provided by the school, countering the criticism that access to an academic National Curriculum does not provide the necessary breadth, balance and relevance. A whole curriculum should include methodology and the personal, social, moral, cultural and spiritual impact of the full range of teaching and learning styles.

A school's SEN provision is inspected by OfSTED 'through the subject'. Hornby *et al*. (1995) note that inspectors will be interested in members of subject teams with designated responsibility for SEN. Inspectors will make judgements on the standards of achievement, progress, quality of teaching and quality of learning for pupils with SEN. The usefulness of assessment, recording and reporting procedures will also be gauged through an accumulated body of evidence provided by subject-specialist inspectors.

Support, through the role of the SENCo is, of course, available. It is important that, as all teachers face the challenge of a growing number of pupils with SEN, teachers do not feel de-skilled. Opportunities to learn and widen the repertoire of teaching strategies available to staff is a positive response to the challenge:

> All that 'successful teachers' have to do, it seems, is to apply 'good teaching' in a way such that failure is replaced by a sense of achievement.
>
> (Gulliford 1985, p.22)

Subject leaders, therefore, have an important role to play. A knowledge of procedures (decision knowledge) and how these can be applied within the subject department, given the human and material resources available (institutional knowledge), is crucial. The procedures themselves focus on individual needs, which inevitably vary from one person to another. The matching of needs to provision requires and generates a reflective knowledge. Through constant evaluation and reference to individual needs and curriculum provision, the subject leader can develop and modify procedures in order to support the child. SEN provision has always suffered from teachers making generalisations and failing to confront their own ignorance and prejudices (Farrell 1997). It is by having access to effective systems and procedures based on sound knowledge and understanding that a caring and educative SEN provision can be made.

DECISION KNOWLEDGE

Government legislation and documentation provides a framework for SEN provision. The *Code of Practice on the Identification and Assessment of Special Educational Needs* provides a definition of SEN, which requires further explanations. Figure 2.1 represents these definitions.

Figure 2.1   A definition of Special Educational Needs

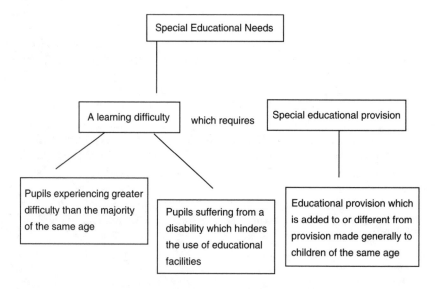

Early identification has been facilitated by the introduction (from September 1998) of baseline assessments. Before facing the challenges of the National Curriculum, four- and five-year-olds are assessed on their concentration span, collaborative and motor skills. The outcomes will serve to inform subject teachers of individual needs. At the other end of the scale, from September 1998 pupils deemed unsuited to GCSE and GNVQ syllabuses may be entered in all National Curriculum subjects for new Certificates of Achievement.

All aspects of educational provision during a pupil's time at school need to be planned. Subject leaders need to have the necessary knowledge of expectations, the curriculum and learning opportunities in order to implement the level of support expected.

SCAA (1996) (now QCA) advised that systems need to be devised which allow for the identification of pupils' specific difficulties, their strengths and weaknesses, and of particular teaching strategies necessary to promote learning. The subject leader's role is to assure subject colleagues' access to information and ideas. The SENCo's role is:

> to be able to advise colleagues on the most appropriate teaching methods, together with the most advantageous learning environments.
>
> (Hornby *et al.* 1995, p.16)

Subject leaders should understand the demands of their own subject, yet also recognise Wolfendale's (1992) point that corporate teaching can be an effective means of ensuring that each child receives their rightful share of teachers' attention and time. Skilful co-ordination requires subject knowledge and a full appreciation from a SENCo's perspective.

Many writers (e.g. Hull 1994, Hornby *et al.* 1995) stress the role of class- and subject-teachers in the identification of needs. The trigger for Stage 1 of the five-stage model contained within the Code of Practice (DFE 1994) is the judgement of the class-/subject-teacher. Teachers are required to identify and record their concerns and to attempt to deal with the problem through increased differentiation.

Activity 2.1   Activities designed to identify learners' needs

Using Hull's list of causes of failure to complete tasks (Hull 1994, pp.7–8), consider activities in your own subject-curriculum which will assist you to identify and provide evidence of pupils' difficulties.

Possible causes	Activities
Behavioural and emotional	
Hearing	
Cognitive (dyslexia, dysgraphic, dysphasia)	
General delay (poor previous teaching)	
Physical/sensory	
Medical (epilepsy, diabetes etc.)	

The role of subject leaders is to understand how an inability to learn their particular subject may manifest a Special Need. The judgement to be made first of all concerns the gravity of the problem. Farrell (1997) suggests the causes of failure may be due to a task being badly presented, the reward for achievement may be unrewarding or the task may simply be too difficult. The challenge is, therefore, to provide support when it is most needed.

Sayer (1987) provides a similar list to Hull (1994), but also includes problems associated with organisation. Many pupils experience difficulties in these areas, but are able to compensate for shortcomings in one area by emphasising strengths in another. The subject leader therefore needs to devise a method of gathering information which shows that such deficiencies have a detrimental impact upon the pupil's performance in their own subject. In order to do so, Hornby *et al.* (1995) recommend cross-referencing to pupil's attainment in terms of the National Curriculum class-based tasks, the outcomes of standardised tests and samples of work included in a Record of Achievement. All serve to illustrate the level of performance attained.

Continuous, detailed record-keeping allows for a child's needs and progress to be monitored. If a teacher is unable to meet the needs of a particular pupil, the pupil may be classified as being at Stage 2. It is at this point that the information gathered may be used to develop an Individualised Education Plan (IEP). Hull (1994) points out that it is also at this stage that the SENCo takes the lead in assessing, planning and monitoring by working with fellow teachers. An IEP is rarely specific to one curriculum subject. It is through a detailed understanding of a subject that subject teachers are able to match pupil's needs with particular subject provision.

Subject leaders should be able to take the lead in demonstrating how, for example, the learning of their subject in a particular way can contribute to the development of study skills and a more positive attitude to learning.

Activity 2.2   Using subject-specific activities to enhance social and study skills

1   Scan through a Scheme of Work for a unit.
2   Identify the core activities.
3   Against each activity, list the study and social skills required in order to complete the task.

Hornby *et al.* stress strongly that an IEP should build on the curriculum that the child is already following, and that:

> the plan should be implemented as much as possible within the classroom, and make use of the programmes, activities, resources and assessment techniques available to the child's teacher.
>
> (Hornby *et al.* 1995, p.36)

Evidently, the teacher may need support in terms of increasing their own repertoire of subject teaching strategies and techniques.

Activity 2.3   Supporting study and social skills through subject-based provision

Using the outcomes of Activity 2.2, note against each core activity ways in which support for a lack in study and social skills can be provided.

In order to direct colleagues, subject leaders must be aware of what an IEP should contain and to what extent these contents can be implemented in their subject. The IEP is essentially built around the concerns, supported by evidence, provided by subject teachers. Bliss and Timbrell (1997, p.37) list what an IEP should contain:

- the nature of learning difficulties
- action and special provision
- targets and time-scale
- extra care
- review arrangements

Hull insists that effective IEPs include precise curricular priorities and teaching requirements. The SENCo will benefit from an understanding of what can be done and how in any given subject, which can only be provided by the subject leader. Hull (1994, p.12) lists the types of alternative provision which can be made:

- a reduction or increase in the amount of work set
- peer tutoring
- daily reports
- individual instruction
- before/after school help
- adaptation of teaching materials

It is for the subject leader to consider the appropriateness of each.

Activity 2.4   Finding out about different support methods

Using the list of support activities above, collect examples of what teachers in your subject team actually do from day to day. Where are there gaps in provision? Which learning activities best lend themselves to each type of support?

The IEP must contain details of a review. This review demands that evidence is collated, in order that progress can be assessed against the criteria and targets contained in the IEP. Mechanisms need to exist in order that the effectiveness of the IEP can be judged and further stipulations may be added (Bliss and Timbrell 1997).

The information to be gathered will, of course, relate to the individual pupil, but will also relate to a range of curriculum subjects, one or more specific subjects, and social and behavioural aspects. Failure by the pupil to respond in a positive way may lead to Stage 3 and subsequently Stage 4, when the school prepares an application for a statement which may be granted by the LEA. Hull (1994) explains that the decision to proceed with a statutory assessment demands evidence of full staff involvement and a consistent approach to managing the provision for a particular pupil's needs. Once again, record-keeping is a key to acquiring support. Records include factual data and accounts of health problems, sensory impairment, speech and language difficulties, attendance, home problems and emotional and behavioural problems (DFE 1994). A demonstration of the pupil's lower levels of attainment shows the negative influence of the pupil's problems. The annual review for Stage 5, statemented pupils, requires considerable information, in terms of ongoing assessment of SEN pupils on an individual basis. An appreciation of the types of information required enables the subject leader to devise subject-relevant procedures which facilitate the collation and analysis of relevant data.

The need for accurate assessment records is supported by the less than informative outcomes of IQ tests. Farrell argues that pupils should be assessed on what they have been taught in order to gain a clear picture of their educational performance:

> An IQ score tells us nothing about a pupil's performance on basic skills related to the curriculum. It therefore offers no suggestions for individual programme planning.
>
> (Farrell 1997, p.33)

IQ tests are intended to measure potential, yet clearly they do not indicate why a pupil is having difficulty, nor what type of learning processes are posing problems.

Diagnostic assessment within a particular subject area, on the other hand, will enable particular difficulties to be highlighted. Teacher assessments can be related to the results of Standard Assessment Tests (SATs). Target-setting is made more manageable if the targets are related to performance in a particular subject.

SCAA (1996) accepts the need for performance to be measured in a range of different ways. Teachers need to be sure that assessment methods are valid and reliable. Particular objectives need to be assessed in particular ways. A full range of response types should, therefore, be deployed. Questions should be easily understood and pupils allowed to respond in a way which both challenges them and also enables them to demonstrate knowledge and skill. Newson (1993) argues that careful planning of assessment enables a wide range of factors to be accounted for. She includes observation of group work and play as one assessment technique; one which allows the gathering of evidence which is pertinent to the list contained in Activity 2.5.

Activity 2.5   Matching activities to assessment criteria

For each aspect below list activity types which require competence on the part of a pupil:

- social behaviour
- ability to follow instructions
- communicative skills
- problem-solving ability
- co-ordination

Figure 2.2 is an adaptation of SCAA's assessment model. Subject leaders need to be aware of how the full range of subject activities can be assessed and for what purpose. In understanding such a model, recording methods can be devised.

From Year 9, annual reviews must contain a Transition Plan for statemented

Figure 2.2   The purpose of common assessment activities

Activity	Purpose	How to record
General classwork (Observation, questioning)	Inform planning Set targets Identify progress	IEPs Mark book Reports
SATs	To relate scores in different subjects Identify strengths	Reports Reviews Evaluation
Internal tests	Focused diagnostic assessment	Reviews Reports
Reports on school activities, including extra-curricular	Celebrate success	RoA Reviews Reports

Source: Adapted from SCAA 1996, p.58.

pupils. This involves the consideration of skills and attitudes which the pupil will need to develop as an adult. Social skills and vocational aspirations must therefore feature on the IEP. It is for the subject leader to consider how their subject contributes to this broader aspect of the curriculum. Farrell considers that the context of learning is crucial to pupils with learning difficulties. He explains:

that pupils with learning difficulties generalise their learning more effectively if they are taught in natural contexts.

(Farrell 1997, p.65)

Teachers, therefore, should contextualise learning, thereby facilitating the
application of knowledge at a later date. Once again, subject leaders require a
good subject and pedagogical knowledge in order to facilitate effective planning
and differentiation. It is the ability to break component parts of learning down
into simple, realistic steps, which simultaneously improve subject-related and
general cross-curricular skills that, in turn, enable problem diagnosis and the
monitoring of learning in its widest sense. Through their knowledge and understanding of the set procedures for dealing with SEN and of their own subject,
subject leaders are able to develop a type of 'Portage Checklist'. Developing
such a cumulative list of abilities and knowledge which lead to eventual task-
completion is only attainable if the writer (subject leader) has a detailed
knowledge and understanding of the subject curriculum.

Activity 2.6   Developing a curriculum-based 'Portage Checklist'

Take an activity and break it down into component parts, in terms of
knowledge, study and social skills. Can you use this 'Portage List' as a
form of diagnostic assessment? An example for Modern Foreign
Languages is provided below:

Learning the twenty-four-hour clock
1   Recognise numbers 1–20 (listening and concentrating on the teacher,
    memory and identification of sounds)
2   Say numbers 1–20 (working with a partner, co-operating)
3   Recognise numbers 20–60 (participating in a game – bingo – led by the
    teacher)
4   Say numbers 20–60 (conveying information to others, reliability)
5   Recognise the time (hours only) using a twelve-hour clock (listening to a
    tape, operating a cassette player)
6   Tell the time (hours only) using a twelve-hour clock (answering peer
    questions in group work, responsibility and discipline)
7   Recognise the time (every half-hour only) using a twelve-hour clock
    (discriminating between own and foreign culture – as half-past is said
    differently, tolerance)
8   Tell the time (every half-hour only) using a twelve-hour clock (recog-
    nising the value of telling and understanding the time outside the
    classroom, ability to generalise)
9   Recognise the time (every ten minutes) using a twelve-hour clock (being
    precise, using approximations as clues to exact meaning, predicting)
10 Tell the time (every ten minutes) using a twelve-hour clock (courtesy and
    etiquette, using language in public situations)

11 Recognise the time (hours only) using a twenty-four-hour clock (reinforcement of above)

12 Tell the time (hours only) using a twenty-four-hour clock (reinforcement of above)

13 Recognise the time (every half-hour only) using a twenty-four-hour clock (reinforcement of above)

14 Tell the time (every half-hour only) using a twenty-four-hour clock (reinforcement of above)

15 Recognise the time (every ten minutes) using a twenty-four-hour clock (reinforcement of above)

16 Tell the time (every ten minutes) using a twenty-four-hour clock (reinforcement of above)

INSTITUTIONAL KNOWLEDGE

The Code of Practice is not intended to be a 'bolt on' (Hull 1994, p.7), but integral to the teaching and learning of all curriculum subjects. All teachers need to work in collaboration, with the support and guidance of the named SENCo, to avoid a scenario where teachers are simply instructed how to deal with one child after another (Hanko 1990). Stakes and Hornby (1997) see the need for a co-ordinated and coherent effort, if the moral and ethical values held by the school as a whole are to be translated into practical management strategies. First, then, subject leaders must be aware of and understand whole-school values.

The system of a staged response to pupils in need of a Special Educational provision is to be co-ordinated by the SENCo, but, as Hull (1994) states, such a system can only operate effectively if all teachers are able to generate evidence and information enabling the monitoring and review of each pupil's IEP. Such a level of co-ordination requires set policies and procedures, with which a subject leader must be certain to facilitate and to enhance the teaching and learning of their own subject. Once again, the subject leader must be aware of the contribution their subject makes to a pupil's overall educational needs.

Activity 2.7   Tracking individual progress

In subject team meetings report on the performance, progress and behaviour of one pupil in detail. Invite suggestions how teachers might react to the evidence you present. Relate the outcomes to the pupil's *general* educational needs. In what ways does your learning subject contribute to the pupil's particular needs?

It is then for the SENCo to collate the views, judgements and teaching strategies across subject areas. From this informed position, the SENCo is able to discuss the possibility of adapting teaching and learning strategies, the deployment of specialist equipment and support to assist particular pupils. Evidently, from the first baseline assessment, through to planning and provision, and lastly the assessment of outcomes, all procedures must be manageable in terms of staff expertise, time and available resources. These institutional concerns are obviously essential forms of knowledge for the subject leader.

Baseline assessments must be useful. Lindsay (1993) recommends that they be accurate, valid and reliable, but also of use to subject teachers. If, for example, a pupil displays poor co-operative skills, the subject leader must be able to recommend teaching approaches which appeal to and support the learner within the context of the subject. It is through a sound knowledge of the range of teaching and learning styles which are applicable to the subject, and an awareness of which of these can be implemented by teaching staff, that subject provision can be matched to learners' needs.

Subject teachers are also required to identify pupils with particular needs, to gather evidence and to provide differentiated learning programmes to address learners' difficulties (DFE 1994). The subject leader has to appreciate what failure to achieve particular tasks or an inability to engage in learning activities actually means. Knowledge and understanding therefore include an appreciation of the impact of learning (content and processes) on the learner. Such a sophisticated process of assessment cannot be developed in isolation: subject teachers need to devise methods which fit into whole-school approaches. Hornby *et al.* (1995, p.47) have produced a checklist for assessment policies, in order that leaders and co-ordinators can review and evaluate existing procedures. The list is adapted in Activity 2.8.

Activity 2.8   Evaluating a whole-school assessment policy

Evaluate the school and subject assessment policy against the following criteria:

- Does data generated contribute to whole-school requirements?
- Does the assessment system identify and record success?
- Are teachers able to specify concerns?
- Do teachers collect relevant assessment information?
- Do the assessment records contribute towards the production of IEPs?
- Do IEPs set out learning difficulties?
- Do IEPs set out objectives and targets related to needs?
- Are targets given time-scales?
- Do IEPs identify key subject teachers?
- Do IEPs set out specific programmes?
- Do IEPs allow progress to be monitored and rewarded through subject teaching?
- Do IEPs set out effective teaching and learning strategies?
- Do IEPs specify the potential uses of specialist equipment and learning materials?

The outcome of successful assessment is therefore an individualised learning programme, broken down into component parts. First, the subject leader must know if the recommendations can be implemented by colleagues with or without support. Second, for the impact of classroom efforts to be appreciated fully, reference in teachers' plans should be made to National Curriculum levels, the range of strategies deployed, links with other subject areas (content and processes), how additional support will be used and how the impact of measures taken can be evaluated (SCAA 1996).

The content, processes and their effect on the learner in a broad educational sense need to be known and articulated, in order that the subject leader can contribute to the overall SEN provision.

All teachers need to respond to an IEP. Systems must be devised to allow for the dissemination of the content of an IEP. Bliss and Timbrell (1997, p.9) suggest three ways by which knowledge and understanding of an IEP can be achieved:

- pupils carry the plan from teacher to teacher and lesson to lesson
- subject leaders contribute to the development of IEPs, building on evidence generated by subject teachers
- departments draw up and work to their own IEPs, which relate to the more generic form

For primary teachers, this process is easier, but teachers will need to provide coverage of pupils' contributions and performance in all subjects. Whatever the method, subject leaders need to know and understand the system in order to be in a position to offer support.

SEN pupils on the register at Stage 2 or above, according to Farrell, should be following an 'objectives-based curriculum' (Farrell 1997, p.93). The objectives must be related to the core curriculum in order to guarantee equal access to a broad, balanced and relevant curriculum, and also to desired outcomes which are related to the individual's needs.

The core curriculum should include the development of cross-curricular skills, such as communication, social skills, and personal and moral development. Subject leaders need to audit the subject provision in order to appreciate the full educational benefits of their particular subject provision. Any such audit must be realistic, in terms of what actually happens in classrooms as opposed to the potential learning opportunities offered by colleagues. Inevitably the actual picture is ever-changing, as colleagues learn from experience and relevant professional development activities.

Westwood (1987, p.136) suggests that all subject teachers should contribute in the ways listed in Activity 2.9. Such a set of requirements does serve as a useful auditing tool. Re-phrasing of 'what a regular teacher needs to know' into questions directed at a subject leader enables an analysis of how well a subject team actually does address issues related to SEN. The range of teaching skills is vast. Wood (1984) has categorised these skills into assessment (diagnostic and formative), analysis, behaviour management, motivation, communication, evaluation and human relations. The audit questions in Activity 2.9 provide guidance on the classification of activities.

Activity 2.9   Auditing the subject provision for SEN

- How can course objectives be translated into specific individualised objectives?
- Can the content of the course be assessed in a diagnostic way?
- What measures are taken to integrate pupils with SEN?
- How are social skills developed through the subject?
- Are assessment tasks personalised?
- Do pupils develop self-management and independent learning skills?
- What communication exists between the subject team and SEN staff?
- Do you use support materials?
- How do/can you use adult assistance?
- How do you measure the quality of provision in the teaching and learning of your subject?

Wolfendale (1992) presents issues associated with provision and the need to give learning a purpose. Teachers need to understand the purpose of learning tasks in terms of what task completion can lead on to, and also what failure tells the teacher about the learner. Systems therefore need to be devised to record pupil performance in terms of their behaviour, attitude, progress and attainment. Simple marks in a mark-book are not sufficient:

> Records kept and regularly completed as an intrinsic part of the teaching process are the most economical way to obtain cumulative information about a child ...
>
> (Hull 1994, p.13)

Subject leaders need to advise colleagues about what to record, but also how data and information can be gathered. Wyllyams (1993) acknowledges the role of the support team in gathering records which assist in the individual planning of learning programmes. Notes on when support staff have to intervene to explain a task, remind of prior learning, address bad behaviour or refer to support material all serve a purpose in problem diagnosis. Observation of pupil behaviour to measure attention span, levels of concentration and application provides evidence of the nature of learning difficulties. Support staff can provide encouragement and immediate rewards with enthusiasm, in a way recommended by Farrell (1997). Knowing how to use support staff is an essential element of managing SEN provision in a subject department.

Activity 2.10   Using support staff to clarify pupils' learning difficulties

Ask a support teacher to make a note of every intervention they make to support a child over a series of lessons and to consider why the intervention was necessary. Discuss with the support teacher what action can be taken to avoid the need to intervene in the future.

Monitoring and assessment serve a real purpose if they contribute to future learning. Farrell (1997) recommends target-setting in the form of 'performance language'. Pupils should demonstrate learning through the completion of tasks related to the subject curriculum. Careful wording in the form of 'write', 'note', 'say', 'read', 'listen' etc. are more meaningful if pupils are able to attach the target to particular task components. Success at some of the demands must be recorded, even if the whole task is not successfully completed. Once again the subject curriculum has to be broken down into very small steps.

This degree of focused assessment can be achieved in part by support staff. However, subject teachers must also recognise their own expertise. The support staff also have a role to play in maintaining class discipline whilst subject teachers give time and attention to individual pupils. Good provision, therefore, requires an understanding of which activities for larger groups do not require specialist supervision.

Activity 2.11   Using learning support assistants to generate time for the subject specialist

Scan a scheme of work. Which activities/tasks do not require the supervising adult to have specialist subject knowledge? Could the activity be supervised by a learning support assistant?

The provision of clear instructions to support staff also requires an understanding of the theory underpinning the learning activities with which the assistant is assisting. Bloom's (1978) guidance for peer tutors is also applicable to learning support assistants. Subject leaders should, in collaboration with colleagues, articulate:

- clear directions on what to do and how to do it
- the uses of specific materials for specific tasks
- examples and models of good practice

and also offer opportunities to:

- practise under supervision
- modify the activity if necessary

Understanding the role of support teachers in the classroom is crucial. Knowing individual support staff's potential underpins any policy. Wyllyams (1993) propounds a four-faceted role for support staff which, if discussed with subject teachers, can provide useful information and ideas. These four functions are:

- representing the class teacher to pupils
- offering suggestions on behalf of pupils
- observing
- intervening to maintain the flow of a lesson

Suggestions for action to support pupils' learning will include the mention of specialist equipment. Any proposals should be considered by subject staff, particularly in view of Warnock's (1978) recommendation that access to the curriculum also includes access to a full range of equipment and resources. A knowledge of what equipment exists, and how it can be used, is valuable support for all subject teachers.

The DfEE (1997a) sees a role for the LEA in monitoring and improving schools' provision for pupils with SEN. The features of a good provision are noted by Stakes and Hornby (1997). Underpinning these characteristics are knowledge and understanding of how each is manifested and/or operated within the school. Subject leaders must understand the school's vision and strategies designed to meet the challenge of wide-ability classes. A sensitivity to the degree of autonomy enjoyed by individual teachers must be balanced against the recognition of a need for change. The potential and actual involvement of colleagues in ongoing development and change through the evaluation and analysis of assessment data is necessary to maintain and sustain the momentum of quality provision. Subject leaders need to know their curriculum, their staff and the procedures for the assessment and provision for pupils with SEN.

REFLECTIVE KNOWLEDGE

Much of what has been presented under decision and institutional knowledge is underpinned by the need for reflective knowledge. In SEN provision there are no blanket answers to questions and problems. Ware (1994) raises the question of whether all learners follow similar learning paths (which developmental curricula assume). Teachers do need to consider learners' learning styles and gauge the appropriateness of a step-by-step subject curriculum. The introduction of baseline assessments from September 1998, and the constant need for review and monitoring of progress, places assessment evidence at the core of strategies. Teaching and learning techniques are best developed as an outcome of analysis and choice based on pupils' needs (Mintzberg and Quinn 1991). Hanko recommends that staff work collaboratively and reflect in an informed way on developing a corporate and consistent approach to teaching pupils with SEN:

> As we saw, individual support consists of the staff group jointly exploring the opportunities that exist for them as individuals to meet special learning and adjustment needs in their classrooms through sensitive curricular adaptations.
>
> (Hanko 1990, p.139)

Taking account of the individual pupil perspective, how classroom activities and contexts of learning influence learning outcomes, and to what extent colleagues can assist, all require degrees of reflection. Stakes and Hornby point out, however, that:

> the quality of reflection depends upon a base knowledge for comparison and values. Increased awareness of SEN teaching and learning strategies and support mechanisms is therefore essential to improve the quality of special needs provision.
>
> (Stakes and Hornby 1997, p.144)

Subject specialists are best placed to reflect on evidence and subject leaders must be able to present a range of strategies and ideas as alternative solutions to problems which arise from the processes of reflection.

A knowledge of what can affect pupil performance is therefore essential, if ideas are to be generated to solve problems as they are perceived. Lindsay (1993) clarifies four key influences: background and ethnicity, home process (i.e. if teaching is undertaken at home), school and teacher variables (expectations, curriculum opportunity) and pupil variables (attitudes, personality). When such information is available, in conjunction with baseline assessment data, subject leaders are able to introduce institutional factors into the process of reflection. These factors include, according to Reason (1993), classroom organisation and ethos, curriculum content, formative assessment procedures and assessment of the potential for active participation by learners.

The need for reflection is increased by the obvious series of possible conflicts inherent in the policy of inclusion. The policy must demand the promotion of a broad, balanced and relevant curriculum, and pupils should only be withdrawn (or the curriculum modified) in exceptional cases. At the same time, a degree of alternative provision should be made for pupils with Special Needs, which (as Hornby *et al.* suggest) may include:

> a range of teaching strategies, differentiation and special arrangements such as in class support and withdrawal.
>
> (Hornby *et al.* 1995, p.21)

Subject leaders do, therefore, need to consider to what extent SEN pupils share equal access to the subject curriculum with other pupils.

A second conflict arises from the comparison between the outcomes of cognitive tests and attainment in relation to National Curriculum tasks and tests. Cognitive tests generate scores which are often regarded as a measure of potential. National Curriculum-related performance measures attainment. When both sets of scores are standardised, there is an opportunity to gauge (Tod *et al.* 1998 claim) whether individuals are in fact fulfilling their potential.

Activity 2.12   Using assessment data to identify learning needs

1   Relate (with SEN) a pupil's scores in cognitive tests to the class average.
2   Relate the pupil's scores in National Curriculum-related tasks/tests in your subject to the class average.
3   Relate the pupil's National Curriculum scores in other subjects to the class average.

In which part of the curriculum do they have most problems? Can you conclude that it is methodology or content which poses difficulties? How can you use this data to improve provision in your subject?

Reflection on an individual basis may well lead to crude conclusions that pupils' and/or teachers' expectations are too high or too low, yet many would argue that too many assumptions are made. The relationship between learning ability and intelligence is questionable: low scores in cognitive tests do not signal, necessarily, an innate disability, but might indicate poor concentration skills, bad memory skills or simply a lack of interest. The greater the evidence-base in terms of what pupils can and cannot do, the greater the opportunity to make objective decisions and judgements.

Teachers should be encouraged to experiment with a range of strategies and Gross's (1993) suggestion that staff list aspects of current practice which are in accord with the values and principles underpinning the school's SEN policy is extremely helpful. SCAA (1996) takes the suggestion further, arguing for strategies and techniques to be evaluated in terms of their usefulness in accounting for differences in age, maturity and ability. Farrell (1997) urges that all teachers should experiment and monitor the effectiveness of techniques with particular types of children. The range of variables is, of course, enormous and SCAA (1996) provides a useful – if long – list of variables. Subject leaders would gain from examining subject-specific strategies which lend themselves to the categories identified in Activity 2.13 and using such information as a basis for how provision can be adapted to suit particular SEN pupils.

Activity 2.13   Investigating opportunities for differentiation

Scan these schemes. Complete the middle column by inserting the ideas you develop. The left-hand column lists alternative strategies. Refer to a pupil's IEP and discuss with the SENCo which particular activities will support the pupil's learning.

Range of strategies	Subject-specific activities (alternative means of fulfilling teaching objectives)	Tick if relevant to particular pupil
Separate tasks		
Group work with individual roles		
Didactic approach		
Discovery methods		
Varied types of response: verbal non-verbal movement		
Varied use of time		
Using support staff		
Using pupils as a resource		
Simplifying instructions		
Clarifying objectives		
Using range of equipment		
Encouraging and supporting		
Celebrating success, step by step		
Providing support material		

The process of analysis, reflection and action in order to monitor and adapt practice to suit learners' needs is reliant upon the constant generation of evidence. Farrell (1997) commends behavioural methods as the process of learning is observable. The analysis of behaviourist process by Farrell concludes that there are three key factors which influence the behaviour of the learner. First, evidence must be available for teachers to recognise 'antecedents'. These include prior learning experiences and achievements. Records passing from teacher to teacher and from school to school should include details of the content of learning programmes as well as pupil's reactions and attitudes to particular teaching and learning methods. There is no doubt that some generalisations can be made, which will influence the new teacher in terms of Farrell's second key feature: 'contexts' for learning. The contexts will include grouping of learners, ground rules, pace, variety of activities and the level at which the teacher should pitch lessons. Third, in evaluating lessons, teachers will want to note the 'consequences' of learning in terms of behaviour, knowledge and skills.

Reflection on the process will not result in generating causal links, but is likely to produce ideas which could be related to different pupils and different classes. In this way teachers can plan in a way that ensures that:

> the situation is seen in terms of the need to modify teaching strategies in a non-threatening way, rather than as an indication of the innate disability of the child.
>
> (Farrell 1997, p.143)

A criticism of a behaviourist approach is that learners find it difficult to generalise what is learnt, and cannot transfer skills and knowledge from one context to another (Farrell 1997). It is crucial that opportunities are built in at relevant moments to allow for interactional learning. By engaging in problem-solving activities and peer group discussions, teachers are able to identify learning. Reflection is necessary in that:

- appropriate moments for full learning need to be identified
- pupils need to be made aware that learning has taken place and been demonstrated
- teachers may need to intervene to support learning

Observation of teaching by other specialists supports this process of reflection. Several researchers (e.g. Tizard and Hughes 1984, Wood 1988) note that although due attention appears to be paid to (for example) teachers' talk, the impact on learners is not great. What teachers say, and what they do, do not always match. Observation allows for the focused discussion of the impact of different strategies on pupils and also generates evidence for inclusion at future reviews of IEPs.

Activity 2.14   Observing colleagues

Observe a colleague and make a note of all the different activities which take place during the lesson. Afterwards discuss with your colleague how the completion of one activity assisted with the next. Is your perception the same as that of your colleague? How can you improve the consistency and continuity in lessons?

Lewis (1991, p.3) suggests the types of evidence which inform practice and which are 'observable'. The types include:

- activity types which help the pupil to concentrate

- activities which the pupil values
- activities in which the child is confident
- preference for particular resources and materials
- most productive time
- impact of different groupings
- preferred methods (teaching and learning)
- preference for noise and quiet

Reason (1993, p.5) adds other elements to the list, arguing that child-centred activities allow for teacher observation. She adds:

- level of involvement
- ability to share and co-operate
- level of dialogue

Teaching and developing policies to support pupils with SEN is, to a degree, a balancing act. To ensure a sense of equity and fairness, Wolfendale (1992, p.53) suggests that the constructs listed in Activity 2.15 merit consideration and reflection. There is no doubt that generally applicable answers are not to be forthcoming, but, for a subject leader, knowing what merits consideration, reflection and noting is crucial.

Activity 2.15   Personal approaches to dealing with SEN

Compare and contrast your approach to dealing with several pupils with SEN. Ask colleagues to undergo a similar task.

The constructs contain two extreme positions. Circle a number which best represents your views in relation to a particular pupil.

Integrate into mainstream	1	2	3	4	Differentiate to the point of providing a separate curriculum
Develop strategies which work for you	1	2	3	4	Co-operate and collaborate with colleagues
Breadth and balance	1	2	3	4	Focus on particular learning skills
Help the individual meet own interest	1	2	3	4	Focus on socialising
Simplify language	1	2	3	4	Perseverance with subject-specific terminology
Variety to maintain interest	1	2	3	4	Develop concentration skills

SEN is concerned with providing for individuals. Individuals – if the provision is effective – develop and change. The reflective knowledge base is therefore ever-changing. Teachers will need to react and respond to new situations, and subject leaders should note and reward reflective knowledge as it is generated in order to provide a support framework for colleagues in their teams.

CONCLUSION

OfSTED (1996) notes improvements in SEN provision and some of the judgements made include better staff awareness of SEN, more effective planning and provision, identification and assessment, and improved use of IEPs. The report does also note, however, room for further improvement in terms of strategic and operational issues. SEN provision requires the involvement of all staff and, particularly, assessment arrangements demand support from subject teachers. In order to monitor provision, and to develop systems to generate and communicate relevant information, subject leaders must be involved. Values and attitudes should permeate the whole of SEN work and few would argue with Farrell's view that:

> All professionals ... should interact with people with learning difficulties in a manner which promotes dignity and respect, and this comes from providing a curriculum similar to other people of the same age.
>
> (Farrell 1997, p.103)

It is crucial that subject leaders are aware of the types of problems manifested by pupils, how school systems can offer support and how, through subject teaching, many aspects of the curriculum (in its broadest sense) can be made accessible. The aim is integration of SEN pupils into the school without running the risk of narrowing learning experiences down to perceived needs in terms of preparing learners for the next stage or employment. The arguments against a purely utilitarian curriculum apply aptly to learners with SEN. All learners have an entitlement to a broad, balanced and relevant curriculum, and the need to celebrate success at every level is a positive way of encouraging inclusion. Subject leaders, therefore, need to have an understanding of policies and procedures and also to generate and act upon knowledge which emerges from the experience of working with pupils with learning difficulties.

3 The place and value of cross- and extra-curricular work

INTRODUCTION

The Education Reform Act (DES 1988b) states clearly that one of the aims of a National Curriculum is to provide a preparation for the opportunities, responsibilities and experiences of adult life. The National Curriculum Council (NCC 1992a, 1992b) reminds readers that there is a statutory requirement to provide balance, breadth and relevance through an education which enables spiritual, cultural, moral, mental and physical development of individual pupils, and also of society as a whole. Lawton's (1983) studies of the curriculum led to the identification of three types of curriculum: classical humanism, progressivism and reconstructionism – he advocates the latter as the most valuable in modern times. He recognises reconstructionism to be 'society-centred', which implies that relevant knowledge must be transmitted so that individual learners can develop the skills and knowledge in order for all to live harmoniously within an ordered society. In addition a relevant curriculum, West (1995) argues, must be of immediate interest and meet what pupils see as their present and prospective needs. This complicated view of the curriculum therefore contains multifarious aims:

- to equip pupils with the tools of learning (e.g. numeracy, literacy and oracy)
- to provide opportunities for practical and realistic application of knowledge
- to assist pupils to learn how to co-operate
- to set high expectations
- to enable the development of self-esteem, self-confidence and self-discipline

(Adapted from 'Curriculum Guidance 1', NCC 1990a, p.2)

Considerable emphasis was placed, in the early 1990s, on cross-curricular dimensions, themes and skills as a means of ensuring a full curriculum entitlement. However as Inman and Buck (1995, p. xi) point out, little mention has been made of such work since the Dearing Review (1994) recommended the 'slimming down' of the National Curriculum. Theorists such as Nias *et al.*

(1992) have always seen the 'curriculum' as a comprehensive term embracing content and teaching and learning methodologies. Even the DES (1989a) noted that foundation and core subjects constitute the minimum scope of the curriculum, and that cross- and extra-curricular work should figure in schemes of work which, in combination, comprise the whole curriculum. The NCC is very clear that the core and foundation subjects alone are 'not enough' (NCC 1990a, p.90).

An adequate curriculum is, then, the combined efforts of the core and foundation subjects, and also the provision of cross-curricular dimensions, themes and skills. It is, then, imperative to understand that:

> the full potential of the ten subjects will only be realised if, in curriculum planning, schools seek to identify the considerable overlaps, which inevitably exist in content and skills.
>
> ('Curriculum Guidance 3', NCC 1990a, p.3)

For the subject leader, then, there is first a need to recognise how the particular subject links with other core and foundation subjects, cross-curricular themes, skills and dimensions, and also with other agencies which have an impact on pupil's learning (see Figure 3.1).

The whole curriculum is complex and in need of careful planning. Subject leaders need to be aware of and to understand the influence of their subject on learning as a whole. The whole curriculum must serve a purpose, if this understanding is to be achieved across all subjects. Hicks (1995) argues that at the core of the curriculum is conquering nature and industrialisation which runs the risk of creating unbalanced and one-dimensional people. Orr (1992) prefers a post-modern interpretation of the curriculum, one which aims to connect, liberate and empower individuals. Certainly, Inman and Buck (1995) argue in favour of preparing learners for the future in terms of providing opportunities to learn decision-making skills through experimental learning. Young (1995) dispels the myth that education serves a purely economic purpose by asserting that there is no hard research evidence to link educational and economic success.

Burke (1995), on the other hand, argues that at the core of the curriculum should be the personal development of the learner, that increasing self-esteem and confidence is a means by which learners can take responsibility in society. Personal growth requires an understanding of societal and even global contexts, which consists of not just the absorption of knowledge, but also the skills of critical analysis and application. It is through gaining and using knowledge that the learner can make important decisions and also learn to respect the autonomy of other individuals and cultures.

This apparently liberal interpretation of the whole curriculum is not divorced from the National Curriculum. The core and foundation subjects provide essential knowledge, but it is through the application of knowledge that the learner can develop as a person. It is for this reason that methodology is so

Figure 3.1 Subject links with the whole curriculum

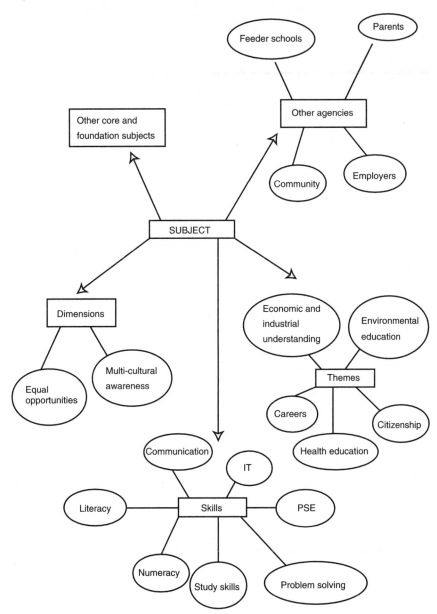

important, and that quality of learning should not be sacrificed in the name of equality of outcomes (Riley 1994). To place 'process' only, though, at the heart of the curriculum is to ignore the reality of the world outside school. Learning to co-operate is essential, but to focus only on this one aspect of education for citizenship is not a good preparation for induction into a competitive outside world. While the post-Dearing National Curriculum has not retained such an emphasis on cross-curricular elements, their influence – Inman and Buck (1995) insist – must not be underestimated. Breadth, balance and relevance include the understanding and application of knowledge of contemporary society, but also that pupils are prepared for entry into a future society through the development of learning skills and an appreciation of social values. We cannot escape the fact that values are asserted through the selection of content and guidance which pupils are given in terms of social and moral behaviour. Schools provide guidance and provision, both of which demand that values are asserted. As Richardson states:

> Schools are not powerless; they are not doomed to be mere victims or pawns, nor bound merely to breed dependency and passivity amongst their pupils.
>
> (Richardson 1992, p.181)

DECISION KNOWLEDGE

As middle managers, subject leaders are bound to implement statutory orders within their own subject areas. As leaders, they are entitled to interpret the orders in order to provide learners with the skills to use knowledge productively. The National Commission on Education (1993) noted that all workers need knowledge and applied intelligence for Britain's success, and also for individuals' own sense of success in society. To achieve this goal, those organising the curriculum must recognise the place, value and potential of all that is contained within their own sphere of influence.

It is of course important to bear in mind the NCC's guidance:

> No single subject can provide the full range of knowledge and understanding required.
>
> (NCC 1990b, p.9)

If personal development is at the heart of the learning experience, leaders must recognise that learners need to understand their own identity and culture before broadening the context. Personal and social education (PSE) therefore assists in the preparation for adult life. Adult life, as the Swann Committee Report (DES 1985a) claims, involves living in a multi-cultural society. Harrison and Rainey (1994) insist, therefore, that equal opportunities and multi-cultural education should play a major role in PSE. Subject leaders must be certain that teaching approaches promote tolerance and understanding, and avoid stereotyping which can easily be associated with their own subject. Lee (1996) quotes the DES report *Better Schools* (DES 1985b) when he explains that science education is concerned with developing skills and attitudes which are transferable throughout the curriculum. Transferability must involve a sense of equity and justice if racial and gender stereotyping is to be avoided.

Activity 3.1 The transferability of skills

Note activities contained within teachers' repertoires in your own subject area, which help pupils to develop strategies for:

- reading
- writing
- listening
- speaking
- decision-making
- problem-solving
- use of technology
- numeracy

Consider how the development of strategies and process skills might assist the pupil in other subject areas.

National Curriculum cross-curricular dimensions build on such themes. Health Education, Bennet and Pumfrey (1994) explain, should make explicit health issues which, if left implicit, can lead to bias and prejudice. An examination of foreign eating habits, for example, can therefore open up opportunities for enrichment, rather than close the doors of racism. Diet can, of course, provide an insight into alternative faiths, values, beliefs and cultures. Careers education, too, has generic qualities (Inman and Buck 1995) which also permeate the whole curriculum. Decision-making and problem-solving are cross-curricular skills, which when placed in the context of careers education have immediate and obvious relevance. Education for citizenship is concerned with the preparation of pupils to participate in the family, the community and pluralist society.

Smith (1994) adds a further relationship. People must interact with nature and the environment, and environmental education allows for the development of a concern and sense of responsibility regarding the impact of human decisions on the environment. Individual pupils must, therefore, be aware of their own impact on global warming and the destruction of the ozone layer, for example.

Survival in contemporary society, as much as in the future, relies on individuals understanding basic economic concepts and being able to base economic decisions on costs and benefits (NCC 1990b). Economic and industrial under-standing is part of personal development and can be taught through all foundation subjects.

Activity 3.2   Cross-curricular dimensions

Which topics within the subject curriculum contribute directly to:

- economic and industrial understanding
- health education
- careers education and guidance
- environmental education
- education for citizenship?

The cross-curricular dimensions provide a context for learning, an opportunity for learners to apply new knowledge to immediately recognisable problems. Decision knowledge is first and foremost knowing what is meant by 'cross-curricular' – in terms of skills, themes and dimensions. Each and every subject should therefore address the issues. Indeed, subject leaders would undoubtedly claim that their own subject does just that. What is, of course, important is that the curriculum coverage is systematic, one which reinforces 'a common school viewpoint, which will guarantee a consistent approach' (NCC 1990a, p.4).

First, in one sense, 'cross-curricular' is the aspect of education which involves all teachers, regardless of the subject taught. The NCC (1990f) places morals and values at the centre, aspects which can be applied to all areas of the curriculum. Teachers should be concerned through their subject teaching with the development of independent thought, respect for others and for reasoned argument, a concern for human rights and decision-making. It is, then, for subject leaders to examine the provision of their own subject to ensure that such attitudes prevail.

Activity 3.3   Subject provision and personal development

Does the methodology within your subject area contribute to:

- the development of independent thought
- respect for others
- respect for reasoned argument
- concern for human rights?

Please specify other aspects of personal development that you feel are relevant.

Give examples of activity types which are commonly deployed.

Second, the content of subject syllabuses must allow for the themes of health, the environment, citizenship, economic and industrial understanding and careers to be covered in full through a combined effort with other subject areas. Third, the skills of communication, numeracy, study skills, problem-solving and use of IT need to be developed if the concepts of rights, duties and responsibility are to be developed.

The role of subject leaders in primary and secondary schools may well diverge at this point. A project-based approach to curriculum coverage is often favoured in the earlier Key Stages (SCDC 1987). The task for subject leaders in such cases is to plan, implement and monitor the role of the subject within the project. The risk of such an approach is that continuity and progression within the subject can be lost as the focus is on processes and knowledge more readily associated with the cross-curricular dimension for teachers of secondary pupils, although the reverse usually is the case. Evaluation procedures might involve the consideration of how effective each type of approach is.

Activity 3.4   Assuring progression in the subject within topic-based teaching (primary subject leaders)

Write the title of a topic in the centre circle. In the outer boxes, detail subject-related tasks which enable pupils to progress in the subject. You do not need to complete every box.

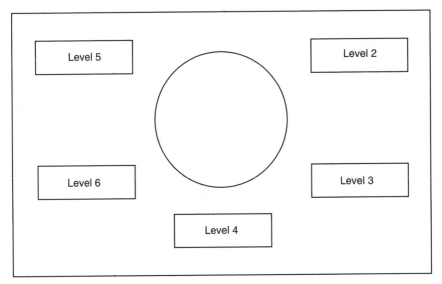

Compare the outcomes with a fellow subject leader.

Activity 3.5   Auditing a unit of work in the subject in terms of cross-curricular dimensions

Write the title of a unit of work in the centre circle. In each of the outer boxes, demonstrate how the unit contributes to the cross-curricular dimensions.

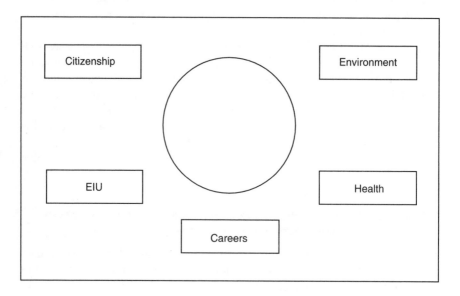

Compare the outcomes with a fellow subject leader.

The multi-disciplinary organisation of the curriculum can lead to aspects of a 'common' curriculum (SCDC 1987) being lost. What is required by all subject leaders is, of course, a detailed curriculum audit, in order that subject content, skills development and opportunities for personal growth can be structured and sequenced. It is essential that subject leaders recognise and can articulate the interrelationship of their own subject with other statutory curriculum requirements.

These interrelationships are complicated. Strands of the curriculum, however, must cross at certain points. Inman and Buck recommend simplifying the issue:

> Central to our understanding of pupils' personal development, then, must be the classification of the present society in which pupils live, and the nature of the future society in which young people will be adults.
>
> (Inman and Buck 1995, p.87)

Subjects should share a purpose and be built on common values, aims and attitudes; for pupils to recognise the coherence of a learning programme there must be co-ordination. Inevitably the content of different subject areas will differ. However, Nixon (1992) points out that the whole curriculum is an amalgam of method and content. The co-ordination of method is much simpler. Teaching styles and approaches for each subject must be overt and understood by teachers from all subject areas. The provision of a full range across subjects is, of course, desirable (see Activities 3.1, 3.2 and 3.3). Nasta (1994) presents a model for curriculum planning, which serves to articulate the need for a course, as well as aims, objectives, methods and means of assessing. Cross-reference between subjects is therefore made easier.

The co-ordination of content is more complicated, but is nonetheless possible. If subject leaders are able to identify points of time when key issues of education (physical, sexual, moral, social, spiritual and vocational) are being covered, then adaptations to sequencing of learning can be made to promote greater consistency and coherence. It is subject leaders, as the authors of the whole curriculum, who should be aware of colleagues' subject content.

It is with this knowledge and understanding that subject leaders can then consider a range of models of implementation of cross-curricular dimensions. The NCC Curriculum Guidance booklets, which remain at present the only source of guidance, present several methods, not as alternatives but as possible complementary approaches. Interestingly, the NCC also provide lists of the advantages and disadvantages of each approach. The assumption is that a combination of methods maximises the advantages. Each approach does, of course, require the subject leader in each case to have the knowledge and expertise to assure effective implementation of both the subject and the cross-curricular dimension. Figure 3.2 represents this relationship between models of implementation and subject leaders' knowledge.

Figure 3.2   The relationship between models of implementation and subject leaders' knowledge

Model of implementation	Knowledge required by subject leader
Permeating the whole curriculum	An understanding of continuity and progression within the cross-curricular dimensions
Separately timetabled subject	An awareness of the impact of the cross-curricular dimension on the subject, and vice versa
Part of PSE	An awareness of the PSE programme in order that concepts and skills can be introduced at appropriate times
Part of a pastoral / tutorial programme	As above
Through opportunities arising from other activities	An awareness of how and when the subject can contribute to the programme of learning

A thorough understanding of the impact of teaching materials used is also of great importance. Plackett (1995) recognises the need to relate reading levels contained within textbooks and other teaching materials to pupils' levels of literacy.

Activity 3.6   Scrutinising teaching materials

Examine texts used in your subject which you use at given National Curriculum levels. Ask a colleague from another subject area to do the same. Compare the levels of literacy and numeracy in each subject. Do your own teaching materials appear more or less demanding? Can they be adapted?

Coping strategies deployed in one subject must be transferable to others if the full impact of learning is to be achieved. This simplistic example is also applicable in more abstract domains. OfSTED (1995b) guidance recommends inspectors to seek examples of spiritual development through approaches to teaching the appreciation of art, literature, music and history. Similarly, moral development is contained in the representations of human relationships, resources, the environment and the impact of technology on the quality of life.

All planned experiences represent the whole curriculum, but pupils do also learn from unplanned experiences. An appreciation of the influence of daily routines and behaviour management practices or, for example, health education is of interest to all teachers. The implementation of subject-related policies therefore requires close scrutiny. Subject leaders need to develop policies with learning in mind.

The inclusion of work experience on the curriculum of all secondary schools since the days of the Technical and Vocational Education Initiative (TVEI) has highlighted the value of extra-curricular and other 'out of classroom' activities (Lee 1996). Participation in major cross-curricular events improves the status and profile of curriculum subjects, through pupils' first-hand experience of the relevance of learning. Subject leaders ignore trips, outings, exchanges, industry days and other such activities at their peril.

Activity 3.7   Cross- and extra-curricular events

Look through the school calendar. How can 'subject time' be devoted to preparing pupils for whole school events such as:

- sports day
- religious services
- careers fairs
- outings and visits
- school plays and musical productions

- presentation days/evenings
- industry days?

    Please add to the list.

Participation in and the organisation of such events do carry considerable responsibilities. Subject leaders do need to know set procedures for the planning of extra-curricular events. Schools must have policies and procedures to protect teachers and pupils, and also to assure quality provision and safety. Subject leaders must be aware of policies on payment for trips, travel arrangements, insurance, supervision, discipline, safety and health issues, and liaison with parents and the local community. Activity 3.8 is designed to assist subject leaders in discovering both legal and institutional policies, procedures and requirements.

Activity 3.8 Legal requirements and institutional policies for extra-curricular activities

Read the school's policies and procedures for extra-curricular activities and summarise the key points under the following headings:

- payment
- travel
- insurance
- supervision
- discipline
- safety
- health information
- itinerary
- liaison with parents
- reporting to the governing body

    Add any other issues of importance stemming from your reading.

INSTITUTIONAL KNOWLEDGE

The distinction between decision knowledge and institutional knowledge is not fully clear in relation to cross-curricular concerns. The subject leader is compelled to know and understand in outline what is delivered, and how, in other subject areas without being a specialist. It is, therefore, inevitable that the subject leader's understanding will represent the specialist interpretation of colleagues. Indeed a detailed and impartial view of other subject curricula is not necessary; it is the actual practice which provides the whole school curriculum with an 'internal coherence' (Nixon 1992, p.57). What is necessary is an understanding of how the curriculum is understood by the learner. Nias *et al.* point out:

> A school is not, in fact, a monolithic organisation. Rather it is a composite of many different parts (people, buildings, teams and groups, beliefs and values) which all need to be accommodated or reconciled before they fit together. The 'whole school' needs to be understood in terms of the complexity and number of its constituent parts.
>
> (Nias *et al.* 1992, p.216)

The overlap and repetition within the curriculum is not, however, a weakness. The NCC's 'Curriculum Guidance 1' (1990a) states simply that decisions need to be made if the repetition of themes and content is to lead to reinforcement rather than conflict. Teacher co-operation is indeed a way forward, and one means of crystallising ideas and combining effort is through an input into the school development plan and key policies. Indeed, Verma and Pumfrey (1994) argue that PSE can and should have a unifying effect on a school. To have the personal development of the learner at the centre of the curriculum facilitates a process of curriculum audit. Cross-curricular skills, themes and dimensions are all part and parcel of pupils' personal growth. Understanding how and when others contribute to a single strand of educational development provides a structure and direction to the curriculum.

Activity 3.9   The subject contribution to PSE

Read through your school's policy and schemes of work for PSE. Having identified key aspects, consider in what way your subject makes a unique contribution and also how it contributes partially to the fulfilment of the aims of PSE.

Nias *et al.* conducted research which contained the conclusion that headteachers recognise in their staff a wish to 'do the best for the individual child' (Nias *et al.* 1992, p.37). Such a motivation transcended, it seems, an interest in the subject at primary school level. The challenge for subject leaders is to offer support and guidance to colleagues to enable this to happen. The cross-curricular themes can provide this framework. It is through providing a context for subject work that the themes and skills can be developed. Subject leaders, therefore, have to ascertain staff interests and expertise in order to channel their efforts into the appropriate dimension. A detailed audit then provides a picture in terms of appropriate balance. As middle managers, subject leaders then need to negotiate between themselves how best to fill any gaps.

Verma and Pumfrey (1994) note the complexity of the task of co-ordination. Identifying the part a subject can play in each cross-curricular theme is not difficult, indeed the Curriculum Guidance booklets provide many examples. The challenge is to provide consistency, coherence and continuity. It is not enough to identify when topics touch upon cross-curricular dimensions. Subject leaders must relate the engagement with the content to skill development. In this way teachers are encouraged to be 'connective' as opposed to 'insular' specialists (Young 1995, p.170) (see Activity 3.5).

For primary teachers the issue is often the reverse – identifying the subject-based outcomes in topic work (see Activity 3.6). The problem, however, of continuity and coherence remains the same:

> Although sometimes of high quality, topic work more often than not lacks continuity and progression, or any serious attempt to ensure that adequate time and attention are given to the elements said to comprise the curriculum.
>
> (HMI 1988, p.11)

The school must therefore provide the curriculum with a structure. Subject leaders must be aware of this and recognise how messages conveyed to learners through teaching styles, pupil–teacher relationships and the informal life of the school, must be explicitly affirmed elsewhere in the curriculum.

Activity 3.10   Learning through the informal life of the school

Observe some colleagues in your subject area. Consider to what extent the following contribute to pupils' levels of response, progress and attainment:

- behaviour management
- teaching and learning styles
- pupil–teacher interaction
- teacher–pupil interaction
- pupil–pupil interaction
- opportunities to take responsibility
- homework policy

In terms of skills, attitudes and values, schools must practise what they teach. As 'citizenship' encourages active participation in the community, the school as a community must offer pupils the opportunity to become involved and to take responsibility for decision-making. Decision-making, respect for group rules and active involvement also feature as aspects to be inspected by OfSTED as part of the 'Spiritual, Moral, Social, Cultural and Personal' dimension of education (OfSTED 1995a). Broadbent (1995) emphasises the need to build relationships with adults, the need for exploration of values and beliefs and of how people reach decisions as key aspects of moral education. Plackett (1995) urges all teachers to take responsibility for children's development of language-use as a tool for learning.

The subject leader's interest must extend beyond the content of the curriculum. The impact of staff behaviour on learning is much wider than in the classroom alone. Any review, therefore, of provision should, as the Kent Curriculum Support Unit (1992) recommends, contain an audit of:

- staff expertise and interest
- staff needs
- curriculum coverage and continuity
- pupil access and experiences
- school policy
- resources and materials

The danger of separate reviews is that it can lead to what Inman and Buck refer to as 'bureaucratic integration':

> Connective integration accounts for the impact of the curriculum on individual learners. Subject leaders will do well to track individual learners in an attempt to identify commonality and conflict in terms of curricular provision.
>
> (Inman and Buck 1995, p.xiv)

REFLECTIVE KNOWLEDGE

The examination of the whole curriculum has involved a consideration of the overall educational intentions and the place of cross-curricular skills, themes and dimensions as a means of achieving this end. The synoptic view of general purposes, underpinned by values, serves a useful function as a means by which the effectiveness of methods can be evaluated. The cross-curricular dimensions and themes have the potential to be political 'hot potatoes'. Burke reminds us that: 'Education is not and can never be neutral' (Burke 1995, p.7). Evaluation of the curriculum must be ongoing, therefore, and judgements should be based on whether values, beliefs and attitudes are or are not being reinforced.

The Kent Curriculum Support Unit (1992) reminds teachers that whole-curriculum planning should transcend subject boundaries and that reference to cross-curricular themes serves to provide all teaching with a clear direction and purpose. Reflecting on whether the cross-curricular objectives are being met on a regular basis is to generate reflective knowledge. Subject leaders need to monitor learning in terms of performance in and enjoyment of the subject, but also on behalf of the whole-school curriculum planners.

This evaluation role is not simple. As Lynch (1992) remarks, society outside school is ever-changing. Given the responsibility of curriculum planners to offer a preparation for future adult life, social changes must be taken into account.

Lynch notes six key changes which have occurred in the last decade alone, which inevitably alter the perception of future adult life:

- greater democracy
- a decline in East/West conflict
- greater competition for world resources
- environmental decline
- more attempts to solve Third World problems
- the increasing importance of education

To these we can add the greater significance of the European dimension and the increasing importance of information technology. It is against this background that the relevance and breadth of education must be appraised.

Activity 3.11   Plus ça change ...

Which of the following influence the content and processes which are adopted within your subject:

- the decline in East/West conflict?
- greater competition for world resources?
- environmental decline?
- more attempts to solve Third World problems?
- the increasing importance of education?
- the European dimension?
- the importance of information technology?

To what extent should such issues influence the curriculum?

There have also been lessons to be learnt from the recent past. The TVEI project was designed to increase learners' employability and Lee (1996) claims that the more student-centred approaches associated with the project increased motivation and improved personal social and communication skills. It is precisely this type of investigation which generates knowledge which should inform future planning of subject curricula. Day *et al.* (1993) are more specific in their claims. They equate intellectual growth with confidence, realism, problem-solving, reflection, collaboration and peer-centred planning and discussion. The evaluation of teaching and learning clearly generates data for planners (subject leaders) to reflect on.

Cross-curricular approaches and discussions of curriculum overlap among teachers themselves also give rise to creativity and new ideas. Gorman comments:

Discussion of values and exchanging views on controversial issues is suitable subject matter for cross-curricular work on specific Attainment Targets.

(Gorman 1994, p.112)

Teachers discussing content with non-specialist colleagues are inevitably productive. Again, advice from the Kent Curriculum Support Unit actively encourages cross-subject discussions, which it claims lead to:

more harmony and revealed hidden talents. … More cross-curricular work could utilise hidden staff resources and skills.

(Kent Curriculum Support Unit 1992, p.18)

Opportunities to discuss and to work alongside each other are therefore productive. Subject leaders need to provide opportunities for this to occur and should also provide a forum for presenting the outcomes of such collaborative work.

There is, of course, a need to structure such discussions and projects. The NCC's 'Curriculum Guidance 3' (1990a, p.10) offers advice in the form of sequenced questions which have been adapted in Figure 3.3.

Figure 3.3   Planning collaborative projects

- Where do cross-curricular dimensions and themes appear in the curriculum?
- Where are the gaps?
- Where is there duplication?
- Is there a place for a co-ordinated approach?
- Where should the specific responsibility for a collaborative project lie?

Are the essential subject components embodied within the project?

The responses to such questions, will inevitably broaden and enhance teachers' understanding. The implementation and completion of a project or co-ordinated approach to covering cross-curricular elements must be evaluated. A similar list of pertinent questions, drawn and adapted from a structured framework provided by NCC's 'Curriculum Guidance 3', can be seen in Figure 3.4.

Figure 3.4   Evaluating collaborative projects

- Have the objectives been met?
- What were the successes/failures?

- What changes could be made to overcome the weaknesses in the approach?
- Is the time-scale realistic? Can the pace be accelerated?
- Is the breadth and balance accessible to *all* pupils?
- Is there any other data/information which will inform developments?

Knowing how to generate useful data and understanding the significance of the outcomes is, of course, reflective knowledge.

Activity 3.12   Planning and/or evaluating collaborative projects

Plan, implement and evaluate a cross-curricular project using the structured questions in Figures 3.3 and 3.4.

The approach, this far, is teacher- or at least adult-centred. Consideration must be given to the pupil perspective. Day *et al.* (1993) recognise the need for pupils to feel confident, to have high self-esteem and to enjoy lessons. Teachers of all subjects should consider the place of different stimuli within their own subject. Enquiry work on the place of, for example, role plays, songs, poems, visits and presentations by members of the local community must take place. Teachers of all subjects have much to learn from the impact on learning of activities associated with other subject areas. Activity 3.1 provides categories for activities, which subject leaders can share. There is evidently a need for subject leaders to familiarise themselves with the aims, content and methods contained within the schemes of work in other subject areas.

Such research is less demanding for primary teachers who often teach a full range of subjects. Nevertheless, the task is not simply one of familiarisation, but also one of justifying the teaching and learning techniques in a broad educational sense. Once again, the completion of this research is facilitated by relating the justifications to the cross-curricular themes and dimensions. OfSTED recommend to inspectors that judgements of subject provision should be based on:

- whether the provision promotes intellectual, physical and personal development
- the impact of learning on equality of opportunity
- whether provision is enriched by extra-curricular activities
- the impact on the subject curriculum of careers education
- the effectiveness of study as a preparation for future education and training

(Adapted from OfSTED 1995b, p.78)

CONCLUSION

Young comments:

> Making personal and social development a whole school curriculum priority for all staff places new demands on senior managers and teachers, especially those whose training and experience has been as subject specialists.
>
> (Young 1995, p.169)

Subject leaders must lead the way. The whole curriculum does not imply adding to subject teachers' load, but individual subjects must be seen to make their own contribution to a single whole-school curriculum. Undoubtedly the provision for the key skills of reading, writing, speaking and listening is assessed by OfSTED and subject leaders need to be aware of the full implications of this. 'Reading', for example, includes the reading of maps, charts, graphs, tables, diagrams and even foreign languages (Plackett 1995). The use of computers must take place in all subject areas and teachers need to vary methodological approaches to suit all learners' needs. Cross-curricular learning does take place whether it is planned or not. The most effective means of co-ordinating the approach are to make use of the published cross-curricular skills themes and dimensions as points of reference in planning and evaluation documents. Subject leaders are curriculum planners and monitors, and consequently need to plan all aspects of learning as well as to organise the contents of their own subject areas.

Part II
Strategic leadership and the improvement of the school

The contribution of the subject and the subject leader

Teaching & learning with Understanding.

INTRODUCTION

This section of the book is devoted to examining the way in which staff that lead and support subject areas can and do contribute to the overall improvement and effectiveness of the school. We will argue that successful subject leaders act strategically in that they work systematically over a period of time to achieve long-term goals that are shared with all subject staff and are congruent with the overall aim of their school. We begin this process by briefly exploring some basic principles relating to how schools perform as organisations. This will enable subject leaders to understand more fully how leadership and strategic planning are essential components of school improvement. This discussion will also relate the subject area/department to the whole school and will link whole-school improvement with improving a subject area/department.

A strategic planning model will be presented that will be explained in detail in the chapters that follow. This will enable subject leaders to inform their thinking and structure their strategy. (Subject leaders can develop a questionnaire to use as the basis to prompt and record their strategic planning.)

SCHOOLS AS ORGANISATIONS

In order to determine how a subject may make a significant contribution to the overall success of a school, it is first necessary to understand the organisational context in which subjects within schools exist.

But what are organisations and what do they do? How do they know if they are being successful? These are questions not automatically asked by subject leaders. However, the answers begin the strategic process since they seek to describe why any school or subject exists. Huczynski and Buchanan describe organisations as 'social arrangements for the controlled performance of collective goals' (Huczynski and Buchanan 1991, p.7).

Organisations are gatherings of people who take inputs (things they bring into the organisation) and convert them into outputs (things produced by communal effort) to achieve a given purpose. Any organisation, including a school, takes a number of different ingredients (e.g. people's skills, money, raw materials) and manipulates them through a range of processes which add value so that what is produced at the end is more desirable (and therefore worth more) than the separate ingredients. This definition can apply equally to businesses, which have a profit motive, and to not-for-profit organisations, such as state schools whose outputs, though less tangible, are nevertheless expected to be better than their inputs. However, it is easier to understand the value-adding features of a factory process (e.g. making cars) or a restaurant process (e.g. making pizzas) or the conversion of a raw material (e.g. making gold jewellery). In all of these the basic raw materials are much less expensive than the finished article and value that is added is determined by the effectiveness and efficiency of the production process and the perceived quality of the end result. In not-for-profit schools, determining the accrued added value at the end of the input–output conversion process is much more difficult. The principal reasons for this are twofold: it is often less clear what the end added-value product is, and it takes a very long time to see the benefits (outcomes) of the process. We deal with each of these below.

Clarity of purpose

First, there is still huge disagreement about the purpose of schools and the relative value and purpose of the subjects that are vehicles for the 'conversion' process. Do schools exist for children (and thereby their parents) or for the state and society in general (i.e. citizenship and commerce)? Or can they serve both and enable children to succeed in a successful society? This lack of clarity concerning purpose is a major reason why it is so difficult to ascertain what value has been added and whether or not input resources (e.g. teachers and materials) and conversion processes (e.g. teaching and pastoral care) have been used efficiently and effectively.

In addition the focus of attention, in terms of added value, is much more upon the 'process' that produces the added value than the 'product', however it is defined. This is because education, like many other industries which focus on people, is concerned principally with the quality of service that the process produces. A correlation is therefore assumed between quality of process and quality of outcome. This is the subject of the school-effectiveness research exemplified by Sammons *et al.* (1995) whose worldwide search for empirical data on school effectiveness produced eleven observable characteristics found in the most successful schools:

- firm and purposeful professional leadership
- shared vision and goals
- a secure learning environment
- concentration on teaching and learning

- purposeful teaching in all lessons
- high expectations from all
- positive reinforcement of success
- systematic monitoring of progress across the school
- emphasis on pupils' rights and responsibilities
- strong home–school partnerships
- a learning organisation

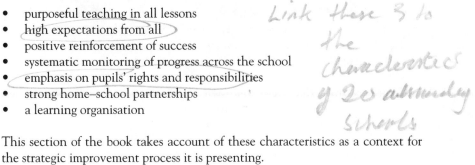

Link these 3 to the characteristics of 20 already schools

This section of the book takes account of these characteristics as a context for the strategic improvement process it is presenting.

Activity II.1   Analysing school effectiveness

Create a checklist by dividing a piece of paper (or flipchart) down the middle and write school above one column and the name of your subject above the other. Now write numbers 1–11 down the side. With colleagues, go through Sammons *et al.*'s (1995) characteristics of effective schools and determine whether or not the characteristics are currently present in your school/subject area.

Use the outcomes of this activity later when we discuss what you might change/improve.

Long-term change progress

The length of the educational 'conversion' process and the difficulty of assessing its added-value-to-life effect cause the second problem. In commercial organisations, goods that are produced on any one day can be sold immediately (e.g. in a pizza restaurant) or within a few days (e.g. via shops selling other food products) or to a wholesaler who will sell them on to retailers in the short- or medium-term (e.g. clothing or electrical goods). Thus cash soon flows back into the business and profitability and customer satisfaction can be assessed relatively quickly.

Schools, on the other hand, deal with children who might go to school for up to thirteen years and into higher education for a further three or four years. Although it is possible to determine very specific 'bits' of short-term learning in this period, it is impossible for any one teacher or one school to know what longer-term impact this will have on the growth and development of the individual over their lifetime. Successive governments, via the introduction of published league tables, have put a great deal of stress on measuring the short-term gains, but have not devised any satisfactory strategy for assessing 'longer-life-term value added'. Equally, OfSTED's system for measuring efficiency (value for money) is based on these short-term measures: inspectors divide the average pupil-funding unit into the average Standard Assessment Tests (SATs) or General Certificate in Secondary Education (GCSE) points score. They then compare the result with similar schools and declare whether or not the school is more or less efficient (education's equivalent of profitability).

The danger here is obvious and much debated. If we merely link success with testable learning outcomes there is a danger that we only assess one part of the reason why schools exist. Indeed some businesses, while accepting the need to make money, stress that measuring their success merely by profitability is also too narrow, claiming to be equally driven by a desire to provide public services or provide goods which add value to people's lives.

There is another advantage in taking a dual measurement of effectiveness: it enables different types of schools in different demographic contexts to strive for goals which best meet the educational demands of their environment. In other words, they can differentiate themselves from other schools by the purpose they aspire to. By focusing merely on quantitative measures of success, the government is denying huge numbers of schools these opportunities.

The paradox is that clarifying the true purpose of any organisation is an essential prerequisite to setting up efficient input and conversion strategies for the effective achievement of that purpose (which is why business organisations have a mission statement and corresponding aims and objectives) (Mullins 1996). Similarly, setting out to 'improve' an organisation like a school requires that the stated purpose of a school is reviewed and re-clarified before any action is taken.

'Effective schools are marked by a clear sense of purpose that is shared by all members of the school' (Harris *et al.* 1996, p.27). Without a very clear definition of purpose that is understood and accepted by all employees, the first principle of what describes an organisation vanishes. Many schools, and the subject areas within them, struggle to become effective organisations because of a failure to move beyond this point.

SUBJECT AREAS AS ORGANISATIONS: THE SUBJECT'S CONTRIBUTION TO SCHOOL ACHIEVEMENT

Subject areas and departments are sub-organisations of the school and also require clarity of purpose. However, the stated purpose of a subject team will need to take account of the overall curriculum objectives of the school. It is generally accepted that the school's curriculum is intended to prepare pupils to succeed in their lives and in society. The material that finds its way into the curriculum comes from a school's or subject leader's analysis of what an individual needs and what society requires for success (Howell *et al.* 1993). This analysis is a key role for the leader and subject team, even in the context of a National Curriculum, since it fundamentally affects everything that follows.

For any subject area, a statement of purpose may be a combination of intended outcomes related to the acquisition of subject skills/knowledge and dynamic outcomes related to the subject's contribution to how pupils learn. In setting this out the team are defining what contribution the subject is going to make to the overall development of the pupil and the school (and to society in general). This contribution may be a unique one and, in some cases, may be very different from other subjects in the curriculum.

It is not the purpose of this section of this book to debate the uniqueness and necessity of particular subjects. However, subject leaders should be aware of the work of Howard Gardner (1983) in multiple intelligences and Honey and Mumford (1983) in learning styles. This kind of research has done much to emphasise the need for all pupils to experience a range of different types of subject content and ways of learning. It will therefore be possible for the subject team to draw upon such research in their statement of purpose and show clearly how their subject supports and extends the school's curriculum.

The statement of purpose will also contain attainment targets for pupils, which relate to the school's overall targets. Other sections of this book deal with this issue, but it is important to note that clearly defining the pupils' attainment targets will be an important feature of strategic planning and its underpinning processes.

THE ROLE OF SCHOOL AND SUBJECT LEADERSHIP

According to the Teacher Training Agency's *National Standards*, the core purpose of a subject leader is as follows:

> A subject leader provides leadership and direction for the subject and ensures that it is managed and organised to meet the aims and objectives of the school and the subject.
>
> (TTA 1998a, p.4)

The *National Standards* are therefore describing two different types of role for the subject leader: providing leadership and direction, and managing and organising. This kind of separation often raises the question: what is leadership and is it different from management? Drucker (1968) made a distinction between these two roles in writing that leadership is about 'doing the right job', while management is about 'doing the job right'. This pithy definition of the difference shows that, while leadership in organisations is usually associated with defining, clarifying and communicating the long-term purpose and direction of the organisation (i.e. setting long-term goals), management is more concerned with planning and implementing to achieve that purpose. We therefore often describe leadership as being strategic and management as being operational. However, both are key aspects of a subject leader's role and are so interrelated in practice that it is usually impossible (and unhelpful) to try to tease them apart.

However, it is the concept of strategic leadership that is more fully explored in the following chapters of this part of the book. A series of discussions and activities will be presented that will enable the subject leader to enhance their knowledge and understanding of this dimension of their role and guide them towards a range of actions they can take to become more effective. We start this by briefly examining what difference subject leaders make to their subject's success.

What can subject leaders do to make a difference?

Effective subject leaders make a difference by 'adding value' to the conversion processes that take place within their department or subject area. In the main, their impact should enhance the quality of teaching and of learning. The *National Standards for Subject Leaders* (TTA 1998a) suggest that subject leaders are effective in raising standards if:

- they possess a high level of subject knowledge essential to the curriculum that pupils are following
- they are able to relate their subject to the curriculum as a whole
- they are very good teachers who can and do model best practice
- they have an overview of how the learning needs of pupils can be served by the teaching needs of the subject
- they have a secure grasp of the strategic development needs of the school and their own subject
- they can lead staff by inspiring them to believe that pupils can achieve better results
- they can communicate effectively and build relationships with staff, pupils and parents
- they know how to plan and implement change
- they manage resources effectively
- they monitor staff and pupil performance and give objective feedback whenever possible

Activity II.2   Analysing skills and attributes

Examine yourself honestly against these skills and attributes (maybe ask others for their opinions). You may wish to categorise your answers into three columns:

1. Can and do well	2. Can and sometimes do	3. Not a strength – don't do

Decide what you are going to do about the things you have written in Columns 2 and 3.

What is the role of the subject leader in subject and school improvement?

Many books have been written about leading and managing change, yet very few books deal with managing the *status quo*. One conclusion we might draw from this is that it must be less important to manage the *status quo* than to lead and manage change. The act of leadership defined by the TTA implies that the leader is involved with movement in a particular direction for a specific purpose. It implies that leadership is necessary because schools, like all organisations, exist in a context where things are not fixed and some things are changing all the time. This is not to suggest that leaders should look to change things for change's sake, but that the most effective leader has insights into what should be changed, when, how and for whom.

However, teachers and pupils live in a world where social and political change, together with the impact of technology, promise to revolutionise our work and our home life. It is therefore vital that subject leaders recognise and react to these imperatives by thinking ahead and trying to 'second guess' the future. Today, we expect leaders in all organisations to have 'a vision' of what their organisation (or their part of it) should be like. Clearly, for subject leaders any vision they construct must be closely related to the whole-school vision expressed and understood by the headteacher, senior-management team and staff so that all leaders and their teams in a school are working towards common goals (albeit that they are taking different routes to get to them). If subject leaders do not take goal alignment into account as part of their strategic thinking then it will impair their potential to be successful and could contribute to their school becoming less effective.

Lack of a common goal is a major cause of organisational ineffectiveness, even in quite small organisations like primary schools (Mullins 1996). Disparity often occurs when new headteachers or subject leaders take over schools or subjects (especially when the previous headteacher or subject leader held the post for some time). In these cases staff may have a very clear idea of what they are trying to achieve, based on their relationship with the previous leader. The new leader may have a different picture in their mind to that of existing staff. While this situation is perhaps understandable for new leaders in the short term, it often comes as a surprise to longer-serving leaders to discover that some staff may not be aware of their vision and goals or to find that not everyone in their school is working towards the same goals. This is because longer-serving headteachers and subject leaders sometimes assume that the staff know what their goals are because, when they joined the school, they invested time and energy presenting their ideas to the staff in order to gain their commitment and support. One can expect that in subsequent years some staff leave and are replaced, others are promoted or change roles, and that the governing body changes and the DfEE and LEA policies change. In fact, many more things might have changed – and even if external elements stayed the same long-serving staff become older and wiser! It is hardly surprising that under these circumstances some staff may not be sure of what their headteacher's or subject leader's vision is. Understanding the strategic process that follows will enable subject leaders to enter a dialogue with their teams that should both ascertain where staff are in their thinking and introduce a process of alignment.

Creating a culture of collaboration

School and subject improvement should start with the leadership expressing their expectations of a future desired state and then collaborating closely with staff to build a common vision and agree a set of goals that all staff can work towards.

> Collaboration should mean creating a vision together, not complying with the head's own. ... The articulation of different voices may create initial conflict, but this should be confronted and worked through. It is part of the collaborative process.
>
> (Fullan and Hargreaves 1998, p.123)

Chapter 4 describes how leaders might harness the power and creative energy of vision-building and goal-setting as they and their staff work their way through the strategic planning process.

THE STRATEGIC PROCESS (WHY? WHAT? HOW? WHO? WHEN? HOW WELL?)

What is the strategic process? Is it different from planning?

> The goal of strategic planning is to produce a stream of wise decisions to achieve the mission of the organisation. Emphasis shifts from product to process. Just as the planning process builds in flexibility for adaption to changing conditions in and out of the organisation, it also accepts the possibility that final product may not resemble what was originally intended.
>
> (Patterson *et al.* 1986, p.23)

Strategy is not just planning. Strategy starts with having a clear view of the intended end-result: the vision or goal; it is more associated with long-term campaigns in which few of the precise steps to reach the vision are visible at the outset and the actual product may not be clearly identified. This is not to suggest that strategy does not contain planning, but it allows the process to begin without being absolutely sure of how the end-result might be achieved. Peters and Waterman quote an executive of Cadbury's who summed this up as:

READY – FIRE – AIM

> (Peters and Waterman 1982, p.119)

This suggests that it is as impossible to improve a stagnant organisation as to steer an immobile car or a stationary boat: it must be moving before the leader, driver or helmsman can begin to alter its direction to get to their destination (Everard and Morris 1990). Sometimes, to continue the car analogy, the route to the destination is known at the outset, possibly because the journey is a familiar one so back-routes and short-cuts are planned. On other occasions, journeys are begun to unvisited locations. While it may be clear on the map that the destination is achievable via the marked roads, what exactly will be encountered *en route* will be much less certain and the streets nearest to the destination might not be marked at all. In this case the strategy might be to stick to well-signed motorways and A-roads to get as near as possible and then ask. The important thing is to set off and solve problems along the way (learning, as it were, to cross bridges as you come to them).

In the case of subject improvement, the ultimate goal may be very clear (e.g. to achieve a set of learning targets for pupils). The broad strategy may be equally clear (e.g. to improve the quality of teaching, procure better learning resources and enhance substantially the learning experience). The subject leader may have a fairly good insight into how these strategies might be translated into a two- or three-year plan. However, at that moment their ability to plan in detail more than a few months ahead might be impaired by a number of issues beyond their control. Peters and Waterman's message can be summarised as: don't wait, start the improvement process and have the confidence to adjust the plan as things become clearer (Peters and Waterman 1982, pp.118–21).

The strategic subject leader will gain people's commitment to setting off towards the goal before the precise means of achieving these objectives is known. This often needs a good deal of clear communication from the leader who may need to share with their team the value of the end-result while being unable to set out a detailed action plan. This requires staff to have faith in their leader. Leaders with a good track-record of strategic planning and successful implementation enjoy the trust of their employees and are often able to show that (although the precise detail may be relatively unclear) the broad goal is both desirable and achievable. Newly appointed leaders may need to demonstrate their capabilities on smaller, more obviously short-term projects in order to build the confidence and gain the trust of their staff.

However, all good leaders instinctively think longer-term even if they do not immediately share their vision with all their staff. As will be discussed in Chapter 5, their capacity to see, share and move towards worthy end-results is a key determinant of their success as a leader.

Strategic analysis

Communication of the worth of an idea may be necessary to begin the improvement process, but it is not enough to achieve the goal. To do this successfully, the subject leader also needs to have analytical skills. This is because once the goal or vision is identified, the second ingredient of strategy is accurate analysis (Weindling 1997). Strategic analysis is primarily concerned with asking:

1   What are the organisation's internal strengths and weaknesses in relation to achieving the goal?
2   What are the external opportunities and threats that exist in the environment concerning the goal?
3   What factors/resources might help or hinder the achievement of the goal?
4   What are the priorities for action that emerge from the above analysis?
5   What should therefore be the long- or medium-term strategy?
6   What is the time-scale for the strategy's achievement?
7   What specific action needs to be undertaken to achieve the goal?

The answers to these questions are the data from which a strategic plan can be constructed and will be discussed more fully in Chapter 6.

Towards a strategic planning model

The strategic process we are presenting can be broken down into a number of distinct stages, illustrated in Figure II.1.

The chapters that follow take the reader through ten stages, asking questions that are fundamental to strategic planning. Each of the stages and questions is underpinned with text that enables the reader to consider their own and their team's responses.

Figure II.1 The strategic process

Why?

Stage One: Establishing our purpose and clarifying our values

Stage Two: Forming our vision

What?

Stage Three: Defining our end results

Stage Four: Defining what we want
the pupils to achieve

Stage Five: Defining what we want
staff and others to do

How, who and when?

Stage Six: Analysing our performance
and our environment

Stage Seven: Prioritising our actions

Stage Eight: Planning for change

How well are we doing? Who shall we tell?

Stage Nine: Monitoring, evaluating and
reviewing our performance

Stage Ten: Reporting our success
to stakeholders

4 Establishing the purpose and place of the subject in the curriculum

INTRODUCTION

> Without a sense of alignment behind a purpose we drift aimlessly. It cannot be any old purpose either. It must be one that galvanizes, energizes and enthrals people.
>
> (Bennis and Goldsmith 1997, p.xiv)

The first part of the strategic management process is concerned with establishing the purpose of the organisation or the activity. Without a clear statement of purpose it is impossible to plan for its effective achievement or determine whether or not it has been achieved.

Therefore, one of the key roles of a school and subject leader is to question continually, re-define and communicate the purpose of the school/subject area. A headteacher may ask: 'Why is it important that this school exists?' The subject leader may ask: 'Why is it important that we include this subject in the curriculum?'

STAGE 1: ESTABLISHING THE PURPOSE OF THE SUBJECT

There are two things to consider when subject leaders and their teams consider the purpose of teaching and learning their subject:

(a) The added value that your subject makes to the pupils' quality of life in the short-, medium- and long-term.
(b) The values that you, your team and others hold about pupils' learning and development.

Considering added value (product) and values about learning (process) together will enable subject leaders to arrive at a balanced view of their subject. This raises the issue about who is included in the consultation. Obviously, all teaching staff who teach the subject will need to be involved, but a case must be made to canvass the views of other significant stakeholders, such as parents, governors, the business community and, of course, pupils.

We shall refer to the first of the two questions above briefly, because other parts of this book offer more comprehensive debate about this topic.

Determining added value

What is the added value of subject knowledge?

Knowledge enables us to do things. Subject leaders should be able to describe what it is that knowing the content of the subject will enable the pupil to do that cannot be achieved from gaining knowledge in other subjects. In broader terms, they should be able to describe to parents what contribution will be made to their child's life through acquiring the foundations of knowledge in the subject.

Hirst (1974) and Gardner (1983) both give the subject leader insights into possible answers to this question. Each explains that different bodies of knowledge contribute essential things that we need to know, and develop specific and often unique skills that enable us to become better thinkers and doers. National Curriculum guidelines for each of your subject areas also offer reasons why particular subjects are in the school curriculum.

Knowledge gives us confidence and raises self-esteem. Many pupils have different types of learning difficulties connected with learning different types of subject knowledge. An important point to clarify in discussion with colleagues is the extent to which knowledge of your subject raises pupils' confidence in their ability to be successful in their lives.

Knowledge also enables us to test pupils' ability to learn through remembering and applying their knowledge (Lindsay and Desforges 1998). Different subjects examine particular aspects of pupil aptitude. This might be of great significance to those organisations that are to receive pupils following schooling (e.g. higher education or employers). A subject leader may therefore ask: what aspects of pupils' aptitude does testing knowledge of my subject assess that other subjects may not test?

What is the added value of the subject learning process?

One of the arguments for exposing pupils to a diverse range of subjects is that we know human beings learn in different ways and at different rates. Most subject leaders have studied their subject in depth for many years and are therefore confident that they understand how the processes involved in learning their subject help pupils. However, can they explain to other staff, pupils and parents what the long-term learning benefits are from learning the subject? Subject leaders may also have to argue their case for resources over and above other subjects and therefore inform senior managers of these unique learning benefits. See Chapter 11 for more discussion on this topic.

What is the added value of the teaching methods employed?

Teachers use different methodologies in teaching different subjects. This is most obvious when comparing essentially physical subjects (e.g. PE) with more desk-based subjects (e.g. history). However, even within these two examples there are opportunities for history to be taught more actively through field research and PE to have knowledge-based sessions taught in classrooms. We argue that the choice of method must lie with the individual teacher, who decides upon the most appropriate pedagogy to deliver the content.

However, there will be a fundamental pedagogy that underpins subject teaching and its unique value may need to be explained to pupils, parents, non-specialist staff and others. Neville Bennett (1976) examined teaching methods and learning and offers insights into the link between teaching approaches and pupil outcomes. Part III returns to this theme.

What is the total added value of your subject?

The answers to the previous three questions provide a picture of the total added value of the subject in the curriculum and therefore the reason that the subject exists. The next task is to summarise the answers into a set of words that can be understood by teachers and all the other stakeholders, especially pupils.

Activity 4.1   Ascertaining added value

With your subject team, summarise the total added value to the curriculum associated with your subject. Write a short statement presenting this that can be easily understood by pupils and parents.

Clarifying values

> The responsibilities of educational leadership are to build educational institutions around central values.
>
> (Grace 1997, p.212)

Values are often difficult to express and even more difficult to write down. Sometimes it is easier for people to say what it is that they believe in and from that deduce their underpinning values. The key issue here is that subject leaders, staff and other people who are going to influence and direct the work of pupils have an opportunity to express their values in order to further clarify their overall purpose. For many teachers, it was these values that brought them into teaching and it is still these values that motivate them, especially when the going gets tough.

Often too, in selecting teachers and other people with similar levels of expertise to work with pupils, headteachers and subject leaders will discriminate between applicants based on an assessment of their values such as their commitment to the children. Leaders would expect these values to be translated into the actions practised by existing staff (e.g. in the teaching style and their conduct in disciplining children). OfSTED inspectors also look into these areas of a school through their observations, interviews and perusal of school literature, and rate their impact on the spiritual, moral and social aspects of the school's curriculum.

An investigation into the purpose of a subject must always include gathering data about the values that people hold. In the case of determining a subject team's purpose, the following more philosophical sets of questions are useful to consider.

What values do you and your staff believe in?

This is an essentially philosophical question and leads to a good deal of discussion amongst staff. Often, in the business of dealing with pupils, parents, resources and the daily act of teaching, values and beliefs can be forgotten. Yet these are often the driving forces that cause many subject leaders and staff to take up teaching in the first place.

What values are held about pupils, people and life generally?

Are pupils, parents and staff seen as an asset or a nuisance? McGregor (1987) created his 'Theory X and Theory Y' construct to illustrate two opposite positions that he believes organisations and those leading them adopt:

1   Management in Theory X-type organisations see people as inherently lazy and assume they dislike work, that they will avoid responsibility, lack ambition and therefore need to be directed and controlled.
2   Management in Theory Y-type organisations see people as inherently work-seeking, whether for gain or for personal pleasure. They assume people will be committed to values and goals and that given the right climate most will seek responsibility and contribute creatively to the organisation's purpose. People therefore do not need to be controlled, rather they need encouraging to become self-motivated.

Activity 4.2   Theory X or Theory Y?

Examine how your organisation (either whole school or subject area) is set up to deal with people. To what extent can you detect aspects of Theory X and Theory Y assumptions?

Are pupils' minds to be controlled so that they can be filled with 'right' knowledge in order that they can go on to lead successful and respectable lives, or should they be empowered and released so that they can investigate and create knowledge for themselves and therefore influence the kind of society that they want to live in? Are people in general free to exercise their will or should everybody live in accordance with society's norms?

What values are held about the concepts of education and schools?

Subject leaders may wish to explore the extent to which subject staff see education as an entitlement for individual citizens, so that they can fulfil their own definition of potential. On the other hand, staff may see education as a function of the state that has a right to prescribe and control the outcomes of the education system. In other words, does society or the state have any right to determine what people should know and can do? Illich (1972) believed that modern society was, through its compulsory schooling of individuals, perpetrating a game on the individual. He believed it effectively brainwashed people into believing that, because the state put a high value on their outcome measures of education, these really mattered to the individual. In an argument for 'de-schooling' he describes how, through schools, individuals are trained

> to confuse process and substance. Once these become blurred, a new logic is assumed: the more the treatment is [i.e. schooling], the better are the results; or, escalation leads to success. The pupil is thereby 'schooled' to confuse teaching with learning, grade advancement with education, a diploma with competence, and fluency with the ability to say something new. His imagination is 'schooled' to accept service in place of value ...
>
> (Illich 1972, p.1)

Activity 4.3   Are schools necessary?

Examine whether Illich's view of what schools do to individuals really does apply to your school and the way in which you are educating pupils in your subject.

Another dimension is concerned with how pupils of different social backgrounds and ability levels are dealt with. Should schools be 'level playing fields' in which all citizens have equal access and opportunity to the best of what is available, or should schools invest heavily in accelerating the prospects of the most able and do what they can with what is left for those less fortunate?

What values are held about teaching and learning?

Research by Harris *et al.* (1997, p.157) indicates that effective teaching and learning is present in classrooms where teachers:

- involved all pupils in their own learning through tasks completed in a range of small-group and large-group situations
- encouraged co-operative learning with pupils working together, in different roles which developed their self-esteem
- enabled pupils to review and reflect on their learning and be involved in action-planning
- developed meaningful, formative, developmental and motivational forms of assessment which reinforced and built confidence

Each of these practices and approaches indicates values held by the teachers concerned.

Activity 4.4   What is good teaching and learning?

1   What do you and your subject team believe is good teaching and learning? What values underpin these approaches? Do teachers always know best or can other adults or the pupils themselves sometimes know better than the teacher?
2   Do you and your staff believe that teaching is the only or best way of helping pupils to learn, or will children learn with or without teachers (e.g. in the school holidays)? Can a skilled teacher accelerate the learning of all pupils or will some pupils never really maximise their potential no matter what a teacher does?

What would you be prepared to fight for?

Sometimes, issues and problems arise that are so fundamental that leaders and teachers are prepared to take dramatic action to defend their position. Fullan and Hargreaves, in their book *What's Worth Fighting for in Your School?* (1998), discuss a number of issues which headteachers, subject leaders and staff need to consider as vital to the well-being and improvement of schools. They work on the premise that

> teachers and heads themselves must ultimately make this [marked improvement] happen. No one else can be relied on to do them any favours in this regard. And they must make this happen despite a number of barriers inside and outside education.
>
> (Fullan and Hargreaves 1998, p.2)

Activity 4.5   Why should pupils learn your subject?

As a subject leader, what issues would you be prepared to resign over? For example, how much of a cut to your subject's time on the timetable or resources to support teaching would you allow before you refused to continue to accept responsibility for the outcomes?

What does the subject mean to you, the pupils, your staff and your school?

It is now being more widely recognised that one of the principal sources of inspiration, creativity and commitment in organisations is the degree to which people feel that they are engaged in a meaningful activity (Beare *et al.* 1997, Bennis and Biederman 1997). Subject leaders and their colleagues may have invested a large portion of their lifetime, considerable amounts of energy and even significant amounts of their own money into studying and improving their subject knowledge (e.g. by buying and reading this book!). They have also taught and championed the subject to pupils, parents, staff, senior management and others over the years.

Activity 4.6   Key principles of a subject (1)

Imagine that you meet someone who has never been to a school or who never studied your subject at school. Could you explain to them why you feel so strongly about your subject? And, just because it's so important to you, why you feel it to be so important for pupils?

From values to policy and principles

The answer to all the questions above will give subject leaders a better understanding of the powerful meaning behind their own, their colleagues' and the subject's purpose. These understandings need to be communicated simply yet powerfully, as a set of principles that will underpin your actions:

e.g. 'In teaching our subject, teachers will … '
    'We believe that all pupils should have access to … '

Activity 4.7   Key principles of a subject (2)

Write down three key principles that could be put onto a wall in each subject classroom, that will communicate the subject team's beliefs about the subject.

Linked to website &
2nd session
The purpose and place of the subject

Creating a mission statement

Your assessment of added value and the principles for managing learning can be combined to set out your subject's purpose. This is best done using active and forward-looking language, and is often called a mission statement. A good mission statement should, in a few sentences or a paragraph, describe the purpose succinctly and clearly to anyone who reads it. It might begin:

> 'The purpose of learning English at our school is … '
> 'History is taught in our school because … '
> 'All pupils who learn Science at this school will … '

Subject leaders will find that the most important part of defining the purpose and arriving at a clear mission statement is not the words that are eventually produced, but the process of arriving at them. It is the series of clarifying discussions with teachers and other stakeholders that both shapes and shares the understanding of what is being set out to be achieved. In this regard, like staff, the more that pupils and parents can be part of this process the more they will be committed to its outcome.

However, the answers to the above questions should also find expression in all the policies that are written in connection with the subject. If the values expressed above do not permeate everything that subject leaders and their subject teams do, then it is unlikely that subject's purpose will be fulfilled.

STAGE 2: FORMING YOUR VISION OF WHAT YOU WANT TO ACHIEVE

The word 'vision' has become an increasingly used term in schools over the past few years, as it has in most corporate cultures around the world.

> Today, vision is a familiar concept in corporate leadership. … A shared vision is a vision that many people are truly committed to, because it reflects their own personal vision.
>
> (Senge 1990, p.206)

or, as a businessman put it recently,

> A few years ago, if I'd have said I'd had a vision I'd have been locked up – now I can't get a job without one!

Teachers might be forgiven for believing that it is merely the latest management-speak fad, but it is not. The capacity 'to vision' (used as a verb rather than a noun) is a basic human ability and has been around for a very long time – it is even mentioned in the Bible, for example:

Without vision man doth perish.

(Proverbs 29: 18)

Vision is a picture of future reality, a vivid image 'in our mind's eye' of the way things are going to be. People use it all the time, for instance when a building is constructed it starts with a picture in the architect's head which is committed to paper and is thereby communicated to the builders. People 'vision' when they plan and execute the decoration of their homes, starting with a mental picture of what they want the room to look like when it is finished. In an even simpler example, people use the technique to cook a meal, having first bought the ingredients using the same kind of mental image of the finished dish to construct their shopping list. In schools, teachers start their lesson-planning with a picture in their mind of the way a lesson will go and what they want the pupils to produce. Display areas and school concerts are similarly envisioned well before they become anything of a reality.

On a larger scale, the capacity to invent and communicate a picture of a better future has enabled military and political leaders throughout time to persuade huge numbers of people to act in ways they would not have done otherwise (unfortunately history has shown us that this has not always been for positive reasons). In fact, we often tend to associate strong leadership with the capacity to inspire through an ability to think clearly and communicate effec-tively, as in Martin Luther King's 'I have a dream ... ' speech.

What is interesting is that in most of the famous orations there is very little description of 'how' things are to be achieved. What is present instead is a vivid picture of the desired future state, a verbal description of the way things will be when we have 'got to the promised land'. So it appears that it is not the expla-nation of the way that the vision will be achieved (i.e. the plan) that energises people to act, it is the significance of the end-result to those that it is being communicated to. In fact, the leader may already have a plan in mind, but revealing it at the same time as the vision focuses the listener on the organisa-tional logistics of the idea, sometimes bringing forth the 'it'll never work here' comment. Martin Luther King did not inspire a generation of black Americans by saying 'I have a strategic plan ... '!

The reason human beings are galvanised by vision may be explained by an application of the Gestalt school of psychology, founded earlier this century in Germany by Wertheimer (1945). According to this branch of psychological theory, human beings require that the world appears complete to them, and therefore understandable, according to each person's perception of what this means. Each person has a picture of normality stored in the subconscious. This perception of normality is gained through the many and varied experiences of life, including what is taught by parents, educators and others who inform us about the facts of our existence. As a consequence, providing feedback is received through the senses that the *way things are* matches the perception of the *way things are supposed to be*, the individual is contented. However, should one perceive through the sense of sight, hearing, touch, taste or smell that something is not as expected, then it is disturbing and more often than not it energises one to rectify the mismatch – i.e. to change things in the environment to match the internal image (Kohler 1964).

A simple example of this is the way very few of us can resist straightening a picture that hangs crooked on a wall. In schools, many teachers have a very clear picture of the way that they want their classroom set out. Pupils, and sometimes other teachers who use the room, do not always share this image. As a consequence, teachers spend a lot of time tidying things up because their teaching room is less tidy than they would like it to be or because it has been re-arranged in their absence (i.e. when they come back into the room what they see does not match their internal image of the way the room is supposed to look).

Our actions are often triggered automatically and sometimes we may not even be consciously aware that we have done something. This is because the image of the way things are supposed to be is programmed into our subconscious and we therefore do not need to be conscious of any mismatch in order to act. In schools, teachers use this subconscious ability to control a class. Consciously, a teacher may be talking about a particular topic but subconsciously the teacher's mind is scanning the classroom for any pupil's behaviour which deviates from their idea of what is considered acceptable. Thus teachers are able to keep the pupils in order with a look or a change in body language (things they have learned are effective and are also programmed in to their subconscious) while maintaining the flow of dialogue. Indeed, often experienced teachers are unaware of what they have done and genuinely cannot remember. We normally refer to this subconscious ability to act in a way that brings about effective results as being 'skilful'.

Another example of how this works is found in the way we use our subconscious skill to enable us to drive – subtly correcting our position on the road to match our internal picture of the correct position which we have learnt to be safe. And we often do not realise what we are doing. How often have we even driven to work in the morning yet cannot remember doing so?

When our subconscious 'skill' to change the environment to match our internal image is applied to the idea of visioning and goal-setting, the results can be dramatic. Figure 4.1 demonstrates the process.

The Gestalt process is triggered by the mismatch between these two positions. In the earlier example of the crooked picture, most of us have been conditioned to believe that the top of a picture should hang parallel to the floor so we simply adjust it until it is. The important thing to note is that the way we want things to be (the straight picture) is the dominant image in our mind – our wish to achieve this state is much stronger than our wish to accept what we see (it hanging crooked). The same is true with our untidy classroom, pupils talking when we are and our car's position on the road. We are galvanised by the need to achieve the image in our mind. Interestingly, we can almost always find the energy to achieve our dominant image even when we are tired. For example, teachers, however exhausted, will not go home and leave an untidy

Figure 4.1   The power of vision

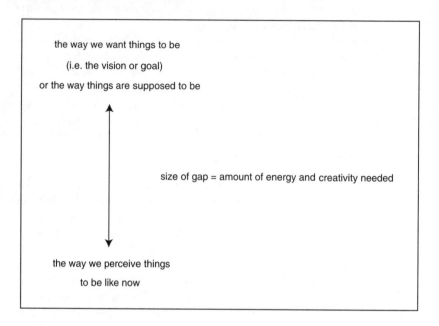

classroom that they will have to walk into in the morning. However, once they have finished the job their energy goes and they cannot wait to sit down (unless they have in mind a better picture, like being at home, in which case they will find the energy to get there, and so on).

The power of the vision works in the same way. When the image of the vision or goal becomes stronger in our subconscious minds than that which we currently perceive, we can find amazing amounts of energy to achieve the new state (i.e. being motivated). Consider how much energy we can find to take our family to a holiday destination, to move house or put on a school drama-production. And we do not just find energy, we also become creative. Human beings are at their most creative when they are trying to achieve something they have not yet achieved (i.e. problem-solving). The greater the need, the greater the creativity – hence the saying 'necessity is the mother of invention'.

Kohler (cited in Child 1973) demonstrated, in a series of experiments conducted in exile during World War II, that problem-solving often resulted from sudden insight (having a 'bright idea') into how to solve the whole problem. He showed that if people saw the problem as a whole they would be more likely to seek and find whole solutions. Interestingly, it also seems from this research that the further the problem or vision is away from that which currently exists the more energy and creativity is found to close the gap. Creativity will be generated (Kohler called it 'insightful learning') according to the seriousness of the problem or importance of the vision to the problem- or vision-owner. It is essential, therefore, that the problem-owner shares the ownership of the problem or vision. This often leads to the problem being solved much more quickly and in a much cleverer way than could have been imagined.

Most subject leaders will already be familiar with arguments about the need to share ownership of goals and planning with their teams. This explanation of why it is fundamentally important to do so brings an additional dimension. In the process being described here, the solution to problems may come from an unusual source (e.g. someone who has little status within the group because of their lack of experience, qualifications or rank) or the solution may be completely novel. Ben Zander, conductor of the Boston Philharmonic Orchestra, in an address to 600 headteachers at the Queen Elizabeth II Conference Centre in London (February 1999), urged them to 'think outside the box'. He asked heads to consider ideas and solutions that were unusual and from people who were not normally considered as experts in education. Similarly, Charles Handy (1989) called for what he termed 'upside down thinking' to bring about the most useful forms of long-lasting change.

The implication for subject leaders is that they need to consult with as wide a range of people as possible within and beyond the subject, and even the school, in order to formulate the vision, the analysis of the *status quo*, the generation of ideas and the finding of new resources. If they are to do this then they need to be comfortable with the idea that they might not recognise or value every contribution they receive back. They need to have an open mind to alternatives from beyond their own experience and be willing to give credit to suggestions from whatever source. In this way they will promote a great deal of learning in those around them.

Problem-setting and vision-building actually promote learning within the organisation. The amount of learning which occurs depends upon the scale of the problem or the distance the vision is away from the *status quo*. Leaders can encourage and promote the amount of learning that takes place in the organisation through the way they approach this aspect of their work. Unfortunately, many organisations and teams which are not aware of the potential of the 'gestalten process' are less than complimentary about leaders who have ideas about what things might look like in the future but are unable, at that moment, to set out clearly how they intend to achieve them.

If a vision is imagined and at the same time the visionary attempts to draw up a plan (i.e. before the gestalten process has had time to work) then it is likely that the plan will be pragmatically attached to current resources and current ways of doing things. Periods of gestation are necessary to allow the psychological process to work and to find the answers (i.e. the 'how?').

Paradoxically, if the vision is an ambitious one, it is unlikely that any clear way will be seen to achieve the vision within a reasonable time-scale (particularly where finances are involved). As a consequence, the more practical members of the organisation will be able to find many questions which cannot be answered. This often leads to the vision being dismissed as 'pie in the sky' and the visionary as a dreamer. If the team can accept the vision and make it the stronger picture (i.e. overlaying the vision of what they want things to be like on their image of the *status quo*), then the group's gestation processes will be activated. The team therefore needs to understand how the visioning process works, particularly the need to allow time between setting the vision and working on a solution to close the gap (i.e. allow a period of gestation). Figure 4.2 describes the process that subject leaders might use to engage their teams in setting and clarifying vision and goals.

Figure 4.2   The Gestalt problem-solving process

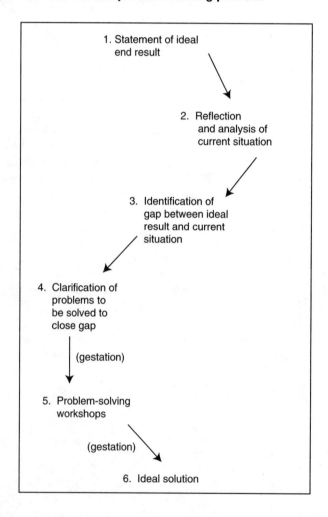

In summary, subject leaders need to help staff to create a 'group vision' that includes *their own* vivid images which describe how things are going to be in the future (i.e. *their* end-results). It is important that the vision statement accurately describes what things will be like in the classroom and/or school when the job is completed. These are not targets that the team is aiming for, they will come later, the vision statement needs to describe the whole picture that will trigger gestalten processes.

The role of the subject leader is to help the vision, whatever its source, to become embedded in the combined subconscious of the subject team or department. This is best achieved by encouraging and empowering the team members to think big, to have faith in the power of the team to achieve their goals by finding creative ways that they might not have thought of to date.

Walt Disney, acclaimed by many as being one of the most creative people this century, had a simple motto for his workforce:

If you can dream it, you can do it.

Activity 4.8   Creating the vision

Create your vision for your department or subject area. Imagine that time, money and appropriate staff had been made available to you and you had therefore done everything that you believe needs doing. What would it be like?

5 Creating goals for teaching and learning

INTRODUCTION

> We cannot exaggerate the significance of a strong determination to achieve
> a goal, together with the conviction, passion, and unique point of view that
> establish the energy and direction of the leader.
>
> (Bennis and Goldsmith 1997, p.xiv)

In Chapter 4 it was recognised that teachers are being urged by the government
to become end-result orientated in a limited way. That is, they are being pressed
to define the outcome (added value) of their work only in terms of eventual
pupil attainment and not to include any other benefit that pupils might have
gained from the process of getting there. This is problematic for teachers since,
as was discussed, there are wide disagreements about what the end-result should
be. Many teachers and educationalists (Broadfoot *et al.* 1994, p.1; Grace 1997,
p.97) believe that current governmental views about pupil attainment are too
narrow, in defining end-results merely in terms of externally validated outcomes
of pupil achievement (e.g. SATs and GCSEs, reported via league tables).

However, becoming end-result orientated does not mean that headteachers,
subject leaders and staff have to take this narrow perspective of what constitutes a worthwhile output of a year, a Key Stage or a phase of primary or
secondary education. It does mean, though, that subject leaders and teachers
must have a clear view of what pupil outcomes should be and be able to (1)
explain them to others, (2) plan and work to achieve them, and (3) say
whether or not they have been achieved. In our view, it is the absence of
strong public articulation by schools of their intended pupil outcomes that led
to external policy-makers deciding and publishing what satisfactory outcomes
for pupils should be.

The purpose of this chapter is to examine the concepts and theories underpinning end-result thinking and suggest how subject leaders can use these to
unlock creative potential within their subject areas to achieve what they aspire
to. The key to unlocking this potential is to be very clear about the end-result
the subject leader and their team wish to create. The greater the clarity, the

more obvious the gap between the ideal and the current situation. This in turn will lead to more accurate analysis of the gap, more specific problem-solving and a better plan of action. It will also enable a subject leaders to know with more assurance whether they have achieved their ideal situation or not.

STAGE 3: SUBJECT END-RESULT STATEMENTS

Activity 5.1   What could my subject be like?

Ask yourself and members of your subject team to write a statement under each of the following prompts:

1   This is what my/our subject will be like when I/we have got things the way I/we want them to be.
2   This is what pupils and staff will be doing when I've/we've succeeded.
3   This is what the response to my/our success will be like.

The prompts in Activity 5.1 may generate much discussion and it is worth spending some time on writing statements under each of the areas. It is important that the statements are written in the first person (so that they are personally owned) and in the present tense (so that they describe a future reality and are not merely wish statements).

The sum of these statements will give you an insight into what the overall vision might look like when translated into the classroom. It can be written down as one or a series of statements related to the subject's overall vision:

e.g. 'In our school, Music is a highly prized part of the curriculum and now that we have acquired all the instruments we need every day at least half the pupils in the school participate successfully in making music.'

'If you come to my classroom you will find all the pupils enthusiastically completing their numeracy tasks, brilliantly supported by well-trained Learning Support Assistants.'

'As a result of the OfSTED inspection, and since our school's achievements were so well reported in the local paper, we have had enormous practical and financial support from parents and the community.'

It does not matter how many statements are produced. As before, the most important thing about these is not the words themselves but the quality of the discussions between staff that produced them. The more that staff can become accustomed to having these discussions and arriving at these kinds of statements, the more the subconscious of all the staff will be informed about the end-result the subject is trying to achieve.

Defining the end-result

Having made the case for the need to become end-result orientated, we need to examine more closely what these end-results are likely to be. This section will look at what pupils and staff might achieve.

Since the introduction of OfSTED inspections to secondary schools in 1993 and primary schools in 1994, more and more schools have used elements of the OfSTED inspection framework and associated criteria in the internal review of their school. With the move to a heavier reliance on internal review verified by less frequent and 'light touch' inspections, it is anticipated that all schools will use the OfSTED framework to monitor, evaluate and review their provision, including the use of the layout of the post-inspection Action Plan for school annual improvement planning. For this reason, we recommend the use of the OfSTED framework to help define pupil and staff end-result achievement.

STAGE 4: DEFINING WHAT PUPILS WILL ACHIEVE

Activity 5.2   Defining pupil achievement

Pupil achievement can be broken down under three broad headings. Use these to define the ideal end-result you wish to achieve.

1   What will pupils attain (i.e. what pupils achieve at the end e.g. knowledge, attitude to the subject, physical skills)?
2   What will pupils' progress be (i.e. what pupils achieve on the way e.g. amount, rate)?
3   How will the pupils respond in lessons and around the school (i.e. what pupils behave like e.g. compliance, application, team and social skills)?

These headings in Activity 5.2 correspond to those identified in the OfSTED framework, and found on their Lesson Observation Forms (LOFs) and in their reports. For our purposes, behaviour is preferred to 'response' since it involves a broader definition of pupil activity beyond lessons. It is not our intention here to discuss exactly what different pupils might achieve at different stages of their school life. Instead, each of these headings has been introduced in order to facilitate discussion of what kinds of end-result targets staff may want to envisage. To support this process, it is suggested that subject leaders consult a range of documentation readily available in school (e.g. OfSTED reports, PANDA, LEA benchmarking data).

As suggested above, we are using the word 'achievement' in this context to describe the end-result of the educative process for your subject. This incorporates the attainment, progress and response of pupils, and other goals which the subject team have included in their vision and goals. When the point of assessing achievement might be, will depend upon which phase, Key Stage or year a subject leader or teacher happens to be responsible for. It follows, therefore, that traditionally any definition of an end-result must always start by defining the end-point at which the measurement will be made. However, it is worth remembering at this point that target-setting is most 'fruitful' when it involves the learner too (Gipps 1994, p.73). Of course, setting a specific attainment level and time limit should not necessarily prevent targets being achieved faster than was hoped for. However, there is always a danger that having set an expected time-related achievement target children will perform to the prediction both in terms of level and time. This is an issue that will be discussed in more detail in Chapter 7.

Learning objectives

As suggested in Chapter 4, in order to trigger 'gestalten processes', what is being encouraged here is a much broader definition of overall pupil achievement. We are therefore recommending that subject leaders examine the work of Bloom (1964) and his formulation of a taxonomy of education objectives. Bloom and his team classified educational objectives into three major domains:

Cognitive – with emphasis on remembering, reasoning, concept formation and creative thinking
Affective – with emphasis on emotive qualities expressed in attitudes, interests, values and emotional biases
Psychomotor – with emphasis on muscle and motor skills, and manipulation in all kinds of activities (such as handwriting, speech, physical education and the like)

Bloom argued that it was the interrelationship of these that produced overall achievement and that concentration on one to the exclusion of others would limit the potential for intellectual development. Others, such as Gardner (1983), have made similar claims.

Furthermore, within Bloom's taxonomy there is a hierarchy of cognitive factors which demonstrate that objectives are cumulative and that higher thinking skills build upon lower thinking skills. The hierarchy is presented in six levels, Level 1 being the lowest (see Figure 5.1).

Figure 5.1   Bloom's taxonomy

Level 1   *Knowledge* – involves those processes which require the recall of facts, terminology, conventions. Without a fund of knowledge one cannot operate cognitively.

Level 2   *Comprehension* – represents a low level of understanding sufficient to grasp the meaning of verbal, written or mathematical material for the purpose of interpretation or extrapolation.

Level 3 *Application* – employs remembering and combining material to give generalisations for use in concrete situations.

Level 4 *Analysis* – means the breakdown of material into its constituent parts in order to find relationships between them. This can only be mastered once the previous levels have been achieved.

Level 5 *Synthesis* – necessitates the putting together of the constituent parts by re-arranging them so as to give an arrangement not apparent before.

Level 6 *Evaluation* – requires value judgements about materials, methods and so forth. To perform this operation successfully would require all the skills of knowledge, comprehension, application, analysis and synthesis for a valid judgement to be possible.

Attainment

It is possible to overlay Bloom's concepts onto a particular subject curriculum and deduce what we would want pupils to attain in each domain at certain time-periods, and to examine what cognitive level different aspects of the curriculum required. From this evaluation of curriculum requirement, a clearer picture will emerge of what, ideally, pupils will be doing and achieving.

Activity 5.3   Applying the taxonomy

1   Take a portion of one attainment target that might typically be taught within the subject curriculum over one term. Use Figure 5.2 to map out which aspects of the topic and its learning processes fall into the taxonomy. Also enter the aspects of attainment that are to be assessed in their appropriate boxes.

2   What is your evaluation of the range of your topic and its learning processes in terms of the pupils' overall development?

As suggested above, for the purpose of filling out and clarifying your vision, the identification of pupil achievement will be wider than the mere identification of targets related to end-of-Key Stage tests or external examination results, although targets of this sort may be included in the statement. What is required here is a broader picture of the summative achievement of pupils. This may be achieved by mapping the content of your subject curriculum onto Figure 5.2 (or an adaptation of it).

Another way of expressing overall pupil achievement might involve describing pupil attainment levels in comparison with other similar schools or even with other subjects within your own school. This 'benchmarking' of pupil attainment is helpful in that if it is included in the vision it ensures that pupils'

Figure 5.2   Using Bloom's taxonomy to map subjects

	Cognitive	NC Level
Knowledge		
Comprehension		
Application		
Analysis		
Synthesis		
Evaluation		

Affective	*Psychomotor*

achievements are always closely related to those of 'competitors' (however they might be defined). This is important as the staff's 'gestalten processes' (i.e. tension caused by an intense desire to close the gap) will be triggered into action whenever they perceive a gap between their school's/department's attainment levels and those of other schools/departments. As we shall see later, when discussing strategic analysis and planning, keeping a wary eye on the competition is essential to creating a successful organisation.

Benchmarking information is now readily available via your school's Performance and Assessment (PANDA) and the Pre-inspection (PICSI) data used by OfSTED inspection teams. When OfSTED judge pupils' level of attainment in lessons or across a school, they always use the national benchmark to decide on their grading, irrespective of the background of pupil or environmental factors affecting the school. While this sometimes causes anxiety at the school level, it is essential for OfSTED to do this since it is the only way they can judge standards consistently around the country.

Individual schools may feel that in the future they too will have to use this same methodology in the interim between inspections to ensure that they are working consistently to national norms and that there are no surprises when OfSTED return after four years! This system has worked well in other places, such as Guernsey (for obvious practical reasons), and in other sectors, such as higher education.

Progress

In some ways, progress might be considered to be more straightforward since, on the face of it, teachers might not need to have the kind of value-laden debate that deciding what attainment should be tends to promote. In fact, determining pupil achievement in terms of progress is equally problematic.

In OfSTED terms, progress can be defined as the amount learned over a given period. To measure this, we would normally examine where a pupil's level of attainment is at a fixed point (e.g. as in Baseline Assessment in Year R) and then measure their attainment again at a later point in time. This is called *ipsative* assessment and, while these individual scores are recorded and used to determine individual progress, an aggregation of pupils' results cannot be used in the same way (because the aggregated averages mask individual progress). Inspectors will comment upon the learning that has taken place either within an individual lesson, or maybe across a term or a year. The judgement will depend upon the rate of learning. Sometimes, if there has been a low starting point, the rate of progress can be judged as good while overall attainment may be considered poor. Schools often find this difficult to accept but, for reasons explained above, it is an essential position for OfSTED to take.

There are, of course, other ways of judging progress. A pupil's progress can be compared to performance criteria that were set for that pupil at the beginning of the year (criterion referenced) or against performance of other pupils (norm referenced). In addition, as well as looking at the amount of progress, we can look for the rate of progress. In terms of fleshing out your vision statement, having a picture of all pupils learning at an accelerated rate *for them* might be a more powerful trigger for creative thinking than trying to predict and set targets concerning the amount of progress. The reason for this is that, rather like the situation with setting attainment targets, having a specified target amount might limit teachers' and pupils' aspirations and have the effect of slowing down the rate of progress to achieve the target amount on the due date.

Response

Whatever targets for progress are set, it is essential that teachers do have a clear picture of what successful pupil behaviour will look like. As we shall see when we discuss 'Strategic monitoring, evaluation and review' in Chapter 7, if feedback activity is to work it must be informed by very clear images of what is desirable behaviour (whereas many teachers only transmit to pupils clear pictures of what is undesirable).

Normally schools have clear policies on pupils' conduct, but it is sometimes necessary for subjects to have specific behaviour policies as well (e.g. science, physical education). In terms of classroom behaviour, how children respond to the teacher is closely related to teaching styles and to the quality of interaction between pupils and teachers. It is therefore impossible to isolate objectives for pupil behaviour from objectives for staff behaviour.

OfSTED look closely at how pupils respond to teachers in lessons and at how they generally behave around the school. They also judge pupil attitude and the way pupils interact with each other. On their own, none of these aspects of behaviour can be deemed appropriate or inappropriate. What determines appropriateness is the definition of what behaviour is required to achieve the desired outcomes. Subject leaders should therefore be spending time looking at what effective pupil behaviour is for high achievement in their subject and then building that picture into their vision. This will subsequently translate itself into subject policies.

STAGE 5: WHAT STAFF AND OTHERS WILL DO

As we have seen, it is impossible to separate how we want pupils to respond to teachers without describing how we want teachers to behave towards pupils. However, it is not our purpose here to examine the qualities of effective classroom management, but to look at issues that affect staff performance in relation to their involvement with the strategic process.

A major problem with policy-makers determining what staff might do in a particular situation is that, because they are often working apart from the 'chalk-face', they make inaccurate assumptions about what behaviour is appropriate. These misjudgements may well lead to plans being devised which simply cannot work.

However, techniques are available to enable policy-makers to investigate fairly accurately what staff behaviour will be required. One example of this is 'backward mapping'.

Forward and backward mapping

The concepts of forward and backward mapping are described by Elmore (1979) who attempts to show why many policies and plans are implemented ineffectively in many organisations, and how a different approach to implementation could bring more effective results. For us, the concepts provide a useful way of analysing the needs of those who are to become involved in implementing policy. The concept of backward mapping is introduced here to clarify what those who might be involved in supporting pupil achievement will need to do and what resources may need to be available. Once identified, necessary actions can be further refined to form the basis of clear policy and an operational frame-work understood and owned by staff.

Before looking at how backward mapping can help the policy-maker it is useful to consider its antithesis, so as to gain a better understanding of the construct. We shall also return to forward mapping when examining how resources can be best allocated to support innovation.

Figure 5.3   Forward and backward mapping

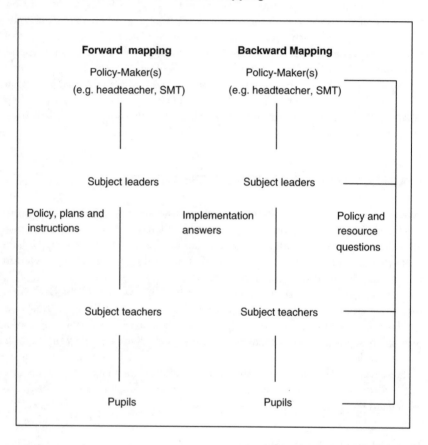

Forward mapping

Forward mapping (see Figure 5.3) describes the way in which senior policy-makers move from policy creation to implementation through a series of pre-planned activities that move down the organisation from top to bottom. In forward-mapping organisations, objectives are drawn up for each layer within the organisation and rules, constraints and penalties are introduced to ensure that each layer complies with the orders issued from the layer above them.

Management therefore assumes that, by and large, each layer of 'subordinates' will conform to whatever demand is made of them and implement the policy as management intended.

This kind of operation is commonly found in military and civil-service organisations, but many businesses, hospitals and even schools were also (and still are) run like this. 'Top-down' management has largely been discredited in professional organisations because it is impossible for senior managers to know with any certainty whether or not subordinates are complying with instructions, since they largely work unsupervised by their 'line manager'.

However, its biggest flaw is not with making people work like this, but it lies in the assumption that senior managers who create policy know, at any given moment, exactly what is required on the 'shopfloor' to implement their policy. History, especially in the case of military and government examples (the Charge of the Light Brigade is often quoted as an extreme example), shows us that in most cases senior managers were not aware of the real needs of subordinates and as a consequence either the planned activity produced a disaster, or shopfloor-level subordinates changed the plans to suit best what they could achieve. In either case, the original policy is never implemented as it was intended. There are many examples of both of these in education. The demise of appraisal, once the subject of bitter debate between the government and the teaching profession, is a good example of a forward-mapping strategy. Interestingly, the government's Green Paper (DfEE 1999a) has now resurrected the debate within the profession by implying that more forward-mapped policy on appraisal will be even more rigorously implemented.

Of course there are contexts in which taking an autocratic, forward-mapping approach is essential. Crisis situations and other circumstances in which safety is an issue often require things to be 'done by the book', for people to follow orders without questioning them or making any alteration to set procedures. The recent spate of terrible incursions into schools by people intent on harming the pupils has led to a tightening of security procedures all over the world. Few teachers would argue against this kind of forward-mapping policy-making and implementation.

Similarly, when managers need to know with certainty that something will be delivered to an exact customer specification then forward mapping might be appropriate. However, it is rarely appropriate in stages of developing what processes and specifications should be.

The obvious problem with this approach to staff behaviour in classrooms is that, except on rare occasions, senior managers cannot know exactly what staff behaviour is needed at any given moment. Managers can and do lay down guidelines about corporal punishment and other forms of barred behaviour, but for most of the time they have to trust to the professional judgement of their staff. In fact, they more often than not adopt a backward-mapping strategy.

Backward mapping

When backward mapping (see Figure 5.3), the school leader takes the view that people in the best position to assess what policy-implementation actions are needed are at 'chalk-face' level and at the level immediately above that.

Backward mapping therefore begins in the *first stage* by policy-makers asking: what objectives will it be possible to achieve in view of the existing context of the likely implementer? The answer to this question may alter some of the objectives in the short-term, until the policy-maker has improved the context for the implementer.

In the *second stage* the policy-maker considers, often in conversation with implementers, the current behaviour of the implementer and asks what changes to this behaviour will be needed to achieve the policy objectives. In asking this question directly to the implementer, the policy-maker may also gain two other vital pieces of information:

1   suggestions of alternative and maybe more effective ways of achieving the objectives
2   some idea about the exact nature of resources that will be needed to make the necessary changes

The *third stage* takes this information and asks: what is the current ability of the implementer's immediate senior to support the changes planned for the implementer? Again, if asked directly, not only will this ability to support change be analysed, but new ideas may be generated and details of resources needed are collected.

This analysis backs up through the remaining layers of the organisation until the question is asked of the most senior manager (i.e. the policy-maker).

When the analysis is completed, the senior management can devise an appropriate plan containing the elements needed to achieve the objectives at each level of the organisation. The planning process should also include a consideration of what resources should be delivered to which people in order to have the greatest effect. Thus a resourcing plan should be developed that may well be forward-mapped through the organisation.

In both of the models, the policy-maker sets and retains the responsibility and accountability for policy-formulation and objective-setting. However, in the backward-mapping process, there is a recognition that while the ability to manage the whole organisation is located among the senior management team, the expertise needed to complete the objectives rests at levels closely involved with their achievement. There is a reciprocal dependency on the part played by both senior management and shopfloor, with a mutual respect for each other's talents.

Activity 5.4   What should staff achieve?

Describe desirable staff achievement in relation to the following questions:

1   What will teachers and other staff be doing to facilitate pupil achievement?
2   What will other people in the school (e.g. subject leaders, senior management) be doing to support teachers and other staff?
3   What will other people outside school be doing to support pupils and staff?

Now, complete Activity 5.5.

Activity 5.5   Applying Elmore's concept

1   Examine Figure 5.3. Take one part of the subject vision or goal as it impacts on staff behaviour and ask the three stages of questions outlined in Activity 5.4.
2   Take the answers gained from this process and produce a plan to forward map actions and resources to the points where they are most needed to bring about the policy change.

Communicating and spreading ownership of the vision

> ... leadership involves providing or offering a sense of direction for the school. It is to do with vision and mission, with goals and priorities. It is also about the leader's ability to articulate these pathways and to explain them to colleagues. Leaders need to be able to present descriptions of where the school is heading and to account for why this is important.
>
> (Southworth 1998, p.34)

The importance of introducing the concept of backward mapping into this part of the book is that links are being made between subject leaders' ability to formulate and share their vision and their ability to see the vision's objectives implemented.

Backward mapping provides a structured process for communicating vision (i.e. the 'what'), while enabling staff to enter into shared ownership of it by asking them to provide the answers to the 'how?' questions. The process will also enable leaders to trigger the kinds of gestalten processes in their staff described earlier. This is because backward mapping facilitates internalisation of the vision and its objectives and draws attention to the gap between future and current behaviours. Additionally, by involving staff in debating 'how?', creative energy is released for the resolution of the problem and implementation of the solution.

Activity 5.6   Communicating your vision

Write down a plan for how and when you are going to share your vision and goals. Who will you talk to first? Will you tell everyone everything? Will you commit this to paper or just talk, say, at a meeting?

The questions at the beginning of this part of the chapter are intended to encourage subject leaders to engage in the backward-mapping process. Clearly, much of what is being asked of staff will involve new classroom behaviours and require class-level resources. However, subject leaders may find that, through backward mapping, much greater things are achieved than even they can envisage.

6 Towards a strategic plan

INTRODUCTION

The overview to this part of the book introduced the concept of *strategic analysis*. It was presented as an activity which comes *after* the vision and goals have been set and not before. This departs from other planning models (e.g. DES 1989b, 1991) which start with a review of the *status quo* and then set targets for improvement (see MacGilchrist *et al.* 1995).

The DES approach produces a number of incremental steps over a long time-period to achieve improvement. Its flaw is that it is impossible do things dramatically differently or improve standards very quickly using this method. This is because under this system each stage of target-setting takes existing practice and resources and moves them on a bit for pragmatic reasons. Thus current staff expertise or the amount of budget available in a particular financial year will determine the type or scale of objective set. It is a forward-mapping model that relies on an audit by senior management to determine priorities that they turn into a School Development Plan.

This approach also has limitations in that it assumes that schools will only do a bit better next year than this year. This means that it actually closes down 'gestalten processes' rather than opening them up. This is because the closer an objective is to what already exists the less we see it as a problem to be solved. In addition, we are unconsciously driven to want to make 'meaningful assumptions about our environment' (Mullins 1996, p.145), to understand the whole problem so our minds can then work towards its solution. Thus breaking down problems into artificial incremental steps before people have had a chance to picture the ideal end-result (i.e. the vision), does not stimulate our creative forces.

Another problem we believe is that, for many of us, our minds are already conditioned to accept that we live in a 'could-do-better' world. It is quite normal for us to experience the feeling this gives us. We know that we might improve 'if only we … '. We learnt this at school via our school reports and at university when we accepted that a 2.2 was about the best we could hope for given the amount of work we did. We know we could be a bit tidier, be a bit better off, spend a bit more time with our children 'if only … '. Living with a sense of unfulfilled potential is already part of our normality. So finding out through a school review that we 'could do better' is not a surprise to us, nor is finding out, via an OfSTED report, that there is scope for improvement at our school, because there always is.

In fact, when OfSTED have delivered their judgements, teachers often say: 'We could have told them that ... we know what's wrong here, it's just we haven't the time or resources to improve it'. And indeed they have not, because most teachers only have enough time and resources to do what they are currently doing (or, they might concede, perhaps a little bit more). They certainly do not believe that they have much spare time or spare creative energy. So setting a modest target that is only just beyond what teachers acknowledge is their current capability does not constitute enough of a problem to switch on the gestalten process.

There is no criticism of staff implied in writing this. What we are describing here is basic human nature. Most of us, if we have worked for a number of years in an organisation, have already reached the level of performance that we have set in our minds. We have filled our time with about as much work as we believe we can cope with and have expended as much energy as we believe we have available. In short, the perception of our world matches closely the picture in our minds and, as a consequence, our gestalten processes are shut down. We do look to improve things, but only when we are given the time and the resources. In fact, we are more likely to find energy and creativity from within when our stability is threatened, and then often the Gestalt works to keep the status quo – to avoid change.

Fullan and Hargreaves (1998) discuss why some teachers, particularly older and more experienced teachers, are less enthusiastic and more cynical about improvement plans. Among others, they quote Huberman's research (1988, 1992) into the same problem: 'He [Huberman] found that most teachers in mid-to-late career were unlikely to embrace innovation with enthusiasm, and unlikely to make any radical changes in their approaches to teaching either' (Fullan and Hargreaves 1998, p.38). This description from the research can be interpreted as being quite critical of teachers. However, we have tried to show that for most teachers (of whatever age) this kind of 'plateau-ing' is normal. The consequence is that, for many school and subject leaders, school improvement is sometimes a slow grind, an uphill struggle to gain commitment, to engender enthusiasm and to secure changed behaviour from their busy and overworked staff.

The alternative, as we have already discussed, is to enable the staff to see a *markedly* better picture of the ways things can be. To inspire staff to want to share the ownership of an image of a *considerably* improved subject/school that they believe they can create, and to be challenged with problems that are worthy of them using their valuable life's time to solve.

We have described earlier how subject leaders might set out and share their vision and goals for a much improved educational deal for the pupils and how that can be broken down further into more tangible pictures of what pupils and staff will be doing when the improvement has been achieved. Now, in order to trigger the Gestalt, subject leaders need to take a close and accurate look at what is currently happening within their subject area.

STAGE 6: STRATEGIC ANALYSIS 1 – ANALYSING CURRENT PERFORMANCE

In the strategic process, the purpose of analysis is to accurately define the gap between the image of the considerably improved subject/school and the way things really are. Therefore aspects of performance that need to be examined should be the same as those identified in Stages 4 and 5 (see Chapter 5). This is important to make the whole process work. Again, to reiterate points made in earlier chapters, it is the tension caused by the difference between our mental picture of the way we want things to be and our perception of the way things are *now* that triggers the creative gestalten process to bring about change. Therefore, the more accurate and explicit the detail described in the 'gap', the more it will support the next stage in the process.

The methodology for collecting data about current performance will be largely dependent upon the type of performance envisaged. The method of analysis used to determine the level of performance will again depend upon what kind of referencing (i.e. ipsative, criterion or normative) is chosen. However, much of the discussion in Stages 4 and 5 that supports the setting of attainment and behavioural objectives, encourages leaders to define aspects of attainment and behavioural objectives in as wide a way as possible.

The more that objectives move away from things that can be counted (quantitative), the more problematic is their assessment. In some cases, notably at governmental level, this has led to a situation where what could be easily measured was made important (e.g. test and examination results), rather than deciding what was important and finding a satisfactory way of measuring it. However, there is an adage used in industry that states 'what gets measured gets done'. This might imply that it is the outcome of the measurement that is the driving force. However, research has shown (e.g. Drucker 1968, Peters and Waterman 1982) that quantitative or qualitative targets work because they give importance to the task – it is the fact that the employees see the work as meaningful to them that makes the difference. Subject leaders, working co-operatively with senior management, do have an opportunity to define what is important and then find a way of measuring what matters so it gets done. What matters, in this context, must be related to the purpose that was defined earlier in Stage 1 of this strategic process.

Activity 6.1 supports this. Subject leaders may wish to further refine questions to align them with their own vision and goals.

Activity 6.1   Establishing levels of performance

With subject staff, discuss the following questions:

What is our current level of performance – pupil, teacher, others (ipsative or criteria referenced)?

2   How well are we doing compared to (similar) others (normative i.e. benchmark referenced)?

3   What is the gap between our current performance and our vision?

The questions in Activity 6.1 are fairly straightforward, the answers (particularly to the second question) will no doubt create a debate within the subject team. Knowing what to do with the answers will help to focus these discussions and it is therefore recommended that staff are familiar with the processes in Stage 7 before interpreting the above data.

STAGE 7: STRATEGIC ANALYSIS 2 – DECIDING WHAT NEEDS TO CHANGE

There are three key questions that subject leaders and teams need to be able to answer:

1   What are our strengths and weaknesses (e.g. pupils, staff, management, governors, resources) and what opportunities and threats exist beyond the school (catchment area, national and LEA policies, competitors, business, the community)?

2   What and who will help and what and who might hinder (e.g. teacher expertise, stakeholder commitment, availability of resources)?

3   What and who is most important and most urgent to change?

To enable subject leaders to answer these questions, this stage introduces three fairly simple, yet powerful, analytical tools that subject leaders and their teams can use to determine subject strategy. None of them are new and many leaders may have used them before. However, in the context of our ten-stage process they provide an effective link between creating and clarifying the vision and planning for its achievement.

Conducting a SWOT Analysis

Conducting a SWOT Analysis: Strengths – Weaknesses – Opportunities – Threats (Ansoff 1987) involves taking an objective view of the current situation in the school and its environment and laying the analysis out in the way indicated in Figure 6.1. The relationship of the boxes is significant. The top two are for data from inside the organisation. Here the subject leader can see the balancing positive and negative side of the current situation. The bottom two dimensions relate to factors outside the school which have or will have impact on the subject leader's vision for improvement. Although the box is quite small in this book, subject leaders can take as much space as they need to set down their analysis (indeed a separate piece of flipchart paper for each dimension is often needed when analysing a whole subject area).

The example in Figure 6.1 is drawn from a Literacy Co-ordinator who has a number of problems: trying to implement the national strategy, maintaining her own good work in reading, coping with the national focus on the introduction of a numeracy strategy, and co-operating with the school's own SDP priority of ICT development.

Figure 6.1   SWOT Analysis

Strengths	Weaknesses
V. good KS1 results (above N. av.)	Dip in attainment in Y3&4 (below N. av.)
Strong literacy teaching in KS1 and Y6	Boys' under-achievement in KS2
Up-to-date L. policy approved by head	Fairly old resources in KS2
Mrs X (NQT) v. good – up-to-date K & U	Mrs J (KS1) leaving
Good reading scheme well embedded	Mr B (NQT)weak, Ms V Y4 ill
Well trained, keen LSAs	No training days allocated
12 parents + 3 govs help each week	High turnover of parents
Subject leader's own ability	Lack of ICT access
Opportunities	**Threats**
V. good LEA L. adviser	School priority on ICT dev't
LEA L.co-ord. good ideas network	Nat. and sch. focus on numeracy
New ICT policy and resources	Publication of SATs KS results
National ICT training	Lack of school budget for dev't
LEA fund to supplement L. training	Ofsted in 2 years

Assessing internal strengths and weaknesses

Taking the outcomes of Stage 6 it is possible to translate the analysis of pupil and staff performance into a subject's strengths and weaknesses. The analysis should have been conducted using the objectives set within the vision, so strengths and weaknesses will be related to these. It is probable that both strengths and weaknesses will be subdivided into the different categories of objectives envisaged.

When writing the results of the analysis down under the headings, statements need to be clear and specific. Statements such as 'good teaching in Year 8' or 'poor KS2 science resources' are not helpful in preparation for planning. The danger is that these kinds of statements average out variations in quality between teachers, pupils and resources. This is unhelpful because:

- it makes it very difficult to target improvement activity
- it is even more difficult to ascertain later whether any improvement has been made

It is better to be more specific (e.g. name names and list the actual resources being referred to).

Analysing external opportunities and threats

In the example given in Figure 6.1, the subject leader interpreted 'external' to mean beyond her own subject responsibility. Normally, external is taken to mean outside the organisation, although either interpretation can be used depending upon which is more useful to the subject leader.

Looking for opportunities

In organisations, this aspect of analysis is called 'Market Analysis' or 'Environmental Scanning' (Fidler 1996) and is considered an essential element of business planning (Drucker 1968). This is because businesses have traditionally succeeded only in proportion to their ability to understand their market (i.e. what products which customers want at what price) and assess their position in that market in relation their competitors. Senior management continually collect information from their environment to ensure that they are always aware of both current and future market opportunities and business threats. Traditionally, schools have been less involved in these processes.

In state schools, up until the 1988 Education Reform Act, the environment in which individual schools operated was largely controlled by the government and the LEA. Opportunities for school growth (e.g. increase in school roll) lay in the hands of Education Sub-Committees and LEA Officers. Similarly, threatening implications of major government changes in policy (e.g. the move from Grammar Schools to Comprehensive Schools, or the more recent introduction of Grant Maintained and City Technology Colleges) were potentially filtered by LEA policy (e.g. West Sussex went Comprehensive yet had no Grant Maintained schools, while Kent retained Grammar Schools and 50 per cent of its secondary schools were Grant Maintained until April 1999).

With successive changes during the last ten years and the introduction of Fair Funding, the environment that schools operate in could not be more different. The changes have introduced new pressures into schools which

> in their powerful and different ways, have created a range of significant effects on the schools of this country, creating an altogether changed and changing context for work of teachers and their pupils.
>
> (Day *et al.* 1998, p.4)

One of the key areas of change relates to reduction of the role of the LEA. Except for decisions relating to new schools and school closure, SEN and home–school transport, an LEA's only major influence on schools will be related to school effectiveness and school improvement. To all intents and purposes, schools will conduct themselves in the marketplace in very similar ways to businesses.

Therefore, schools will have to become much more critically aware of the environment in which they operate. This awareness will need to take account of the same market conditions as the other kinds of business described above. In the case of schools, 'opportunities' will include (for instance) looking to:

- increase the number of pupils (e.g. because of a nearby house-building programme)
- improve the quality of pupils that come to the school (e.g. because of changes to the rules governing selection)
- diversify the range of subjects or type of courses offered (e.g. pre-school provision because of new childcare arrangements for funding lone parents)
- increase Sixth Form courses because of the increased public confidence in GNVQ
- increase the use of plant and machinery through opportunities to open adult-learning centres or after-school and holiday clubs

Scanning for threats

Scanning for threats may include:

- looking for nearby schools getting better test or examination results or a better OfSTED report
- other schools introducing elements of selection procedures
- schools changing their status or offering an enhanced range of subjects
- schools having new facilities built, promoting themselves as community centres or moving location so facilities are nearer the school or in a more attractive site

Much of this school-level scanning may not relate to the role of the subject leader at an individual subject level. However, its outcomes will have an impact throughout the school. For instance, in the future there will be even more comparisons of school results at the local (and national) level and even more parents will be looking at the SATs and GCSE results in specific subjects as a means of comparing schools. This may lead to some schools making strategic decisions to specialise in order to develop a market niche.

Paradoxically, although it was argued earlier in this book that all subjects are necessary and are of equal value to the child in the longer term, the government (through its direction of the National Curriculum) seems to have publicly declared that some subjects are 'more equal than others'. This introduces significant pressure on leaders of core subjects who now find themselves in the limelight when it comes to public comparisons of school results. This situation brings both opportunities and threats: e.g. the introduction of the Literacy Hour brought the threat of timetable disruption and an additional burden on staff, while at the same time the additional resources that were available gave many subject leaders the opportunity to review and revise their policy, develop more consistently effective teaching across the school and add to their teaching materials.

The above is an example of where external forces and resources influenced internal events. However, even when the imperative for change comes from within the school, the subject leader can use the concept of analysing opportunities and threats as they apply to the internal school environment beyond their subject. The fact some subjects are being singled out nationally for additional attention and resources means that there is a danger that an even greater gap emerges between subject areas and departments within the school. Most subject leaders are no doubt aware of the potential for internal disparity of opportunity caused by the effect of national policies on resourcing.

Yet many of the internal factors that lead to some subjects being more favourably considered have little to do with external forces. Tradition, the subject background of senior staff, staff turnover, the ability to recruit specialist staff in 'minority' subjects and special features of local employment are some of the factors that can influence a subject's role and standing within the school. There are examples of schools that have a national standing by having an acclaimed musical group; a gym club that wins national titles; pupils who regularly win prizes for technological innovation, locally successful debating teams and so on. In these schools, the internal environment must be affected by this success and skilfully handled by subject leaders and senior managers.

For a school to remain a balanced institution it is necessary that all subject leaders work together, sharing their visions and conducting their environmental analysis with mutual concern and respect.

Activity 6.2   Conducting a SWOT Analysis

Conduct a SWOT Analysis of your subject area, or an aspect of it that you wish to develop. (NB: Ensure it is concerned with the achievement of your vision.) You may wish to do this jointly with your subject team.

Force Field Analysis

Force Field Analysis is another tool that is commonly used to support strategic analysis. Its basis is two fairly straightforward questions:

1   What and who will help us to achieve our targets? (Driving forces)
2   What and who might prevent us or slow us down? (Restraining forces)

The answers to these questions are derived from the answers to the SWOT Analysis and are drawn onto a chart (similar to Figure 6.2) presented as a series of labelled arrows. Some analysts find it helpful to symbolise the scale of the helpful or hindering force by drawing different-sized arrows (as shown). This enables the evaluator to see the situation more clearly. The example in Figure 6.2 takes up the case of the primary Literacy Co-ordinator's problems. Only a few of the issues have been entered on to the force-field in order to demonstrate how a complete chart might look.

Figure 6.2   Force Field Analysis

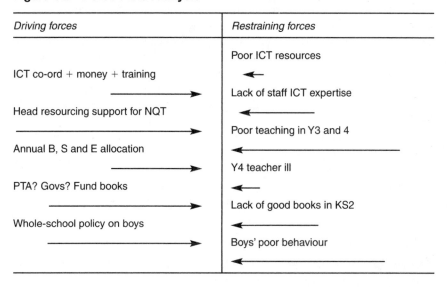

Driving forces	Restraining forces
	Poor ICT resources
ICT co-ord + money + training	←
——————→	Lack of staff ICT expertise
Head resourcing support for NQT	←———
——————→	Poor teaching in Y3 and 4
Annual B, S and E allocation	←—————————
——————→	Y4 teacher ill
PTA? Govs? Fund books	←—
——————→	Lack of good books in KS2
Whole-school policy on boys	←———
——————→	Boys' poor behaviour
	←—————————

It is also useful to have different sections within the force field which relate to each other. For instance, in the SWOT example provided earlier, the need to implement a new ICT policy is seen as both a threat and an opportunity by the subject leader. On the Force Field Analysis this is interpreted by showing that there is a helpful ICT Co-ordinator in the school and that there will be money available for resources and staff training. On the restraining side, the existing poor ICT resources, very limited staff expertise and lack of time in the curriculum mean this is going to be a very difficult policy to implement. However, the purpose of the Force Field Analysis is not simply to identify the scale of the problem and help, it is helpful in showing subject leaders where their priorities are for action.

In the case of the school's ICT policy, there is a need for the subject leader to backward map (see Chapter 5) the problems related to improving resources, staff expertise and curriculum time in order to be able to draw up an accurate estimate of what equipment, staff training and time will be required. Clearly, using the ICT Co-ordinator will be most helpful in this analysis. However, the first question that must be asked by the subject leader is: where does the ICT issue rank in order of priority for action within my subject area? The answer will, of course, depend upon the subject leader's vision and shorter-term targets.

In the example above, although the ICT issue is significant, it is not as important (or as urgent) as the dip in reading attainment in Years 3 and 4 which is having a dramatic effect upon the pupils' (and particularly boys') performance at Key Stage 2. Unless it can be shown that the introduction of more ICT into the classroom would really support the improvement of reading and that this could be achieved within a fairly short time-period (e.g. a term), then the actions to improve reading by more traditional methods should probably be employed.

The Force Field Analysis reveals the problems in this area to be a weakness in the Year 3 teacher (a newly qualified teacher – NQT) and a long-term illness to the Year 4 teacher that has resulted in the class being taught by a succession of supply teachers. In both cases, this has resulted in poor classroom management and a lack of pupil control (especially of the boys). However, as the effects of these problems are not restricted to reading (i.e. all the subjects are suffering) it is to be tackled in the immediate short term by direct intervention of the headteacher. She has decided to allocate all the remaining supply and staff-development budget to support the NQT and provide release for other staff to work with the Year 4 class.

This demonstrates clearly how, because the priority was established, ideas and resources can be found to resolve the issue. It is the clarity of the analysis of what is important and what is urgent that aids the decision-making process.

Activity 6.3   Using Force Field Analysis

Take the outcomes of the SWOT Analysis you did in Activity 6.2 and plot the weaknesses and threats onto a force field chart. What driving forces could be mustered to remove or lessen the impact of the restraining forces?

Determining priorities for action: What is important? What is urgent?

A third tool can be used to help the manager prioritise action. It enables the subject leader to discriminate between those issues which are related to the subject leader's and/or school's goals and those things that appear suddenly – that need to be done 'by yesterday' – and, because of their urgency, seem to be very important at the time to do. This is a vital activity for the subject leader whose time will always be limited and therefore valuable.

> The major strategic decision for leaders is to try to match time to priorities and not be shifted from them even in crisis management. I cannot however escape the view that personal time management is a key to successful leadership.
>
> (Brighouse 1991, p.18)

The Force Field Analysis has shown what needs attention and from where most support (driving forces) can be obtained to overcome difficulties (restraining forces). It should also reveal which are the most important and urgent issues. A matrix can be used to plot these so that an action plan can be produced.

However, the key issue involved with completing a matrix is weighing-up the relative importance of school versus subject demands: namely, to *whom* is it important? The answer should always relate to the subject leader's communicated vision and goals, although there will be times when the headteacher's, other colleagues' or other stakeholders' (e.g. pupils and parents) needs will have to be met first. In a backward-mapping organisation, the senior management will leave decisions about time management to the most appropriate level, since those people are almost always best placed to know what needs to be done in what order.

Criteria

The criteria for making decisions of this kind might well have been discussed and agreed across the organisation and be related to some key principles, such as:

- health and safety for pupils, staff and the public is paramount
- being with the pupils is the most important staff activity
- changing teacher activities should lead to better pupil achievement
- expenditure must be linked with agreed school or subject targets
- any change which saves money without impairing the quality of education available is urgent
- staff development is an important entitlement for all staff providing it links to school improvement

The simple matrix in Figure 6.3 shows four possible positions.

Figure 6.3 Important versus urgent matrix

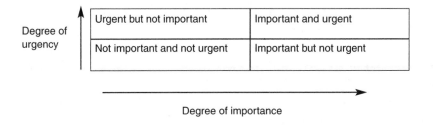

Degree of urgency

| Urgent but not important | Important and urgent |
| Not important and not urgent | Important but not urgent |

Degree of importance

Not important and not urgent

If anything appears in this box then the subject leader may well ask: why am I/are we doing this? Unless the subject leader and team have done everything in the other boxes, then anything written in here should be ignored!

Urgent but not important

This is a situation that often arises when teachers are analysing their own time management. Often people believe that there are far too many urgent jobs to do and urgency can panic people into actions that they otherwise would not take. At school, the issue may not be that important to the subject leader (especially in terms of their long-term goals) but it is important to others (e.g. a pupil or senior management). If the environmental scan has detected an urgent 'external' issue, it may be that it will have to be dealt with immediately, before it does become more important and starts to loom over longer-term plans. The key question to ask here is: can I/we do anything about this *now*? If the answer is 'yes', then do it. If the answer is 'no', then ask: 'when can I/we do something about it?' Then plan an action at that time and put the issue to one side.

Important but not urgent

From our SWOT and FF Analysis, the strategically important, longer-term issues will be identified that can be plotted here. The contents of this box will indicate the issues that should appear on the long- and medium-term strategic plan. The more actions that appear in this box, the more you and your team will be able to act strategically.

Important and urgent

By contrast, although issues which are entered here are going to be ones which you will tackle first, they may be less strategic than the ones above. In an ideal world, a subject leader would never be driven into any action just because of its urgency, however important. However, in the real world, many things happen beyond the immediate control of the leader (e.g. staff leave or become ill, pupils behave unpredictably etc.). If anything does appear in this position, it usually means it is *really* urgent and lack of action might precipitate crisis.

Activity 6.4   Prioritising action

Take the SWOT and Force Field example given above and complete an important versus urgent grid on the subject leader's behalf. Use the suggested criteria.

Activity 6.5   Following up a SWOT, FF and Priority Analysis

Look at a SWOT, FF and Priority Analysis and identify the areas of necessary change in your subject that best fit a gradual change process. Reflect upon the process that will be required and how you will read and manage it.

Preparing to write the strategic plan

At the end of this stage you should have completed a thorough strategic analysis of your problems in relation to your aspirations. It should be very clear to you what and who needs changing and in what order change needs to take place. These actions can be drafted onto a planning sheet. However, before final decisions are made about action, it may be worthwhile to consider how people may react to what is being proposed. In the next section of this chapter, consideration is given to the nature of change and the leadership behaviour that needs to be employed to see it through.

STAGE 8: PLANNING FOR CHANGE

Planning and managing change is nearly always more difficult than planners think. Usually this is because they underestimate how complex it can be and how important change can be perceived to be by those going through it. Change is also 'unsettling, threatening, and unpredictable' (Blandford 1997, p.175), but it also brings opportunities for learning, growth and development. This stage of the strategic process is therefore concerned with examining the concepts of change through three different dimensions: improvement, replacement and re-invention. We contend that these dimensions need different change strategies because the effects of each on the people involved are increasingly dramatic.

Faced with the outcomes of the SWOT and Force Field Analysis, and the important versus urgent mapping, the subject leader will have an accurate idea of who and what needs changing and in what order. The following questions now need to be answered:

1   What/who needs improving? (Continual change)
2   What/who needs replacing? (Incremental change)
3   What/who needs re-inventing? (Revolutionary change)
                              (Adapted from Meyerson and Martin 1997, p.39)

Each of these dimensions is discussed below, so that subject leaders can discriminate between the aspects of change they need to plan for and gain insights into how they might plan the change process.

Improvement (Continual change)

For many schools, 'School Improvement' is an evolutionary process. The exceptions are those schools that are suddenly faced with enormous challenges (e.g. a change of status) or find themselves in 'special measures', in which case the kind of change required is more aptly described as incremental or revolutionary change (see below). The majority of subject leaders are faced equally by the need to improve continually the quality of teaching, the quality (and quantity) of resources and, hence, pupil learning and subsequent test or examination results.

This kind of change is continual in that it builds upon the past and is relatively slow. It often moves at the pace of the slowest, and is resource-constrained, in that what can be achieved has to be linked to the whole organisation and to internal competition for resources. This is not to say that individual subject departments cannot improve greatly over time, but that the improvement will normally be associated with subject leaders' and their teams' tenacious determination to make things better, rather than being the result of a sudden influx of resources, people or bright ideas.

Hopkins *et al.* (1994) have now concluded that this kind of steady, step-by-step process-based change accounts for perhaps 80 per cent of school improvement (with the remaining 20 per cent a result of more incremental or revolutionary activity). This makes sense, since teachers probably spend about the same 80:20 proportion of time, energy and resources on classroom teaching as against other non-classroom activities. It is therefore fairly obvious that change introduced this way will normally drip-feed into lessons over a period of time, the teacher ensuring that it enhances rather than disrupts the learning process.

Changes of this sort normally relate to areas such as:

- planning (schemes of work and individual lessons)
- classroom arrangements (positioning of desks, pupil groupings, resources)
- lesson delivery (teaching style, teacher–pupil interaction, discipline)
- learning activity (tasks, use of technology, active learning)
- assessment (testing, homework, marking)

There will also be other incremental change areas that support classroom activities, such as changes to policies, staff deployment and development. It is likely that as well as being incremental, these changes will probably not be difficult to achieve in the short- or medium-term, since they do not require any wholescale changes. It follows that the largest part of the subject/departmental improvement plan will focus on supporting the driving forces and overcoming the restraining forces related to these areas.

Replacement (Incremental change)

Given that 80 per cent of the subject improvement plan will be related to continual change, most of the remaining elements of the plan will involve incremental change (i.e. doing something new) or revolutionary change (i.e. doing something very different).

However, whereas continual change is more akin to an evolutionary process, incremental change is more a product of organisational culture. Incremental change will often involve innovation and that requires creativity which needs to be fostered and nurtured by facilitating the internal conditions that encourage it. This is sometimes referred to as the organisation's 'climate' (Handy 1993) and the main product of creating an innovatory climate is team-work. Bennis describes how most of the best-known products of innovation (e.g. the Sistine Chapel ceiling, Walt Disney cartoons) were created by what he describes as 'Great Groups' who 'hope to make a dent in the universe' and 'flare like a rocket for a while, then vanish, leaving behind their creation' (Bennis and Goldsmith 1997, p.xi).

Bennis's research shows that one of the key characteristics of the successful leader is to pick 'a small number of good people' (Bennis and Goldsmith 1997, p.119). He describes how one of the most powerful and successful leaders of innovation in the USA aircraft industry had 'an unerring eye for talent. And because he understood why talented people work, he was able to create an environment in which they thrived' (Bennis and Goldsmith 1997, p.120).

A number of other features contribute to creating the kind of climate in which innovation can flourish:

Recognising that things need to change   Change processes are often embarked upon in organisations with significant numbers of employees refusing to accept the need to change – the need to stop doing one thing and do another. Most subject leaders will be familiar with concepts such as 'ownership' and 'getting people on board'. However, if creative problem-solving is linked to gestalten processes then it follows that those people who are required to be creative recognise the internal tension created by the gap between what they want things to be like and what things are like now. They must own the problem and feel the real need to change. In this way, the subject leader gains commitment from all the subject team to finding new ways, for instance, of improving learning.

Commitment in turn promotes another essential ingredient: tenacity in solving the problem by being end-result orientated. It is a key role of the subject leader to encourage the team to hang on to the desired 'worthy' outcome and have belief in the team's ability to achieve it.

Clarifying meaning and purpose   Sometimes comments by staff about the introduction of change are of the 'I'm not sure why we are doing this', 'Why is this necessary now?' and 'What's it going to achieve anyway?' variety. It is hardly likely that these people will be committed to the innovation. This reminds us that, if the team are to put their combined energies behind any innovation, it is essential for the leader to check out the team's current perception.

Activity 6.6   Clarifying the meaning and purpose of change

Ask team members:

1   Are you clear about why the change is important (e.g. to the pupils, to the staff or to the school as a whole)?
2   Can you see how the change activity will bring about this desired result?
3   Can you see how the action you are going to take contributes to the whole effect?

Another important dimension of this is the specific standard or quality of work that is expected of a person. Sometimes, in the complexity of revising practice, quality takes second place to speed and it is not uncommon for lower standards to be tolerated while in this transition period. The leader should be aware that high quality is difficult to re-establish once lost as new working practices are embedded. This is because standards become associated with actions and once people learn what the acceptable standard is they will tend to keep to it.

In order to counteract this effect the leader needs to set clear standards for all aspects of change activity and ensure that they are being met before moving on. Although this means a slower introduction of change and can lead to more tension in the team (particularly between the leader and team members), it reaps dividends in the longer term.

Mutual respect for differences   Innovation is often a product of bright ideas being suggested from unexpected sources. We all know that being too close to a problem can lead to blinkered solutions. The subject leader may well find that people who have an opposite view to prevailing wisdom, or have no knowledge of the subject being discussed, may spark new thoughts and ideas that lead to innovative actions.

It is too easy to dismiss people who are at the wrong level of the school (e.g. LSAs or those who seem to have little experience, such as NQTs). It seems that 'bosses' can sometimes be blind to the cleverness and inventiveness of those lower down the organisation, believing that their own superior experience and wisdom will intuitively tell them whether an idea is good or not. A classic example of this from industry, concerned the 'innovation' of putting zippers in men's trousers in the nineteenth century.

Example

The idea of replacing buttons with a zipper was suggested to the owner of a leading American trouser manufacturer by his head designer. The designer had noticed that the introduction of zippers into ladies' dresses had been very popular and thought men would appreciate this innovation too.

However, the owner was not impressed, believing that men would not find the idea of using something originally designed for women as appropriate. In addition, he was alarmed by the idea that men who were not careful in using the zipper might have an accident and sue the company! To his credit, the designer did not give up, but paid a visit to the owner's tailor, asking him to place a zipper in the next pair of trousers the owner ordered. The owner was delighted and subsequently ordered the introduction of the innovation (which then quickly spread across the whole world).

Flexibility   In organisations there is a need for bureaucracy. This manifests itself in the systems introduced by managers and is locked into place within the organisational structure by the setting out of rules, working procedures, systems and people's job descriptions. A subject leader who is trying to encourage innovation needs to reduce bureaucratic elements as much as possible. This is because it has been found that people's perception of the amount of bureaucracy in organisations has a direct effect on their willingness to share ideas and can also reduce their willingness to give the extra energy and commitment necessary to introduce change. This does not mean abandoning rules and methods that produce effectiveness, but rather means constantly asking the question: is there anything I can do to reduce unnecessary bureaucracy?

If leaders are trying to encourage change then they have to set up an environment where energy and creativity can flourish. Sometimes that means the leader will have to step back from being systematically involved in the generation of new ideas. In researching their book *In Search of Excellence* (1982), Peters and Waterman found that in most top companies there were people and groups working quietly away for little bits of time on projects which were not always officially sanctioned by their managers. They likened it to the 'Skunk Works' invented by Clarence Johnson at Lockhead in 1943 to secretly invent a new fighter (Bennis and Biederman 1997). This kind of semi-official work on new ideas was so-called because the innovators thought that if top management approached it too closely in the early stages, they would find it not to their liking. However, these unofficial projects, if left alone, often produced new products and processes from which the organisation was later able to reap commercial benefit.

Innovation in schools

The parallel with schools is interesting, since the kinds of culture that produced innovation were much more common in the 1970s and 1980s than they are now. With the advent of the National Curriculum has come a dampening of non-conformity. The irony is, that now the kind of non-sanctioned innovation described above has been driven from schools, the government is pumping large amounts of public money into leadership programmes for headteachers and subject leaders in order to galvanise school improvement.

Interestingly, few education leadership and management texts include creativity or innovation in their index (although Day *et al.* 1998 do). However, Day *et al.* also include a cautionary tale of a teacher who was attracted to take a post because of the promise of a climate of innovation in the school but

> very quickly learnt that *in order to innovate, the last thing to do was label the process innovation* because that suggested that the staff view of themselves as radical innovators was in some way flawed.
>
> (Day *et al.* 1998, p.168)

In that school, if a new teacher had an idea, the existing staff who saw themselves as being innovative always considered that it *must* have been thought of before and consequently discarded it as worthless. Anecdotal evidence from newly qualified teachers in their first posts seems to support the teacher quoted here. This 'not invented here' syndrome is not just common to schools, as creativity in many organisations is blocked by staff who think that if they did not think of something (and they know more about the problem than anyone else) then other people's ideas cannot possibly work.

Subject leaders need to aware of the potential problem and discuss the issue openly with staff before any innovation or problem-solving process begins. However, subject leaders also need to bear in mind that the cynicism that sometimes greets new ideas in staffrooms may be symptomatic of a system that considers itself to have been exposed to an innovation overload. The Conservative government of the 1990s were aware of this factor in connection with the post-Dearing National Curriculum, and put a five-year ban on any further reforms.

The current government are nevertheless intent on change. They are also concerned with the level of creativity in schools. This led to the DfEE in 1998 establishing the National Advisory Committee on Creative and Cultural Education, whose remit was to recommend to the government practical ways of enhancing creativity. One of the recommendations the committee published in its June 1999 report (DfEE 1999a) was that government needed to reduce prescription to allow teachers to be more creative in promoting creativity. Ken Robinson, Chairman of the Committee, wrote:

> in our view, creative and cultural development is a basic function of education, not just a separate subject.
>
> (Robinson 1999, p.21)

The committee argues that creative thinking should not just go on in subjects like Art, English and Drama, but be present in all subjects. Subject leaders need to be alert to the possibility that creativity may find its way onto the curriculum as another cross-curricular dimension to be included in their subject teaching.

Activity 6.7 Analysing the creative climate

Using the features of a creative climate, conduct an analysis of the environment in which you and your team operate. After you have evaluated the results, consider what action you and the team could take to improve your opportunities to innovate, particularly in areas related to your vision and goals.

Reinvention (Revolutionary change)

If continual evolutionary change normally accounts for 80 per cent of school improvement and innovation and perhaps a significant part of the rest, then revolution will be neither common nor necessary for most schools and subjects for most of the time. However, there will be elements of a subject leader's work that require drastic action from time to time. This is true too at a whole-school level where a school may have been designated to have serious weaknesses or be a failing school. In such an environment revolutionary change may be necessary.

Handy (1989) discusses how reasonable action will lead to reasonable continual progress. Major change, he believes, is only brought about through acting unreasonably, through what he calls 'upside down thinking'. Others have called this 'thinking outside the box' (see Chapter 5).

In the case of failing schools this kind of thinking has led to ideas about school closure and subsequent re-opening with a new name and new staff led by new management. Another idea is to have the school taken over by external specialist companies. In Surrey, in 1999, an external company was employed to manage a failing school (although its directors are serving and ex-headteachers). The DfEE have now accredited a number of specialist consultancy companies that could perform a similar function with failing LEAs.

At departmental or subject-team level, the effect of revolution will not be so dramatic or far-reaching across the system. However, for the individual, the effect of revolution, or even the suggestion of it, can cause major tensions and traumas. This is because of the same Gestalt factors that we were encouraging leaders to stimulate in Chapter 6. However, in this case the trigger is not the stimulation to pursue a much-sought goal but to hang on to a known situation because of the feeling of fear from or opposition to a suggestion of unwanted dramatic change.

Recognition of the psychological effects of change

Scott and Jaffe (1989) introduced a helpful model, describing what happens when people are faced with change (see Figure 6.4).

Denial   A state of not accepting what is being told or what is being perceived.

Figure 6.4   Psychological effects of change

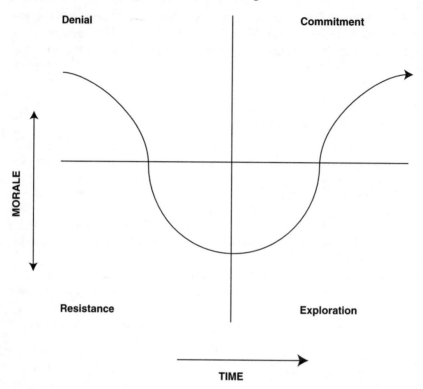

It appears our propensity to deny depends upon two factors: (1) how much of what we are being confronted with is agreeable or disagreeable to us, and (2) how far the new idea or information is from that which we currently believe. For example, on being told we have won the lottery we will still tend to push the news away: 'get away, you're pulling my leg', but we will quickly accept the news once proof is provided. This contrasts with being told very bad news (e.g. that someone has died or that we have a life-threatening disease). In these cases, the feeling of denial: 'he can't have died, I was only talking to him last week' may last a comparatively long time and it may be days, weeks or months before 'the news sinks in'. In some cases, so strong is the feeling and the refusal to accept the news that we say someone is 'living in denial'.

In a school, we are often confronted with news, new ideas or 'changes from above'. We may learn that a pupil has done something very out of character and react: ' no, it couldn't be Sarah, she wouldn't do a thing like that'. Or we may, on being told the date of the next OfSTED inspection, say: 'no, it can't be us yet, they've only just been'. Even good ideas, like being given more classroom resources, can provoke comments such as: 'it can't be for my room, I have some new ones of those already'.

The subject leader's role

The job here is to get the person to accept that the change, or the state they find themselves in, is inevitable and that it is happening to them, now, and that it will not go away. For some people, the introduction of totally new computer technology or a curriculum change (e.g. the Literacy Hour: 'we don't need it – our SAT results are really good') can be as difficult to accept as, say, the breaking up of a relationship. This is because people have strong feelings (akin to loyalty and devotion) about the 'old way' of doing things (remember Gestalt). For this reason, people are often very reluctant to accept that something is finished and gone, or that something new will happen to replace the 'good old days'.

The leader must therefore 'confront' the person in an assertive way. Often doctors have to do this when trying to get patients to accept that they have a serious illness (so that they will take their medication). In schools it is less dramatic, but can be as difficult, and persuading some people of the need to change can be very time-consuming and, sometimes, impossible. Eventually, schools have to decide whether or not a person can be persuaded or assess what the ongoing cost is of employing a person who is in denial. The result can be that the person eventually leaves the organisation.

Resistance A state of not acknowledging that what we are being told will happen or not accepting our own perception of a new *status quo*.

Even if the new idea or current position is to be welcomed, we will feel some kind of resistance to the new order. This is because, whether the change is welcome or not, we feel a sense of dipping morale (see Harris 1995). As our morale dips, our self-esteem weakens, and we begin to feel tense and a range of other emotions: anger, anxiety, fear, panic. The type and degree of feeling is dependent on the specific nature of the changed perspective and our previous belief about it. On being convinced that Sarah really did behave badly, we might feel sad, let down or slightly foolish because we blindly defended her. The imposition of the Literacy Hour might make us feel angry, and the OfSTED inspection might engender the feelings of anxiety and fear we felt last time ('especially when you think of what happened to Mrs X').

These emotions can be grouped into a simpler description of how we feel: we say we are 'stressed'. When we are in this state, we tend to want to go back to the 'old ways', to familiar people, places and things.

The subject leader's role

Assuming that the leader has managed to persuade the team to acknowledge the inevitability of the particular change process, some team members may be feeling unhappy (or even stressed) and need support.

The key issue here is that a leader is dealing with people's feelings and not with their logical or intellectual capacity. Too many leaders faced with resistant team members try to bombard them with arguments about how good the change will be for them and the organisation. When people are upset they need to be listened to, they want to express their real feelings openly without there being any long-term comeback for being emotional.

In New York, the Cromer School Improvement Team have been trying to change practice in very deprived schools for thirty years. They are often faced with difficult staff situations caused by their analysis of what needs to change. Above the inside door of their office they have a sign to remind them of how they should conduct themselves when dealing with people in resistance. It reads:

Remember,

people don't care what you know

until they know that you care.

Good team leaders do care about their people and show them by making time simply to listen.

Exploration   A state in which we are prepared to explore the beneficial aspects of the change.

According to Scott and Jaffe (1989), most people tend to want to see the positive side of things, to look forward to a better future. For most people this side of their character eventually overrides their resistant feelings and they are prepared to see a way forward. Scott and Jaffe (1989) found that if people had an opportunity to vent their feelings within a trusting environment, while at the same time knowing that change or the new state of affairs was inevitable (e.g. it would be if they continued to be employed by their current company), then they would eventually begin to seek an understanding of the benefits of the change.

Of course, if people are faced with tragedy in their personal lives, then this more optimistic state might take a good deal longer to emerge. People do this naturally, but they can be helped by leaders who create a positive and optimistic climate that enables them to see the personal and organisational benefit of changes.

The subject leader's role
Once listened to, people have a tendency to become more positive and optimistic. As people cross over the line from resistance to exploration and begin to climb up the 'U-bend' (see Figure 6.4), their morale and self-esteem rise again, and with it comes creative energy. This mood can be enhanced by the leader

facilitating discussion about peoples' roles and developing ideas about actions they might take in the change process.

However, sometimes people have an almost desperate need to see the way forward, to the extent that they become recklessly impulsive. The danger is that they might latch on to the first idea that is presented. This sometimes happens in brainstorming sessions, when staff can get carried away on a tide of euphoric optimism and settle their ideas upon a list of hopelessly unrealistic actions and timeframes. The result of this is that things are started and not finished or not started at all. The danger is that, in time, the group's optimism wanes as they realise that they are not going to succeed. Their self-esteem and morale diminish and they find themselves back at the bottom of the U-bend or back in resistance. Often people's moods swing like a pendulum back and forth across the line – even to the extent of feeling good in the mornings and then more and more cynical as the day wears on.

The leader's role is to ensure that this stage is successfully completed by carefully nurturing the optimism, but not allowing it to run ahead of what is practical. This is perhaps the most difficult of all the stages, since it requires a loose–tight touch: the leader must show willingness to be flexible and encourage creative thinking, but must also retain control of the framework within which the change is being introduced. The skill is to enable team members to focus upon the key actions that will produce both the key objectives and the satisfaction to the member of staff of a job well done.

Commitment A state in which people are positive about the change and its benefits, are clear about what they have to do and how they will achieve the positive outcomes. Thus, once motivated, they are prepared to give the extra time and creative energy to making things work.

The subject leader's role
Once focused, the leader's role is to establish the operational systems, find and deploy the resources and support necessary for the staff's actions to be implemented. This may involve finding time to continue to support staff or opportunities for staff development, as well as more traditional physical resources.

Long-term commitment cannot be guaranteed or expected, unless the factors which motivate staff to engage in change are constantly reviewed and supported. The leader should consider each and every member of the team's needs on a regular basis. The job of sustaining the momentum of change, while not as difficult as getting it going, nevertheless cannot be underestimated.

Summary: The subject leader's role in managing change

It is clear from this model that everyone who is asked to change will undergo some kind of psychological trauma. The degree to which people might get stuck in any portion of the U-bend (see Figure 6.4) cannot be known for sure. A wise leader will therefore not underestimate the effect that any proposed change will have on the team and will be looking for signs that a person needs help. The kind of action needed depends on which part of the U-bend the person is in. Figure 6.5 summarises the process, showing what staff might be saying in each phase, what the subject leader should do and what staff might be saying when they are moving into the next phase:

Figure 6.5   Reacting to change

Phase	Symptom	Subject leader action	Check success
Denial	'No, it can't be'	Confront: be assertive, press home the message, use evidence/proof	'Am I really?'
	'Not me' 'We don't need this'		'I suppose, if I must'
Resistance	'I'm very angry'	Support: listen, give time and space for their feelings	'I feel better now I've spoken'
	'I don't feel good ... '		'I suppose it won't be so bad'
	'I fear I'll be awful'		
Exploration	'I wonder if ... '	Focus: ask questions, promote discussion, encourage ideas, move to action points	'I'm clearer now'
	'Why don't we ... ?'		'I can see what I have to do next'
	'Could I ... ?'		'It'll be good'
	'What if ... ?'		'It really works'
Commitment	'What's in it for me?'	Motivate: show how their actions will achieve their goals, produce plans with details of resources	'Can I do more?'
	'Will I get the time and help?' 'When do I start?'		'I'm really glad we are doing this'

Activity 6.8   Plotting reaction to change

Take an example of change that is impacting on you and your team now. Examine the methods that were employed to introduce the change, how people reacted and what was done about this. Plot onto a U-bend diagram (like Figure 6.4) where you and your team are now. What can you do to help your team to move successfully through to the commitment phase?

NEXT STEPS

By this point the subject leader should have a good grasp of what they want to achieve, what needs to change and what their own behaviour will be to lead and support this process.

Other chapters in this book discuss issues about writing policies, plans and effectively implementing them. The next chapter will therefore examine the principles of monitoring, evaluation and review, and the reporting of success to stakeholders.

7 Strategic monitoring, evaluation and review

INTRODUCTION

> So what is a successful school? How would you recognise one? Do you need to see the exam results? Or is it sporting success? Is it to be affirmed or denied by the views of the people in the school's locality, the shop keepers in the town centre or the local employers? Is it to be won or lost by the messages and views of the staff who happen not to be teachers at the school – the caretaker, the secretary, the technician, the classroom assistant, the school meals staff, or the parents or governors? Is it to be seen in the behaviour of the children?
>
> (Brighouse 1991, p.1)

Tim Brighouse illustrates the dilemma that headteachers and subject leaders face as they try to determine how best to evaluate their school and get the good news across to the community. It also links our discussion back to earlier chapters, in which we were trying to ascertain the real purpose of a subject. Subject leaders might well substitute their subject title for the word 'school' in Brighouse's series of questions.

This chapter will consider the principles and processes that underpin the evaluation and review of improvement activities, and examine the accountability that subject leaders have for reporting progress and attainment. Subject leaders do not evaluate and report in a vacuum, and what a subject leader does, particularly in relation to reporting, might well be pre-determined by whole-school policies. However, there are decisions to be made as part of the strategic process that subject leaders should make at subject level and contribute to at school level. These relate to Stages 9 and 10 of the strategic process model that we have followed in this section.

STAGE 9: MONITORING, EVALUATION AND REVIEW

We are not too concerned here with the practical details of conducting monitoring, evaluation and review (MER), as this is discussed in Part III. The purpose here is to examine each of the MER dimensions and discuss the strategic issues that subject leaders will need to be aware of when making or contributing to decisions to establish MER systems. It first may be helpful to briefly define each of the MER dimensions.

Day-to-day monitoring, evaluation and review

Monitoring is about the collection of information about an action or activity. The information to be collected has usually been pre-determined and its collection will enable the teacher to check out whether or not the action or activity has been successful. At a day-to-day level, teachers may ask of themselves: 'What happened in that lesson?', 'How did I do?', 'How did Sally get on today?'. Determining the answer may involve collecting relatively simple information that will give the teacher a clear understanding of the event. As a consequence of the answers to their own questions, teachers' actions might change the next time they have that particular class.

Evaluation is the consideration of evidence against criteria, in order to make an overall judgement of the success or otherwise of a series of actions and activities. The evidence that is considered will be the aggregation of the assumptions made as a result of monitoring activity, however informal. In the staffroom or at subject meetings, the subject leader may ask of staff: 'How are you getting on with the new ... ?' or 'Has Sally made any progress this month?'. The resulting discussion will involve formally or informally sifting through the information gathered over the period in question, to arrive at an answer to the question.

Review is the making of decisions about what action, if any, to take as a consequence of the decision reached through evaluation. The subject leader or staff may ask: 'What should we do about this?' or 'Do we need to change the way we plan lessons?' or 'Do we have to alter the way we support Sally for the rest of term?'. The answers enable the subject leader and staff to make decisions about changing aspects of their practice or the way things are organised (e.g. for the next half term).

MER activity can be considered to take place every day at this individual level and subject leaders will no doubt encourage their staff to reflect on their practice and the performance of pupils as much as possible. However, the danger is that if left at this unsystematic level MER will, at best, only have an impact on individual teachers and their classes. In order for subject leaders and teams to be able to review whether or not their collective vision and goals are being achieved, more systematic and strategic MER activity is required.

Activity 7.1 Reflecting on MER activity

Reflect on how you and your staff currently monitor and evaluate classroom activity. Is it systematic? Do staff have a predetermined set of information that they draw on when they evaluate their lessons and dealings with pupils? Do you sit down as a team together and review your evaluations?

Creating a strategic MER system

To consider what the system should comprise, another more strategic view of MER is required. Although the basic questions related to each type of activity will still be asked, the scope and timing of each activity is scaled up across the subject area or school.

Monitoring involves a range of activities to collect data about specific aspects of performance (e.g. quality of lesson-planning, amount of learning by specific children, attendance and punctuality of a class). What gets monitored is usually informed by pre-determined targets and performance indicators. Data can then be analysed to check if targets and indicators are being met (e.g. 'Are our lessons differentiating as much as they should?' or 'Are those four pupils now reading for the amount of time we decided they should and have they improved? If not, why not?' or 'What do we need to do to make sure the teacher meets these targets?'). Decisions can be made to improve those actions which do not meet performance criteria. Monitoring activities usually take place continually, although different aspects of performance will be examined according to a schedule outlined in an improvement plan.

Evaluation involves making judgements about the overall performance of the aspect in question. These judgements are made based on looking across the analysis of monitoring data in relation to the goals or objectives set out in a plan or policy (e.g. to improve the quality of teaching across a Key Stage, to improve boys' performance or for support from learning assistants to become more effective). Judgements are made about whether the goals or objectives are being or will be met and decisions are made about what action might be taken to change a previously arranged activity (e.g. 'Are all lessons being well-planned using specific learning targets and are the pupils achieving those targets regularly in all lessons? If not, what more can we do to support teaching staff and learning assistants next term?'). Evaluation usually takes place when there is enough data to make judgements about goal achievement. Annual improvement plans will usually have points identified when evaluation of progress is necessary.

Review involves taking a broader view of performance in relation to the summative achievement of the longer-term strategic vision and goals. It takes the outcomes of evaluation, seeks to identify trends and patterns, and estimates the longer-term effects that these may have on desirable achievement (i.e. 'Did we achieve what we set out to achieve this year? If not, are there any common reasons why we failed? What are we going to do about making sure this does not happen again next year?'). Strategic decisions can then taken about the allocation of staff and resources or the adjustment of future goals and targets for the subject.

Review is an end-of-improvement-year activity (or whatever time-period was set for the completion of the improvement). It should be programmed into the annual subject-improvement planning cycle. Its terms of reference should be signalled at the same time as the date is set.

Activity 7.2   Strategic planning process

In the strategic planning process, decisions relating to the above dimensions need to be made at the outset. So, take a fairly new subject goal for which you have not yet set up an MER system. With your subject team, answer the following questions:

1   Strategy

- Do we need an MER system?
- What do we hope it will achieve?
- What outcomes and activities will we systematically collect data about?
- Who will be the target group?
- Have we enough time, resources and the knowledge to see this through?
- Who will manage the MER process?

2   Monitoring

- What performance criteria are we going to compare the data with?
- What evidence is already available?
- What else do we need to collect data about?
- How will we collect it?
- When and who will collect it?
- How will it be collated and stored?
- How much data will they need to collect?
- What indicators will the data be judged against?
- Who will analyse the data and what will they do with the results?

3   Evaluation

- What goals and objectives will our analysis of evidence be set against?
- How and when will we analyse and evaluate?
- Who will do it?
- Do we have all the knowledge and skills we need in the team?

- What judgements will we legitimately be able to make in relation to the monitoring data we will collect?
- How will we decide whether or not we are on course for being successful in achieving our goals?
- What will we do with the outcomes of our analysis?

4   Review

- What aspects of our vision and goals will be used to assess our achievements during the agreed MER period? When will we conduct the review?
- Who will be involved?
- Do we have all the knowledge and skills we need?
- How will the results be used to inform future planning?
- What resources might we need to take action as a result of the review?
- How will we report the findings and to whom shall we show them?
- How will we know that we have acted ethically, legally and observed natural justice?

How MER creates a learning process

Essentially an effective MER system provides subject leaders and their teams with the opportunity to learn from their teaching and improvement activity. This is because

> Learning progresses as learners question what they had previously taken for granted or assumed to be part of the natural order of things.
>
> (Nixon *et al.* 1996, p.48)

Teachers do this, we suggested earlier, by continually reflecting upon their experience. However, for many of us, questioning what we have previously taken for granted does not necessarily occur when we reflect. Indeed, it is more likely that our unsystematic reflections will tend to focus on whether or not our current experience matches our perception of normality (this is directly linked with the Gestalt process described in Chapter 4). We do this because our subconscious mind needs to be reassured that our actions are normal for us and that we have achieved our normal outcomes. If our reflections confirm that we have, then we usually cease to reflect because we do not have a problem.

Thus, our usual action and reflection process might be as shown in Figure 7.1. We may not learn anything by this process, since planning decisions which flow from a positive reflection on action tend to be based on doing 'more of the same'.

However, should we receive feedback that our actions were not normal for us or that they have produced an unusual outcome, then we might continue to

Figure 7.1   Reflection cycle

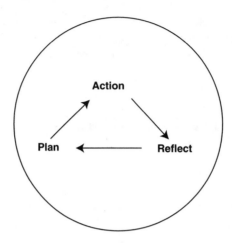

reflect until we have figured out the reason why. It is therefore much more likely that we will learn from reflecting upon a negative experience than upon a positive one. In fact, when we refer to having 'learnt from our experience', we are usually referring to a negative rather than a positive one. We should not conclude from this that we can only ever learn from our unsuccessful actions – Kolb (1985), among others, suggested that if the normal reflection model cycle was extended, real experiential learning could take place.

To do this, he argued, something needs to be introduced into the normal action–reflection–planning loop to interrupt our tendency to merely check ourselves out with our view of normality. We need to disturb our thought process so that we really do question what we are doing and how we could do better. A good example of when we do this is when we go on an INSET (in-service training) course. On a good course our thinking is stimulated: either by the content we are introduced to by the speaker; the processes we are asked to engage in; or the conversations we have with other course members about what they do. The New Leadership Programme for Serving Headteachers (LPSH) that the TTA introduced in 1998 was designed by Hay McBer to have this kind of effect. One of the directors of Hay McBer, Chris Dyson, summed this up in advice to would-be trainers:

> The purpose of a good training course is to comfort the afflicted and afflict the comfortable.
> (Chris Dyson, director of Hay McBer UK, Highgate House, September 1998)

Kolb (1985) suggests that learning can and does take place when our reflections are informed by the introduction of an abstract idea or 'theory' that enables us to step back from our normal reality and take a new look at our

Figure 7.2   Kolb's learning cycle

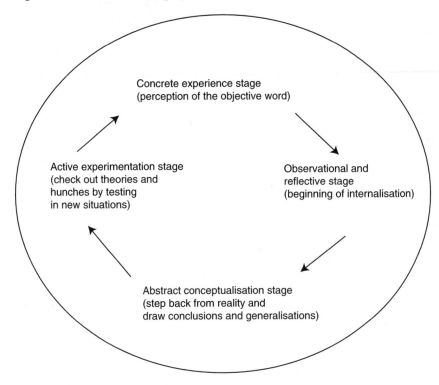

actions. In this way we are able to learn from our actions and plan to try out new actions in future. This is demonstrated in Figure 7.2.

Figure 7.2 illustrates two constructs:

1   Concrete action versus abstract conceptualisation – the need to underpin all our actions with 'theory' that enables us to understand what we did, how we might repeat it and how we might improve it.
2   Reflection versus active experimentation – the need to stop and think about what we have done, try out new actions, reflect again and so on.

Kolb's theory is at the heart of 'action learning' and supports the notion that the teaching profession must comprise 'reflective practitioners' who engage in action research as a systematic part of their everyday role (see Oldroyd and Hall 1991). We contend that a properly constructed and managed MER system can guide and support all staff to engage in active learning from all their experiences and not just the negative ones.

Activity 7.3   Reflecting on Kolb

Reflect on how you have learnt from experience. What were the significant points at which real learning took place? Do you recognise Kolb's model in terms of your own learning experiences?

A good subject leader will strive to use the outcomes of MER to inform formal and informal continuing staff development, either on an individual basis (possibly through appraisal) or through leadership of group-review and problem-solving activities. Thus it is essential that all subject leaders see themselves as being responsible for their staff's growth and development and do not allow this vital function to be taken over by others. This is, of course, more easily said than done, as others may control resources (although, in a primary school, staff will in effect have several subject leaders). In doing this, the subject leader is creating their own learning organisation within the school. This ensures that the subject area, as a learning organisation:

> is geared to change and determined to develop and refine its capacities to move into the future with confidence, curiosity and commitment.
>
> (Day *et al.* 1998, p.19)

Thus MER serves three vital strategic purposes:

1   It enables subject leaders and teams to check out whether or not they are achieving their short-term targets, medium-term objectives and long-term goals and vision.
2   It supports a culture in which organizational and personal learning can take place for all staff.
3   It provides evidence of subject improvement and pupil attainment to the rest of the school and other stakeholders.

It is this last outcome that provides the link to the last stage of the strategic planning process.

STAGE 10: REPORTING TO 'STAKEHOLDERS'

The concept of stakeholders is a relatively new one for schools. Foskett defines stakeholders simply as 'those with an interest in the work of the school' (Foskett 1992, p.7). He describes how Ballinger (1986) had subdivided this rather broad category into four main groups who had a stake in education in general:

• professionals inside education, ranging from teachers to LEA officers

- professionals outside education, such as social workers, industrialists and commercial providers of services
- politically involved individuals, such as councillors and MPs
- consumers of the service, such as pupils and students

Interestingly, parents are not included in Ballinger's analysis, possibly because he was writing in the early stages of the 1980s movement towards a consumerist society. Foskett brings the concept up to date by making a distinction between stakeholders who are consumers and stakeholders who are customers. Whereas in further and higher education students can be both customers (in the sense they make the purchasing decisions) and consumers (in that they receive the product), in schools it is parents (and others listed above) who are the customers, while pupils and students are only consumers. This distinction is helpful in determining to whom teachers and schools are accountable and for what.

The natural partner to the concept of stakeholding is accountability, a concept most famously highlighted in James Callaghan's 1976 Ruskin speech, in which he called for education to be more publicly accountable for its outcomes. Since then, education and most other public organisations have become increasingly and more transparently accountable to the people whose council taxes and rates provide the money to pay for them. These ideas formed the basis of the principles of the government's Citizens' Charter (1999) – principles which are now being applied across the country and which in turn affect schools. Examples are:

1   *Raising public service standards*

- explicitly indicating what can reasonably be expected (publishing attainment targets)
- making these services more answerable to users by taking account of their convenience and views (governors' reports to parents)
- providing appropriate channels for consultation (annual meetings for parents)

2   *Greater choice and competition*

- subjecting more local council services to tendering (cleaning, school meals, grounds and maintenance contracts)
- extending the idea of 'market-testing' in Whitehall (enquiry into the possibility of the Teacher's Pension Agency being run privately)

3   *Independent review of performance and publication of results*

- publicly reporting inspections and audits (OfSTED)
- producing statistics that enable consumers to compare like with like (league tables)

4   *Providing remedies in the event of specific standards not being achieved*

- closing poorly run public organisations or bringing in external management (supporting schools in serious weakness or closing and re-opening with new management)
- financial compensation for un-met targets, such as reliability or punctuality (not in schools … yet!)
- improved complaints and disputes procedures (new powers for governing bodies)

Activity 7.4   Effects of Citizen's Charter

Examine the above list and reflect on how changes introduced by the Citizen's Charter have affected your school and subject area:

1   Which of these principles has added value to your ability to achieve better standards of teaching and learning in your subject?
2   Which of these principles has affected the way that you communicate with stakeholders and report on your subject's achievements?

East Sussex LEA began an accountability project in 1979 and identified three kinds of accountability:

1   *Answerability* to one's clients, such as pupils and parents (moral accountability)
2   *Responsibility* to oneself and one's colleagues (professional responsibility)
3   *Accountability* in the strict sense to one's employers or political masters (contractual accountability)

(Day *et al.* 1990, p.165)

As the project progressed, it was realised that the emphasis of school activity moved from responsibility to self (teachers) through answerability (to parents) towards accountability (to the LEA or government). This shift in emphasis has been further accelerated by the transfer of more accountability to governing bodies:

> The powers and duties conferred on governors by the articles of government have a single purpose, to enable the school to provide good, efficient and appropriate education for all pupils registered at the school. Directly, governors are accountable to the community and to parents.

(Anderson *et al.* 1992, p.67)

Implication for subject leaders

At a subject level, accountability is primarily related to pupil attainment determined by nationally designed assessments. Assessment of subjects within the National Curriculum was devised for three purposes: to be 'formative, summative and evaluative' (Lindsay and Desforges 1998, p.5). These purposes link closely with the types of accountability described in the East Sussex project and to the strategic concepts of monitoring, evaluation and review.

Although subject leaders will be involved with reporting subject achievement and pupil attainment related to all three purposes and types of accountability, they will normally have less direct responsibility over reporting the second and even less for the third level of accountability. However, even though the headteacher and governors will take an increasing role at each level, the subject leader's responsibility is paramount at the first level. This is true for both operational and strategic reasons.

At the operational level, the data gained from monitoring assessment of pupil progress and attainment is vital in enabling the subject leader to give formative feedback on pupils' progress to teachers, pupils and parents. Not only does this enable pupils to see where they must improve, it informs teachers of where they must prioritise their own improved teaching and support.

At the strategic level, it provides progress data that, together with summative data, will enable subject leaders to evaluate and review their subject's effectiveness against their vision and goals, and inform subject policy. In turn, this analysis will inform the headteacher's and governors' evaluation of the school's effectiveness, which will then be translated into school-improvement planning policy.

Activity 7.5   Reporting achievement

Taking account of the issues raised above, use the following questions in a discussion with staff:

1   What and how will we report to subject staff, pupils and their parents?
2   What and how will we report our results to other staff, senior management and governors?
3   What and how will we report to the wider community?

SUMMARY AND CONCLUSIONS

This section of the book has asked four sets of questions of subject leaders:

- Why are you teaching your subject?
- What end-results do you want to achieve?
- How are you doing already and what must you change?

- How will you know if you have improved and whom do you tell?

These questions have been presented as stages in a strategic planning process that 'integrates an organisation's major goals, policies and action sequences into a cohesive whole' (Quinn 1980, p.7). And it is only when subject leaders and teams are able to see the strategic process as a complete picture that it will make sense and drive action forward.

What subject leaders need, though, is a clear picture – a vision – of a time when they have been able to improve the teaching of their subject and the consequent learning of the pupils. Then, while tenaciously hanging on to that vision, they must look objectively at the reality around them, recognise the gaps and plan to close them. Thus, having started the improvement process, the subject leader is able to monitor progress and celebrate attainment. It is this ability to see the cohesive whole that enables a subject leader to be truly effective.

However, for subject leaders there are, in fact, two complete pictures – one inside the other. The first is their vision of the professional leadership and management of a subject that 'secures high quality teaching, effective use of resources and improved standards of learning and achievement for all pupils', but their vision must also be seen within a wider understanding 'of how their subject contributes to school priorities and to the overall education and achievement of all pupils' (TTA 1998a, p.4).

It is this juxtaposition that makes the role of subject leader both challenging and rewarding. For the subject leader provides the bridge between the individual aspirations of pupils and their parents, and the much wider ambitions of headteachers, governors and politicians. Earlier in this chapter we indicated that 'the culture of accountability now empowered in English schooling is corporatist and consumerist rather than democratic' (Grace 1997, p.201). In this culture it is more difficult than ever for a subject leader to create a climate within their subject area where the kind of democratic practice and democratic accountability described in our strategic process can flourish. However, it has never been more important for pupils and their learning that subject leaders keep this issue alive, through enabling reflective practitioners to work within a reflective community.

Figure 7.3   The purposes and value of assessment

Assessment purpose	MER activity	Accountability level
Formative – to publicly report pupils' individual progress and attainment	Monitoring	Answerability
Summative – to inform teachers and pupils of attainment	Evaluation	Responsibility
Evaluative – to provide public information about the effectiveness of the school	Review	Contractual accountability

Part III
Managing teaching and learning

INTRODUCTION

> The government's principal aims for schools are to improve standards of
> achievement for all pupils across the curriculum, to widen the choice avail-
> able to parents for the education of their children, and to enable schools to
> respond effectively to what parents and the community required of them,
> thus securing the best possible return from the substantial investment of
> resources.
>
> (HM Treasury 1988)

Such an edict makes schools accountable to those outside the profession and
clearly makes the link between financial input and educational outcomes (see
also Chapter 7). The growth of large comprehensive schools and the responsibilities deriving from the local management of schools place the onus of
achievement on schools themselves, and Bailey (1986) acknowledges the
impact that heads of department in secondary schools have. He recognises their
influence on subject teaching through staff and pupil control, resource control
and communication (HMI 1984). Similarly, he comments on the value of effective subject heads:

> schools rely more for their success on the dynamism and leadership quali-
> ties of the head of department that on any other factor.
>
> (Bailey 1986, p.8)

Hall (1998) sees the role of managers to include planning, administration,
dealing with people, technical and professional knowledge and personal skills.
The development of such skills enables the key functions of leadership to be
undertaken: planning and organising, co-ordinating, producing and evaluating
(Brighouse 1991).

Such a level of responsibility is matched by accountability, and it is therefore
interesting to note to whom and for what teachers are seen to be accountable.
In Chapter 9, we comment on how the National Standards provide criteria

against which individual subject leaders' performance can be measured. In this chapter we focus more on leaders' interrelationships with colleagues and their expectations. First, then, to whom: Elliott's (1981) research reveals that teachers themselves recognise the need to be held to account to parents and pupils. Government legislation since 1988, and the successful implementation of a National Curriculum policed by OfSTED, places the government itself as a key stakeholder. Governing bodies and senior managers bear the brunt of accountability and consequently middle managers must be required to implement plans and generate data which serves to assure a quality provision.

OfSTED (1993a) suggests middle managers' areas of responsibility, including the organisation, planning and delivery of the National Curriculum. In order to achieve and monitor learning and teaching, OfSTED identify the assessment, recording and reporting of pupil progress, the development and support of subject teaching staff, the efficiency with which resources are used and the quality of accommodation as critical factors.

Throughout the 1990s, subject leaders have, therefore, been faced with explicit responsibilities, which appear to encompass many approaches to management and decision-making. Hargreaves and Hopkins (1991) recognise features of Management By Objectives (MBO), Programme Planning and Budgetary Systems (PPBS) and Critical Path Analysis (CPA) in the work of what we now call subject leaders. Indeed the language of managerialism can at first seem confusing, with the large number of interrelated terms and jargon. Bell (1992) distinguishes between quality control, quality assurance and quality assessment, recommending a Quality Assurance Management System (QAMS) which directs managers towards building checks into the system at all stages of operation. He draws his analysis from the British Standards *Principal Concepts and Applications*, Part O (1987), in which quality is defined as:

> the totality of features and characteristics of a product or service that bear on its ability to satisfy stated or implied needs.

Hardie (1998) differentiates between strategic, tactical and operational evaluation as means of assuring a quality provision from inception to implementation and finally review.

Morrison (1998) stresses the need to conduct general and specific audits to assume the inclusion of strategic areas and visions in operational methods. Bennett *et al.* (1992) note the tendency to break from the established LEA tradition of separating audits from reviews and inspections. They claim that the influence of the Audit Commission is to insist on the assessment of the efficiency and effectiveness of resource allocation in relation to service outcomes.

Subject leadership therefore demands an understanding of the jargon of management. A first priority is to agree a definition of quality. Everard and Morris (1996) track the understanding of quality from a view that it is synonymous with 'excellence' to 'reasonably fit for the purpose' to the more recent interpretation of quality as 'meeting or exceeding the expectations of the customer'. Tofte (1996) extends this view of quality by representing it as providing and surpassing what is actually planned through consensus between all stakeholders. Øvretreit (1992) sees this view as only one aspect of quality: 'client quality'. He adds to this 'professional quality' (recognising the need for some professional autonomy) and 'management quality' (demanding the efficient and effective use of resources). The concepts of effectiveness and efficiency continue to appear in the language of quality. Riches' interpretation matches that of OfSTED which we explain in Chapter 9:

Effectiveness   The extent to which a measurable target is achieved.
Efficiency   The cost for a given level of achievement.

(Riches 1997, p.17)

What becomes clear from the confusion is that quality is concerned with planning in advance, with monitoring provision to answer the question 'Do we do what we say we do?' (West 1995, p.42), with evaluating (making decisions and judgements about practice with a view to improving provision) and review, which is concerned with looking back on provision and assessing whether targets have been met and what action is needed.

To simplify even further, subject leaders have a crucial role to play in assuring quality by considering issues which should occur *before*, *during* and *after* educational provision.

BEFORE

Elliott (1981) recognises the need for careful planning to ensure smooth operations in a number of relevant areas: the curriculum, human resource development, in-service training and support programmes, the use and development of accommodation and public relations. Careful planning is more than setting up clear, step-by-step procedures, but each policy should be founded on expressed and agreed principles and values. The work of Sammons *et al.* (1995) identifies features of effective subject departments. Once aware of such characteristics, subject leaders should be concerned to build them into policies and plans:

- high expectations
- an emphasis on academic performance
- shared vision and goals
- clear leadership
- a sense of direction
- the encouragement of teamwork
- positive relationships with the senior-management team

There is, therefore, guidance on what plans and policies should be based upon and for which issues there actually should be plans and policies. The OfSTED (1994) report *Primary Matters* serves to reiterate such existing guidance and to place it into a primary school context. The report recommends that subject teams develop policies on resource management, long- and medium-term curriculum plans, documentation and advice for teaching. The report stresses the value of policy-writing for two reasons: first, the gains accrued from the process and, second, gains due to the creation of meaningful frameworks and procedures.

The process of policy formulation involves teamwork and collaboration. Hall (1998) warns against paying lip-service to collaboration: it must be meaningful and not simply an attempt to demonstrate political correctness in an age of democracy at work.

Policy formulation is not the only form of 'advance quality assurance'. Indeed Hardie (1998) recommends that analyses of organisational cultures in the form of a SWOT Analysis (Strengths, Weaknesses, Opportunities and Threats – see Chapter 8) should be undertaken prior to the consideration of new practices. Elliott (1981), too, recognises the need to raise awareness as a means of assuring quality. His view of accountability is that provision must fit in with role expectations pre-determined by others. Evidently an understanding of what expectations others have is essential if subject teachers are to deliver satisfaction.

Everard and Morris (1996) recognise the ever-expanding range of stakeholders in education (parents, pupils, employers, government, local community etc., etc.). The need is to plan with the expectations and demands of such bodies in mind. The British Standards BS5750 and ISO 9000 recognise that a systematic approach to identifying market needs and having working methods to suit such needs are crucial signs of a quality provision.

A school is not simply a learning factory, but has a role to play in giving the educational provision a particular ethos and identity. Indeed it was one of the stated aims of the government in 1988. Subject leaders cannot initiate and implement change, therefore, if the nature of the change runs counter to the school's vision:

> Curriculum change is seen to require a whole school response and strategy for implementation.
>
> (Morrison 1998, p.87)

The need to fit in with whole-school aims can be perceived in a much more tangible way too. Bell defines Total Quality Management as 'the means by which agreed customer requirements can be met continuously, at the lowest cost' (Bell 1992, p.5). Within the world of education, delegated budgets may well give 'schools more of a say over real resources, staff, books, equipment and materials' (Bennett *et al.* 1992, p.5). However, the responsibility also means that attention must be paid to financial costs, which implies that educational progress must be linked to financial investment. As Elliott (1981) points out, there is nothing new in tying the management of a budget to educational outcomes. Careful planning at a time of financial audits and education inspection does sharpen such a focus and it is helpful for subject leaders to bear in mind Sammons *et al*'s (1995, see earlier in this introduction) characteristics of effective departments when developing and evaluating budgets.

Budget planning should therefore operate at three levels: long-term, medium-term and at a day-to-day operational level. Development and improvement should be planned in advance and include the full range of financial costs, including staff-time, resources and materials.

Hall (1998) reminds us of the need for teachers to control development and change. Teachers do not respect change imposed by external agents. It is therefore incumbent upon subject leaders to involve staff in the planning and development of policies and activities. O'Neill (1997) warns teachers against resisting the 'making public' of planned future targets. He points out that other professions (medical professionals, dentists and solicitors) make available a professional register in advance of being engaged, in order that clients can be assured of quality before entering into a professional relationship. Teachers should recognise their own powers, exercise professional integrity, yet remain publicly accountable. Careful advice and open planning of curriculum through policy development, budget planning and consideration of staff needs within the existing whole-school culture is a way forward to assuring quality.

DURING

Schools cannot stand still and the challenge is to improve provision continuously. Indeed, as society develops, schools have to respond. New media facilitate individualistic learning and subject leaders need to adapt to maintain at least a constant level of effectiveness. In a similar way to industry adapting to suit the prevailing economic climate, schools and therefore subject leaders have to examine current practice with a view to amending and improving. Subject leaders have to monitor the performance of colleagues, a need which is ever more acute since the 1988 Education Reform Act placed the responsibility for teaching and learning in individual schools and placed each school in direct competition with others (Hall 1998). Staff development must therefore be continuous and related to need. Brown and Rutherford (1996) summarise the subject leader's role in this respect as establishing networks and channels of communication in order to deploy existing staff expertise effectively, and to share views on good practice in order to maintain the momentum of improvement.

Monitoring provision with an ever-changing climate is problematic. Good planning provides subject leaders and teachers with a fixed notion of outcomes prior to implementation. Effective as this is, over-rigidity prevents the development of a capacity for change and improvement. Built into plans and policies should be the opportunity to audit and review. Indeed, all plans – as Foreman

(1998) reminds us – should be consistent with a whole-school philosophy, yet this does not prohibit adaptations. Freeman (1993) maintains that the achievement of quality requires continuous improvement by the surpassing of existing standards. If staff are encouraged to identify problems and share in finding solutions, the quest for total quality becomes a realistic process.

For improvement to be continuous, teachers need to feel responsible and empowered. Oldroyd and Hall (1988) highlight features of school- and team-culture which are conducive to continuous development. A summary of such features includes:

- leaders delegating responsibility
- staff experiencing a sense of ownership of in-service training policies and procedures
- leaders inviting regular review
- leaders drawing on existing strengths to support team members
- good practice within a subject team being shared and celebrated
- leaders leading by example and following professional development programmes themselves

Developing such a culture must be planned and agreed procedures designed to appraise collective performance must be applied continuously. Auditing provision involves checking that systems are in place and that all involved adhere to the procedures. Freeman (1993) recognises teachers' professional qualities and judgements, and recommends that internal auditors should be appointed and be able to develop the necessary skills. It is for the subject leader to make such appointments, and to arrange for a schedule and method for existing systems to be audited.

The process recommended is not about fault-finding and tracking past mistakes. The purpose of an audit is to detect non-compliance with established and agreed procedures, and not to make value judgements about teachers' practice. Non-compliance then raises issues for discussion and may lead to amending the original procedures.

The use of internal auditors is important. The aim is to question current provision and to compare what the subject team is striving to achieve with what it actually achieves. Internal auditors are in a good position to understand the context of subject teaching in terms of pupil intake, school traditions and teachers' roles and responsibilities. The appointment of internal auditors from within the team is a means by which leaders can demonstrate a respect for colleagues' expertise and therefore provide a sense of ownership of issues. It is, of course, crucial that findings are not seen as judgements of the quality of individual teachers and that, as a teacher, the leader is open to exactly the same level of scrutiny.

The outcomes of the audit are related to team, not individual, performance. They are the basis of future action planning. As Middlewood and Lumby (1998) explain, the outcomes serve to reveal existing strengths and identify priorities for future development. A recommended response to an audit/review is, Goddard and Leask (1992) argue, an action plan, designed to improve practice. Audits provide the necessary link between new innovations and a team's capacity for change. Like planning, auditing is as valuable for the climate it generates through the process, as the outcomes themselves.

The process of internal auditing should be as informative for the auditor as for the team itself. For example, West (1995) recommends teaching a pupil, in order to gain an insight into subject provision from a fresh perspective. Hopkins (1989, p.33) is more specific, listing what aspects of provision should be audited:

- whether or not the planned curriculum meets statutory requirements
- gaps between and overlaps with other subject areas
- where overlaps occur, whether they are used positively
- whether cross-curricular work is planned
- the identification of 'non-National Curriculum objectives'
- how and why resources are used
- how effective and efficient use of resources is judged
- how subject-development planning fashions the use of resources
- the use made of staff expertise
- expenditure

Such a coverage must be planned and sequenced. Over a period of time, auditing will assist in meeting the demands of Alexander *et al.* (1992). These 'Three Wise Men' recommended that a key role of the subject co-ordinator is to monitor teachers' work by working alongside colleagues.

Internal auditing as a process is not new. The Schools Council developed GRIDS (Guidelines for Review and Internal Development), which was – as Bollen and Hopkins (1987) point out – designed to help teachers review practice. Bollen and Hopkins recognise the value of a system controlled by professional teachers, but also the place of external help to validate the process. OfSTED inspectors are not so fearsome if treated as a means by which existing self-review methods are confirmed and validated.

Bollen and Hopkins present internal audits, and quote the International School Improvements Project, as a means of developing a culture/climate conducive to improvement and change. Conditions necessary for effective reviews include positive terminology in relation to staff attitudes. 'Happy', 'willingness' and 'accept' are all included in phrases which suggest the professional gain to be acquired from the auditing process.

Auditing/review/monitoring (for definitions, see Chapter 7) is not simply a case of relating examination performance to financial input and planned targets. West (1995) is eager to remind reviewers of their purpose: to identify objectives and to relate these to classroom activities, to assess the enjoyment of learning, and to identify opportunities for future development.

The argument is, therefore, that success can be celebrated, and that failure is not the fault of individual teachers, but rather a sign that common and agreed systems need to be adapted.

AFTER

In terms of assuring quality, HMI (1994) perceives evaluation as the weak links in schools. The report recognises that schools have a clear vision and ethos, that planning on the whole is sound, but that in 80 per cent of schools evaluation procedures are below standard.

Evaluation is part of the accountability system. Teachers should be able to explain and justify decisions and actions undertaken, and draw on objective data in order to substantiate and qualify such explications. Russell and Reid (1997) recommend 'value added schemes' as a means of assessing pupils' progress as opposed to attainment, which they claim sits more comfortably with the concept of improvement. Pupil performance outcomes do, therefore, have a major part to play in evaluation. The measure of effective planning and implementation is appropriate results, rather than the focus being on how sophisticated planning and implementation procedures are.

The use of results alone is a crude mechanism, however, and before considering other evaluation techniques it is important to place the use of statistics in context. Statistical analysis allows comparison. If comparisons are to be made, it is important that equity is assured. Before judgements can be made, three types of comparison are recommended, providing some validity. First, a comparison with the results of other schools is meaningful, if variables are taken into account. Staff:pupil ratios, the number of support staff, the quality of the accommodation, resources for teaching, library provision, the number of pupils on the SEN register and local socio-economic factors are bound to have an impact. Consequently school/departmental comparisons must be made with like schools. The provision of Performance and Assessment (PANDA) reports helps here, but with the range of variables to take into account, no simple judgement can be made on the basis of inter-school comparisons. Second, intra-school comparisons can be made. Pupils' performance in other subject areas provides useful indications of the quality and impact of subject provision. Third, a combination of the above enables points to be awarded in relation to particular factors.

Hardie (1995) insists that evaluation must be comprehensive, systematic, objective, periodic and reliable. The measurement of aggregated assessment scores alone is not comprehensive. Performance in teaching and learning includes measurable factors, such as enjoyment, motivation and future choices (options, further and higher education, careers). More sophisticated devices are therefore necessary to gather qualitative, as well as quantitative data. Hardie (1998) asserts, too, that evaluation should inform practice and that therefore information sought should be useful to curriculum planners. Shipman (1979) adds, however, that evaluation data should inform but not determine decision-making. It is the vision and aims of the whole school that determines choices made and evaluation data may lead to a discussion of broader issues. However, the relationship between effectiveness and efficiency must be borne in mind.

Evaluation, then, can take many forms and serve many purposes. It must therefore be planned and timed appropriately if the information sought is to be available and if corrective action can ensue. Russell and Reid reiterate this point when they state that evaluation should:

- involve formative and summative approaches
- incorporate a wide range of data-gathering techniques
- include as many individuals and groups as are appropriate to the focus
- ensure that evaluation leads to feedback

(Adapted from Russell and Reid 1997, p.181)

Evaluation is, then, the analysis and judgement of both the educative process and product. Education must be focused and evaluators (subject leaders) should not attempt to cover all aspects in combination. It is for this reason that it is important to involve all stakeholders.

West (1995) advocates teachers' self-evaluation as a means of generating quality evidence. The role of the leader is to devise a method of finding out:

- what went well
- what did not go well
- whether all that was intended was completed
- that assessment evidence is used to inform opinions
- that successful learning has taken place

The teachers' role is to implement the mechanisms devised and to communicate the outcomes to the subject leader.

To assure equity between teachers, indicators against which judgements can be made must be agreed. Shipman (1979) identifies three properties of good performance indicators. They must be relevant to the objective under review, be spelt out at the same time as the objectives and there must be specified levels which represent success and failure.

Evaluation does take place at the end of a programme. The methods and measures, however, must not be applied without prior consultation. Not all indicators need be objective. Subjective indicators are expressions of satisfaction, obtained by asking people about aspects of a learning experience. Opinions can be aggregated, but more often than not words provide teachers with more information than a statistical representation.

Evaluation is a sensitive issue. Leaders need to evaluate to inform future action. Teachers, on the other hand, may view the process as threatening. Freeman (1993) advises managers to focus on tasks, not people. Aims, objectives and methods should be evaluated, not the ability of team members. As judgements are made, it is inevitable that strengths and weaknesses will emerge.

As the leader of a team, the weaknesses are those of the team, not of the individual. Evaluation should, as a quality-assurance task, be de-personalised.

CONCLUSION

The burden of responsibility for subject leaders and middle managers has grown enormously. Hoyle and Jones (1995) recognise managerialism as a significant force in schools and there is no doubt that subject leaders are one of the school's agents of control and implementation. Assuring quality is not as simple as it might appear. In 1972 the government recommended 3 per cent of teachers' salaries should be dedicated to long-term in-service training. The abandonment of such a target by the Conservatives after 1979 means that teacher development is largely the responsibility of the school itself. The quality of teaching is of course one aspect, yet the processes of managerial control do allow for greater quality and equality of provision.

For the range of aspects to be fully accounted for, it is the subject leader who must guard against the separation of financial management and educational provision. Through planning, monitoring and evaluating, the subject leader is able to place teaching and learning at the heart of educational quality assurance.

8 From strategic planning to policy-writing

INTRODUCTION

It is the role of senior managers to interpret the government legislation and edicts that regulate schools' curricular provision, and to incorporate these into the school's aims. Subject leaders have a strategic role to play within their own department/team. However, the actual implementation of aims and a school's mission statement are the responsibility of middle managers. Bridges (1981) points out, however, that channels of communication between senior managers and teaching staff are not always clear and managers can be misinterpreted. It is therefore necessary to set up formal channels of communication which are both comprehensive and efficient. Inevitably, the translation of whole-school guidelines into subject-specific policies and procedures is problematic and, therefore, the need is for subject leaders to structure and organise the teaching and learning of their subject according to agreed guidelines (Bennett 1995). Subject leaders are middle managers, in that their primary function is to implement strategies emanating from the senior-management team. At the same time, as representatives of the subject-teaching team, subject leaders also have a role to play in contributing to the overarching philosophy and values of a school.

Activity 8.1 The relationship of the subject with a whole-school ethos

1 Look in the staff handbook and consult the senior-management team. Identify the key features contained within the:

- school vision
- school mission statement
- strategic/school development plan
- whole-school aims

2 Now consider your own subject-related policies. In what ways do subject policies contribute to the fulfilment of whole-school aims? Is the

contribution of a subject to the fulfilment of whole-school aims overt and clear? In what ways do subject policies need to be improved?

Bennett's (1995) research reveals that the key to such a dual function is the management of staff. Such a task is not simple, and indeed Floyd and Wooldridge (1996) see it as involving four main elements. The four elements are not linear in nature, but represent a dynamic, cyclical structure: the completion of one leads on to the next (as illustrated by Figure 8.1).

Figure 8.1   The relationship between whole-school and subject-specific responsibilities

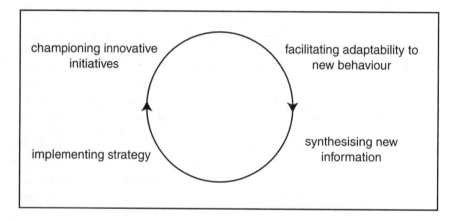

Teachers are professionals and enjoy a degree of freedom. Everard and Morris (1996) celebrate this sense of professional integrity, yet point out the need to invest effort in preparation as a means of assuring quality. They emphasise the sense espoused by followers of Total Quality Management (TQM), who lament the need for correction which is so often necessary when staff follow the human instinct of 'getting on with the job'. Careful planning, through the formulation of agreed policies, serves to combat the negative effects of impetuousness and also to overcome teachers' individualism. On the other hand, to promote individualism is to encourage creativity. Subject leaders have to be certain of when and how to determine teachers' methods and approaches.

Activity 8.2   Consistency through policy

Discuss with colleagues which of the following aspects of practice should be consistent:

Structured	Semi-structured	Independent
Planning		
Teaching and learning methods		
Display		
Assessment		
Evaluation		
Differentiation		
Other (specify)		

Do you have formalised policies on each? Should you? Decide when you feel colleagues' practice should be determined by policy and when colleagues should be encouraged to be creative.

Policies can ease the workload, and develop and foster a sense of collective responsibility, which Elliott (1981) recognises to be a key feature of a successful team (see Chapter 13 for more on teams). The formulation of and adherence to policies is not necessarily a means of managerial control, and need not have the effect of undermining teachers' professional integrity. Indeed, policies can protect teachers from the impact of macro-pressures (social and political change) by providing a sense of stability and security. Day *et al.* (1998) note that micro-pressures (such as devolved budgets, new types of schools, accountability and inspection) also place new stresses on individual teachers. Membership of a team through conformity to agreed structures can provide a safety-net for those who feel they cannot cope at any given point in time.

An essential point to make is that successful policies should be agreed. Cardno (1998) insists that to formulate policy, the team leader must involve all for whom decisions are relevant. It is, after all, classroom teachers who will have to implement policy at the 'chalk-face'.

Activity 8.3 The role of stakeholders in policy-formulation

How much involvement should each stakeholder have in policy-making? Shade in squares to indicate the degree to which you feel each should be involved (an example is provided in Figure 11.2).

What information could each group provide to inform policy-writing? How would you find relevant information? How might each group be involved in the process of policy-writing and represented in the final outcome?

Government		1	2	3	4	5	6	7	8	9	10
Governors		1	2	3	4	5	6	7	8	9	10
Senior Management Team		1	2	3	4	5	6	7	8	9	10
Subject colleagues		1	2	3	4	5	6	7	8	9	10
Other colleagues		1	2	3	4	5	6	7	8	9	10
Learning Support Assistants		1	2	3	4	5	6	7	8	9	10
Parents		1	2	3	4	5	6	7	8	9	10
Pupils		1	2	3	4	5	6	7	8	9	10
Community		1	2	3	4	5	6	7	8	9	10

Figure 8.2   An example of the stakeholders' role in policy-formulation

Government		1	2	3	4	5	6	7	8	9	10
Governors		1	2	3	4	5	6	7	8	9	10
Senior Management Team		1	2	3	4	5	6	7	8	9	10
Subject colleagues		1	2	3	4	5	6	7	8	9	10
Other colleagues		1	2	3	4	5	6	7	8	9	10
Learning Support Assistants		1	2	3	4	5	6	7	8	9	10
Parents		1	2	3	4	5	6	7	8	9	10
Pupils		1	2	3	4	5	6	7	8	9	10
Community		1	2	3	4	5	6	7	8	9	10

By involving others, subject leaders therefore have to clarify the parameters within which decisions can be made. On the other hand, by engaging colleagues in a collaborative effort, the subject leader does not have to abdicate responsibility. TTA (1998a) recognises the subject leader's need to provide leadership and direction by establishing high standards for teaching and learning. Earley's (1998) list of responsibilities: planning, organising, resourcing, controlling, evaluating and teaching, requires a direction and set of values. Policy, West (1995) states, is a course or method of action selected from alternatives, which guides actions and decisions.

Policy is, then, a product of collaboration, which serves to describe and inform practice. Goddard and Leask (1992) acknowledge this as an outcome of subject leadership and middle management, but perhaps more significantly note that the process of policy-making is even more important. The development of policies requires discussion, the sharing of ideas and collaboration. Policies are, therefore, the manifestation of collective ownership.

THE RELATIONSHIP OF POLICIES TO STRATEGIC PLANNING

Individually, subject leaders do not have the authority to create whole-school strategies. Their prime concern is 'the successful implementation of the organisation's strategy' (Earley 1998, p.149). The School Development Plan and mission statement state values and priorities, and should therefore be used to inform policies. This is not to say that subject leaders are victims of set principles, but it is important to recognise the status of policies in relation to strategy. Middlewood (1998, p.15) presents a structure locating the functions of policies:

Mission
Vision
Strategic planning
Development planning
Policies
Annual review
Regular review and adjustment
Action plans
Daily work of the college

It is, then, clear that policies are informed by the work of senior managers, yet must be adaptable in terms of colleagues' evaluation of implementation.

Activity 8.4   Fixed and flexible policies

1   Read through your subject policies. Which parts should be 'set' and which are open to change?
2   Are the 'set' parts consistent across policies and do these aspects relate to whole-school issues?

Goddard and Leask (1992) provide more detail. The impact of strategic plans is to create a framework and to clarify the relationship of policies to other areas of school life. Policies should be built on set principles and values, establish intra- and inter-subject procedures, and enable subject provision to be monitored. Bennett (1995, p.18) explains that school leaders therefore determine 'what' innovation should be put into practice, and middle managers carry the responsibility for deciding 'how' decisions are implemented.

As a consequence, policies should contain vital information, which is handed down from senior managers:

•   a sense of purpose
•   internal and external channels of communication
•   criteria for evaluation
•   the means of involving others in decision-making

(Adapted from Peeke 1994, pp.9–11)

In short, subject leaders must use strategic plans, articulated in a range of forms, to provide a blueprint for their own more results-oriented policies – by which it is meant that a policy should allow for the generation of the tangible outcomes of strategic planning. In doing so, subject leaders spread the understanding of strategic direction, ensuring that all involved are working towards the same objectives.

In the same way that individual teachers are protected by policies, subject leaders are protected by strategic plans; a process which is successful only if they have a sense of ownership of the values and targets for development which inform their own decisions. Earley (1998) assumes that effective middle managers place whole-school aims (strategic plans) before their own subject's short-term goals (policies). This is not to be presented as a dilemma for subject leaders, but as a way of facilitating the process of prioritisation.

Shipman (1979) articulates the issue in simple terms. He explains that an aim should be divided into several objectives. The objectives are derived from the aim and although they may change, the aim itself should not. Shipman's interpretation is one where objectives are represented by policies and the overarching aims by the strategic plan. By retaining a close link with the strategic plan, policies become the means by which aims and values are made explicit in practical terms.

Strategic plans and policies can appear to be the 'chicken and egg'. Goddard and Leask (1992) report on their research into secondary schools in Enfield and observe that strategic plans appear to be collections of departmental policies. This, we feel, is a misconception. The policies are borne out of strategy, not the reverse. In this case, to retain a link with the strategic plans, Freeman lists aspects which all policies should contain:

- their relationship to the organisation's mission
- a description of the management system
- staff responsibilities
- how quality assurance is documented
- the range of functions for which there are set procedures
- how management review operates

(Freeman 1993, p.144)

Activity 8.5   Checking the content of policies to ensure the fulfilment of whole-school aims

Across the top of the matrix, write the names of policies which exist. Using Freeman's (1993, p.144) list as criteria, check the content of the policies.

Policy A	Policy B	Policy C	Policy D
Organisation's mission			
Description of management- system staff responsibilities			
Q/A procedures			
Functions			
Review procedures			

As a result of this analysis, what should be added to your policies to ensure they serve the needs of the subject and of the school?

It is important that policies contribute to the overall ethos of a school, and do not militate against the plans created to achieve the aims and values which actually determine the ethos. Subject leaders must agree with, espouse and ensure the fulfilment of whole-school aims, which are best articulated in the form of subject-related policies.

COLLABORATIVE POLICY-WRITING AS A LEADERSHIP TOOL

Russell and Reid (1997) identify features of school cultures which are most supportive of school improvement and school effectiveness. These include a sense of collegiality, high expectations, a consensus on values, an orderly and secure environment, and a willingness on the part of all teachers to take on leadership roles. They also highlight the positive impact of collaborative work on the development of a spirit of trust and co-operation that is necessary if teams are to respond to the demands of change. Policy-writing, as a collective effort of the subject team, encourages these positive aspects. Indeed, it is the policy which serves as an articulation of common goals and agreement on means of achieving ends. The policy therefore acts as the 'oughts' (West 1995, p.28) of a subject team.

By building policy together, defining the purpose and methods, the subject leader has an opportunity to engage in team-building exercises. The process of policy-writing enables a clear subject-team identity to be built through the sharing of a collective vision, which when implemented will permeate all teachers' work.

Activity 8.6 Sequencing the process of policy-writing

Sequence the following activities to develop a procedure for building policies. Would you add in any other steps?

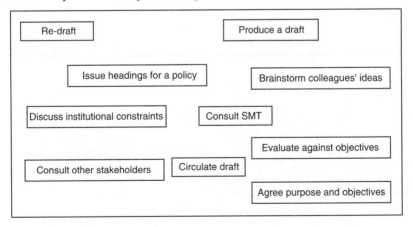

Re-draft

Produce a draft

Issue headings for a policy

Brainstorm colleagues' ideas

Discuss institutional constraints

Consult SMT

Evaluate against objectives

Consult other stakeholders

Circulate draft

Agree purpose and objectives

The subject leader must ensure, then, that all views are contained within the policy, in order to establish within the team senses of value, purpose and integrity. Hall (1998) recognises the need to deal with disagreement in a productive way and the production of departmental/team policies serves as a means of combating the potential conflict between micro-political concerns and collaboration. Individual members should be able to recognise their own input and impact on the practice of the team. In the same way that participation for subject leaders in the production of the school development plan can lead to middle managers realising what an effective job they already do (Goddard and Leask 1992), so an active engagement in policy-writing can lift the morale of classroom teachers.

O'Neill (1997) observes that teachers spend most of their working day in isolation from colleagues. He also asserts that, on the whole, teachers value and respect authority and the opportunity to exert an element of control. This level of individualism is healthy, yet does need to be checked if, as Hall (1996) claims, success hinges in part on providing opportunities for teachers to 'connect' in and out of the classroom. Again, clear agreed polices provide such an opportunity.

There is a potential clash between the need for professional integrity, by teachers as professionals, and the high level of accountability. Bridges (1981) intimates that adherence to a policy does in fact provide teachers with a layer of protection from the judgements of other stakeholders. Not only do policies serve to maximise the impact of individuals' expertise, but they also provide a protective structure. Policies therefore facilitate collaboration, enjoyment, commitment and skill development.

Subject leaders are duty bound to strive for quality, through the sensitive management of staff. Bell (1992) recognises that successful and effective teams rely on the quality of the policies which support them. It is a simple equation to relate the features of successful teams to the contents of policies.

In providing a framework which allows individual input, yet which also bonds a team, policies should contain:

- clarity of objectives
- opportunities for shared decision-making
- clarity of tasks, roles, responsibilities, organisation and time-frames
- opportunities for regular review, designed to inform future practice

For middle managers, completed policies enable the departmental identity to be articulated and provide a basis for review and evaluation. Of even greater importance, perhaps, are the opportunities to gel as a team provided by the collaborative process of policy-writing. Policy-writing provides support, lifts morale, highlights expertise and contributes to the development of a culture of collegiality and collaboration.

POLICIES ON WHAT?

Teachers are faced with the challenges of multiple initiatives (Goddard and Leask 1992). All innovations need to be managed if they are to contribute to the fulfilment of long-term aims. Policies prevent the feeling of fragmentation and therefore need to tie together aspects of provision: subject development, planning, implementation and evaluation. Medium- and long-term issues must be shaped by policy and indeed Bennett illustrates this point in relation to inspections:

> Well run departments, according to OfSTED, are not just concerned with the day to day, but have medium-term development plans which link resources to actions.
>
> (Bennett 1995, p.119)

West (1995) sees a place for an overarching policy which focuses on teaching and learning. He argues that a policy which answers the type of question: 'What do we want to witness in the classroom?' will facilitate (by providing a structure for) other policies.

Bennett (1995, p.21) lists issues which concern leaders and managers: teaching and learning, funding, persuading and motivating (pupils and staff). Consequently policies fall into clear categories:

- curriculum
- planning
- resource (including human-resource) management
- reviewing and evaluating performance
- teacher motivation

Careful planning in each of these areas provides coverage of the main functions of subject leaders.

The categories can be broken down into elements. Overarching policy statements provide the link between each, ensuring a sense of coherence and consistency. Figure 8.3 demonstrates how each can contribute to the general identity of a subject team and also to the whole-school ethos. The overarching policy statements provide reference points for each set of procedures. The policy statement should contain principles, values and, therefore, criteria by which the procedures can be evaluated.

THE CONTENTS OF POLICY

We have differentiated between policies and procedures. The purpose of this is to avoid an overload of paperwork. The system recommended also enables consistency and coherence. Planning is an essential element of

Figure 8.3   Overarching policies and formal procedures

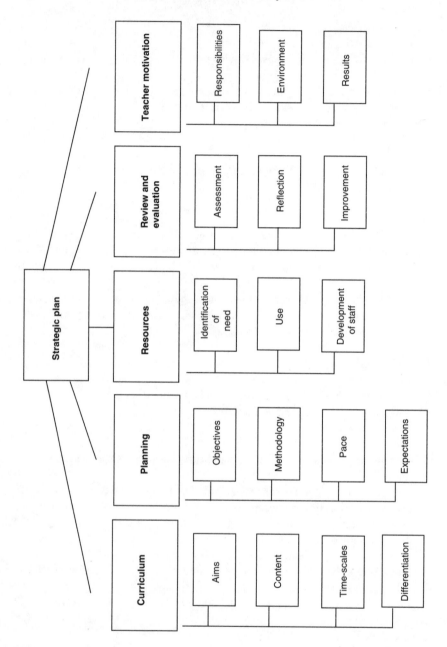

quality assurance, as is evaluation. Plans must be open to scrutiny as much as implementation and the identification of key principles in 'overarching policies' allows for this.

Curriculum

Inevitably the content of a policy on the particular subject curriculum should be shaped by the National Curriculum documentation and/or external examination syllabus. The subject team is, of course, in a position to interpret statutory requirements. The subject provision must contribute to whole-school aims and a policy should identify its unique contribution, and also how in combination with other curricular areas it meets the demands articulated in the aims. Clear objectives should demonstrate how aims are to be met; the identification of content and the sequencing of activities should enable teachers to structure and prioritise. By linking provision and methodology to the aims, subject leaders can ensure that any inclusion in the policy, as Hopkins (1989) insists should happen, will impact on long-term benefits to the teaching and learning process.

A curriculum policy therefore must contain aims, objectives, content and methodology. The inclusion of suitable time-scales and differentiation techniques relevant to the subject enables Hall's (1998) requirements to be met:

- to combine moral purpose with collaboration
- to match individual teachers' expertise to objectives
- to communicate a vision
- to recognise the need for teachers to develop
- to manage disagreement between teachers

Planning

Bennett (1995) reminds leaders that teachers, as professionals, must enjoy some autonomy. A policy on planning should provide an element of individual choice in some respects. Stoll and Fink (1996), on the other hand, recognise that democratic decision-making is not always the best use of time. The policy should therefore allow representation, rather than individualism. Earley and Fletcher-Campbell point out:

> The absolute key to departmental improvement is to involve everyone in everything that goes on. If you can get ideas flowing then you have a structure for making improvement.
>
> (Earley and Fletcher-Campbell 1992, p.187)

A policy on planning must be adaptable and flexible, yet underpinned by a common acceptance of objectives and expectations. Teachers should be guided in pitching their lessons at an appropriate level, drawing on National Curriculum documentation and whole-school targets. Teachers are then in a position to make professional judgements on the pace of learning and the selection of an appropriate methodology. Such independence is only viable if teachers' individual approaches are accountable to the agreed, common elements contained within the policy.

Activity 8.7 Standardising lesson plans

Do teachers in your team use a common format for lesson planning? Can you identify the following in their plans?

objectives – National Curriculum PoS – performance levels – sequence of activities – timing/pace – opportunities for monitoring/assessment of objectives – evaluation

If not, how can you be sure that other teacher's work matches up to specifications contained in the subject related scheme of work?

Resources

A leader has to establish priorities. Team members provide an abundance of ideas, yet it is the team leader who has to co-ordinate these efforts within the confines of existing expertise and budget constraints (Earley and Fletcher-Campbell 1992).

The overview of staff expertise should inform who teaches which classes, whether teachers should share classes or work independently with them. An awareness of teachers' strengths and development needs is therefore a pre-condition for a timetabling policy and the deployment of staff. West (1995, p.30) places the issue in context by asserting that such a policy should provide the answers to three key questions:

- what should characterise learning experiences?
- what should characterise the learning environment?
- what should the major characteristics of teachers' repertoire be in order to achieve high-quality learning?

Activity 8.8 Developing a policy on use of resources

	Daily use	Weekly use	Monthly use	Termly use	Purpose
Text books					
Audio tapes					
Video tapes					
OHP					
Computers					
Whiteboard					
Readers					
Games					
Worksheets					
Cards					
Other artefacts (specify)					

Look at the list of resources above. Ask teaching colleagues to tick how regularly they are used and to specify the purpose of using them. Do these relate to learning objectives? Do patterns of use emerge? Could a policy on the use of resources lead to greater (e)quality of provision?

The use of resources is therefore crucial. A policy should require staff to use resources regularly if, when purchased, they were seen to hold the key to improvement. Staff use and suggestions for use should be closely monitored.

MONITORING, EVALUATION AND REVIEW

A policy which is imposed, regardless of the effect, is counterproductive. All policies should themselves be reviewed. Good teachers respond to evaluation by amending future plans. There must therefore be procedures which allow for the impact on practice to be measured.

Activity 8.9 Developing a policy for monitoring, evaluation and review

1   Under the following categories, devise a list of performance indicators which could be used to evaluate teachers' and learners' performance:

- Assessment
- Pupil enjoyment/stimulation
- Use of resources (regularity and quality)
- Behaviour

2   Which of the indicators are best used to assess performance by:

(a) the teacher
(b) the pupil
(c) an outsider?

3   Draw up a table and ask colleagues to tick who is the best person/people. Do colleagues agree with you? Can a schedule/ programme for evaluation be drawn up? What would you do with the outcomes?

Schools are required to analyse the outcomes of pupil assessment, yet such a mechanistic approach to evaluation is often condemned. Alongside quantitative evaluation techniques, however, allowing teachers to reflect on practice and educational outcomes, a qualitative analysis takes on greater meaning.

The purpose of evaluation is improvement (Goddard and Leask 1992) and therefore procedures need to be in place to allow for the amendment/adaptation of practice. A policy for review and evaluation must provide indicators by which performance can be measured in order that improvements can be made.

Staff motivation

Much has been said about the involvement of teachers in decision-making and policy-writing. A policy must therefore exist to allow teachers to participate, input ideas and evaluate implementation.

Activity 8.10   Human resource management: Towards a policy

1   What can *all* teachers be expected to do beyond basic lesson planning, teaching and marking?
2   Do colleagues agree with you?
3   Do the additional responsibilities match up to what is stated on generic job descriptions?

The culture of the school and, of course, the leadership style of the subject leader must be taken into account. Consequently the degree of autonomy and accountability must be clearly expressed in order that individual teachers can match a professional responsibility to agreed limits.

CONCLUSION

Policy-writing is a complex activity. As West (1995) notes, there are as many different ways of structuring a policy as there are policies themselves. The process of developing policies contributes to school effectiveness and school improvement. A structured approach allows teachers to focus on pupils and their learning, through collaboration. Jayne (1998) comments that an important by-product of this process is that teachers themselves are encouraged to become learners. In these ways the policy serves as a design process, if we regard effective learning as the educational product. Freeman (1993) recognises that careful design is a crucial part of assuring quality.

The Quality Assurance movement advocates close attention to the processes, rather than the product, and key features of this are that procedures should be in place to support the induction of new staff. The subject leader, in a school context, can use policies to monitor compliance to agreed systems and practices. BS5750 or ISO 9000 awards for quality assurance demand that such systems are in place, and also that policies and procedures should be reviewed and updated when necessary. National Curriculum performance descriptions and external examination criteria are well defined, enabling teachers to work towards pre-determined targets. Policies provide leaders with procedures to control and verify the design in the form of plans, implementation procedures and evaluation.

The role of subject leaders includes that of being middle managers. They represent decisions made by senior managers at an operational level. Through the careful management of policy development, they have the opportunity to incorporate whole-school aims, values and ideals (Day *et al.* 1998). The policy represents, therefore, the school as an institution and eases the difficulty middle managers face of compromising teachers' professional integrity for the sake of managerialism and the concept of public accountability. The policy can determine the relationship between individual autonomy and responsibility to the institution. In this way, effective and useful policies provide quality assurance on behalf of the school as an institution, and support and protection for individual teachers.

9 Sustaining an improvement in subject knowledge and in-service training

INTRODUCTION

Four-fifths of a school budget is designated to staff salaries. Clearly the staff must be seen as the most prized asset of a school and therefore the management of the curriculum must include the planning, monitoring and evaluation of teachers' classroom work. Literature on effective schools contains little reference to teachers' subject knowledge. Everard and Morris (1990), however, note that a common assumption underpinning such studies is that teachers can only teach subjects that they know. Goddard and Leask (1992, p.204) note:

> High quality training and regular updating of teachers is essential if standards are to be improved. Even if no other aspect of teaching changed, subject content changes continually.
>
> (Goddard and Leask 1992, p.204)

It is simple common sense that, in monitoring the provision within any subject discipline, the subject leader has a responsibility to assure quality teaching, at least, in part, by deploying staff with adequate subject knowledge.

The updating of subject knowledge and, indeed, all forms of professional competence has in some ways been hindered by the trend towards a 'consultancy model' (Goddard and Leask 1992, p.204) of in-service training (INSET), which involves the cascading of training outcomes by one teacher to others within a team. School-based INSET is an effective means of implementing new policies and procedures through a discussion of institutional opportunities and threats. The danger of this approach is that institutional self-development can lead to the recycling of existing, even stale ideas. The method is, however, relatively cheap, in that currently only 1 per cent of teachers' salaries are devoted to training.

Teachers can be mistrustful of INSET. Low-cost training, at a time of immense (imposed) change, is often perceived as a way of adding duties and responsibilities to teachers' roles and, in fact, serves to detract from teachers' primary purpose of teaching their subject(s). There is then a need to create an atmosphere of motivated learning, when training leads to an improvement in pupils' learning experiences (Dean 1991).

Evidently, the subject leader plays an instrumental role in identifying needs in terms of pupil requirements and therefore in understanding the process of learning *vis-à-vis* concepts, skills and content. At the same time, teachers must want to improve, and must be in possession of the necessary understanding and skills to face future demands with confidence. Goddard and Leask (1992) remark that a major requirement in education is to maintain and enhance teachers' motivation as learners themselves, thereby developing the culture of a school as a learning organisation.

Subject leaders must, therefore, plan professional development. Dean (1991) asserts that success is dependent on three crucial factors:

- the knowledge, experience, motivation and personality of teachers
- the school content and culture
- opportunities for professional contact outside of school

The first point suggests the need to conduct a human-resource audit which, as Knight (1993) insists, must be both quantitative (age, gender, qualifications) and qualitative (knowledge, competence, attitudes, morale). Many commentators (e.g. Dean 1991, Oldroyd and Hall 1991) mention the need for a school culture which is conducive to a sense of lifelong learning. Teachers need to be aware of the intimate link between staff development and school improvement.

Subject leaders must give their subject a high profile in continuing professional development (CPD) activities. It is too easy to allow the focus of training days to be whole-school issues, which may not be seen to address individual teachers' concerns.

Activity 9.1   The focus of school-based training

1   How much time is given over to the development of subject teaching in school-based training days?
2   Does teaching and learning of your subject feature on the agenda for team meetings?
3   How much time is needed to discuss issues related to the teaching and learning of your subject?

The support and expertise of colleagues within the subject area must not be neglected. Even without formalising inter-teacher learning, considerable development can take place through mutual support and working collaboratively.

My experience was typical of my peers. We tended to learn about our professional roles and to acquire the related skills by working alongside other teachers.

(Bell and Day 1991, p.6)

Teamwork and co-operation are opportunities not to be missed. Dean (1991), however, comments that development does not happen simply as a result of years of teaching. Subject leaders need to create an environment in which school-focused INSET is profitable to both the institution and the individual. Morant (1981) identifies features of successful school-based training. By rephrasing features into questions (Activity 9.2), it is possible to identify aspects of a school's culture which are conducive to effective in-school training.

Activity 9.2   Aspects conducive to effective in-school training

1   Do staff recognise that training serves institutional educational needs?
2   Can training opportunities be seen to serve the particular needs of participants?
3   Are training opportunities initiated and planned by participants?
4   Does training take place on the school premises?

The educational potential is not the only justification for school-based training. Schools are able to draw on the expertise already existing within them; the fact that funds are delegated to schools means that resources to facilitate the sharing of knowledge and expertise are available. From a middle manager's point of view, the benefits are obvious. An adaptation of Cowan and Wright's (1990) perception of advantages includes:

- encouraging co-operation
- maximising the use of school facilities
- exchanging ideas on teaching and learning
- highlighting specific needs

Local financial management promotes the recommendations of the Cockcroft (1982) report that middle managers should monitor subject teaching in school, play a key role in professional development of colleagues through in-service training. This then was reiterated in Kenneth Baker's letter to Chief Education Officers (Baker 1990), when he stated the need for middle managers to be involved in appraisal schemes which should be designed to help teachers enhance teaching skills, and also provide help to teachers having difficulty, without resorting to disciplinary measures.

IDENTIFYING STAFF NEEDS AND WANTS

> A teacher must have mastery of teaching material if he or she is to be truly effective. This does not mean knowing all the answers. There are some situations in which teacher and children can find out together. The teacher must know how to make such a search, however.
>
> (Dean 1991, p.12)

Government and press reports since the 1960s have recognised teachers' deficiencies in subject knowledge. This assertion in the Newsom (1963) report was reiterated in the DES's *Aspects of Secondary Education in England* (1979), when HMI added some frightening statistics (22 per cent of mathematics was taught by non-specialists and 10 per cent of science was taught by staff with inadequate subject knowledge). The *Times Educational Supplement* (1991) reported a mismatch of up to 50 per cent between subjects taught and teachers' qualifications. These worrying statistics have not been hidden by teachers. Dean (1991) notes that surveys of what teachers want from INSET focus attention on subject content. Not only is there a need for subject-knowledge 'training', but also it represents teachers' 'wants'.

Subject leaders have therefore to accept that 'subject knowledge' must feature as part of the appraisal process. Leaders have to take responsibility for identifying teachers' weaknesses, as well as respond to requests for further professional development. This responsibility requires sensitivity and, as Oldroyd and Hall (1991) intimate, needs identification should be based on factual information rather than personal judgements.

Activity 9.3   Identifying colleagues' strengths and weaknesses

1   What are the particular areas of expertise of colleagues in your subject team?
2   Under each of the headings below, list aspects which contribute to good practice. Formulate a questionnaire asking colleagues to grade their strengths (1 = weak, 5 = strong). What do the outcomes tell you?

Subject knowledge

	1	2	3	4	5
•	1	2	3	4	5
•	1	2	3	4	5
•	1	2	3	4	5
•	1	2	3	4	5
•	1	2	3	4	5

Lesson and unit planning

•	1	2	3	4	5
•	1	2	3	4	5
•	1	2	3	4	5
•	1	2	3	4	5
•	1	2	3	4	5

Methodology and delivery (including classroom management)

•	1	2	3	4	5
•	1	2	3	4	5
•	1	2	3	4	5
•	1	2	3	4	5
•	1	2	3	4	5

Assessment recording, reporting

•	1	2	3	4	5
•	1	2	3	4	5
•	1	2	3	4	5
•	1	2	3	4	5
•	1	2	3	4	5

3   How does this information help you to structure a subject-related staff-development programme?

Oldroyd and Hall (1991, p.72) consider the means by which needs can be identified. First, teachers should engage in self-review. This can be achieved by individuals being required to relate their knowledge to their job description. Observation of colleagues, a discussion with peers and the completion of a carefully constructed questionnaire related to classroom performance can all facilitate the recognition of subject-knowledge needs.

Second, a subject-team review of performance and a collaborative effort to plan for future projects highlights the collective need for specific subject-knowledge. A sense of anonymity through the production of a combined team needs-analysis exercise in relation to the teaching and learning objectives can furnish the subject leader with relevant and useful information.

Third, Oldroyd and Hall acknowledge the value of whole-school initiatives. Subject reviews which measure performance against quantifiable outcomes can stimulate discussion and the examination of existing subject knowledge. External inspections (OfSTED) can serve to focus discussions.

The above strategies do rely on a spirit and sense of trust and confidence. Subject leaders must centre all needs identifications around the concept of collective development and improvement. Planning and delivery of content will always be improved with enhanced subject knowledge and this gain for teachers will serve to facilitate their day-to-day duties as a teacher:

How many teachers could achieve more with the same effort by planning their work better?

(Everard 1986, p.177)

Needs identification cannot be separated from curriculum development. Goddard and Leask (1992) comment on the inextricable link between professional responsibility and accountability. Without the two existing as equal partners, there is little basis for delivering an effective curriculum. Forward planning will inevitably involve self-evaluation, and an open articulation of needs in advance of implementation is an effective first stage of quality assurance.

Activity 9.4   Matching needs to existing subject-related expertise

Analyse the subject-development plan. Examine to what extent the fulfilment of targets requires new knowledge and skills. Do these new demands match up to existing staff expertise? Are future plans and changes the source of anxiety within your subject team?

Identifying needs must be a shared task between subject leaders and team members. The role of the subject leader is, in one sense, to frame the discussions in order that all are at least aware of what is needed. The worst case scenario is of course that teachers do 'not know what they cannot do' (adapted from Oldroyd and Hall 1991, p.67).

The strategies discussed above, in combination comprise a human-resource audit. An audit, Hargreaves and Hopkins (1991) indicate, must be followed by action. Assessable and sensitive auditing processes should serve to reveal strengths as well as weaknesses, provide a basis for future action and enable the subject team to prioritise needs.

Subject leaders are themselves members of subject-teaching teams and should therefore also undergo the needs-identification process themselves. Dean (1991) lists several activities designed to identify strengths and weaknesses (including group discussions, face-to-face interviews, being observed by peers). Brainstorming also provides a non-threatening opportunity to discuss difficulties and concerns. In such a case, teachers are invited to suggest problems associated with the implementation of a policy or project related to the subject. All contributions are noted down without discussion. A second stage is to categorise the concerns; a third is to rank them. The content of the brainstorm does not belong to individuals, but in categorising and ranking in order of need, teachers will justify and qualify publicly and to themselves the exact nature of the concerns.

A common thread running through needs identification is the consideration of teachers' current and future needs. Team members must be encouraged, and feel confident, to articulate their own concerns openly. Subject leaders have a duty to establish a climate of trust, in which the expression of needs is treated as an opportunity for future development. Subject-team improvement is not about self-interest, fear of threatened disciplinary action and angry reaction (Easen 1985).

Needs identification is, rather, a means to:

1   developing relevant professional development activities
2   initiating change and improvement
3   acknowledging existing difficulties
4   recognising particular strengths which may help to overcome (1), (2) and (3)
(Adapted from Oldroyd and Hall 1991, p.73)

Needs identification and quality auditing is not easy. Teams may not be able to provide an objective assessment of performance. However, individual teachers' perceptions are important. The combined top-down/bottom-up approach represented by Figure 9.1 serves as a synthesis of the process recommended.

Figure 9.1   A top-down/bottom-up process of needs identification

LEA/OfSTED/school senior management analysis
↕
Teams identifying needs
↕
Individuals identifying needs

A subsequent stage to needs identification is needs analysis. The subject leader must lead, but share an analysis of the data and information generated by the quality audit. It is the analysis of needs which serves as a basis for action and implementation of professional development activities.

Activity 9.5   Categorising and prioritising needs

Having identified teachers' needs and wants (see Activity 9.3), can you categorise and prioritise them? On what basis have you ranked the training needs? Activity 9.3 places the issues into categories and we present a model in Chapter 8 to help you to prioritise.

PROVISION

Having analysed needs, subject leaders and their teams have recourse to two types of action. As Bell and Day (1991) point out, INSET can be remedial (designed to address identified weaknesses) or developmental (building on existing strengths). Particularly in the first place, teachers will require human support, which Oldroyd and Hall (1991) recommend can be provided by a range of people: subject colleagues, trainers, advisers, advisory teachers, other colleagues and subject leaders themselves. Support and training also requires practical provision, including funding, time and possibly a reduction in the teachers' teaching commitment. The level of support will, obviously, depend on the level of need. An assessment by the subject leader and teacher(s) involved will determine the type of activity required. Possible options include school-based and organised training, an externally provided short course, visits to other schools, a long course undertaken in the teacher's own time or, in increasingly rare cases, a secondment (Easen 1985).

Activity 9.6   Identifying sources of help

1   List subject support groups which offer INSET. Summarise the types of provision offered. You may wish to contact the organisations for guidance.
2   To what extent do you think you can provide similar levels of support within your own subject team?

Whatever the provision, success will depend on the commitment of the teacher. Day *et al.* (1987) observe that favourable outcomes are related to four key aspects. First, the teacher must appreciate that their own improved competence will enhance the performance of the team as a whole and that the participation in training activities is, in fact, possible only because of the support of fellow team members. Second, the provision must be seen to achieve positive results recognisable by the individual and the team. Third, the individual team member must also recognise that their development will be rewarded by an increased influence as a team member. Last, the subject leader must be appreciative of the teacher's personal investment. The onus is, then, on the subject leader to evoke a sense of trust and respect, as well as to facilitate the implementation of new-found knowledge and skills in the work of the subject team.

Bell and Day (1991) make several recommendations to assure the above:

1   The teacher should be briefed about expectations in terms of improved performance prior to embarking on the training programme.
2   The teacher should produce a detailed action plan, identifying performance indicators in order to facilitate evaluation of the support programme.
3   The subject leader should make arrangements for the new skills and knowledge to be demonstrated.
4   The teacher should have the opportunity to evaluate the support provision throughout the programme.

Activity 9.7   Subject-based policies for CPD

Do you have a subject-based policy for professional development? If so, does it account for procedures listed by Bell and Day (1991)?

 If a policy does not exist, draft one and discuss it with subject colleagues.

An assumption underpinning the whole process is that all involved must be motivated and enthusiastic about the subject in question:

> Learning is often caught as much as taught. A teacher who really cares about his/her subject matter will want to maintain skill and knowledge at a high level. Enthusiasm may also make a teacher ready to work at improving teaching skills in order to share a love of the subject with pupils.
>
> (Dean 1991, p.16)

Particularly at primary level, some teachers may not share the love of a subject with the specialist subject leader. The enthusiasm of a subject leader can be infectious, and the new knowledge and skills provided by a teacher must be treated as exciting and an opportunity for development.

 In order to assume positive outcomes, subject leaders must investigate the full range of provision, including a critique of particular programmes. Criteria by which INSET can be appraised are accessible in general terms. The Manpower Services Commission (1985) provided an analysis of successful INSET that includes the provision of clear objectives which relate to particular needs and which have as a starting point teachers' existing knowledge and skills. The programme is not to be presented as a 'quick fix', but should represent a stage of ongoing professional development.

 Consequently, externally provided courses should not be divorced from in-school activity. Dean (1991) sees the role of the subject leader as instrumental in linking external provision with internal needs and development. Observing teachers, being observed and facilitating peer observation are among strategies recommended. Joyce and Showers (1998) advocate peer coaching as a follow-up to INSET in order to promote focused discussion. They also provide a matrix demonstrating how their research links training methods and follow-up to the impact on teachers' competence (see Activity 9.8). Wallace (1991) also promotes micro-teaching to colleagues as a profitable way of experimenting with and acquiring new skills, as well as a practical means of sharing and discussing new ideas.

Activity 9.8   Complementing course input

Use the matrix, adapted from Joyce and Showers (1998), to ascertain the level of impact achieved by different training methods. Consult with team members to evaluate prior experiences and to assist in the planning of future INSET.

Level of impact / Training method	General awareness of skills	Organised knowledge of underlying concepts and theory	Learning of new skills	Application on the job
Presentation or description of new skills				
Modelling new skills (video or live demonstration)				
Practice in simulated setting				
Feedback on performance in simulated setting				
Feedback on performance in real setting				

How does this information on colleagues' views help you to plan ways of following up on INSET within your team?

A commitment to involve colleagues inevitably places pressure on the teacher undergoing training. This pressure, Wallace (1991) claims, counters the (sometimes false) assumption that teachers want to learn. Critical friendship allows for a less daunting approach, which counters this sense of stress and tension. Discussion of issues with a peer, who is charged with relating ideas to practice, provides a pragmatic focus leading to application in the classroom. The critical friend fulfils a friendly yet assertive role. This very informal type of appraisal serves a formative assessment role, compelling the teacher to consider future action. As Bell and Day (1991) point out, the most effective way of dealing with incompetent teachers is to adopt a counselling approach, rather than to use disciplinary measures in a confrontational way.

Careful planning and monitoring of INSET should impact on individual teachers by addressing their needs and wants, the subject-team performance and the effectiveness of the whole school. Provision is well represented by an adaptation of Oldroyd and Hall's triangular model.

Figure 9.2   A triangular model of in-service support

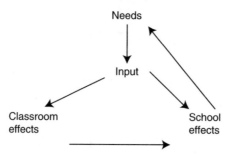

Source: Oldroyd and Hall 1991, p.163

The subject leader's role is then, in short, to maintain the close link between course provision and actual school practice. This is achieved by careful selection of provision, close monitoring and the establishment of procedures enabling the introduction and implementation of new ideas, knowledge and skills.

EVALUATING IN-SERVICE PROVISION

Evaluation is more than an assessment of the content and delivery of a course or programme. A full evaluation is an assessment of the impact of the provision on classroom practice. It is essential, therefore, that the evaluation process is continuous and ongoing. A full appreciation of training is not always immediately obvious. Careful consideration during the provision stage (see earlier) obviously provides a useful beginning. There are, though, other measures which can be applied 'after the event'.

Upon completion of a course/programme, teachers should provide a descriptive account to the subject leader and/or a colleague charged with the responsibility of acting as a 'critical friend'. The subject leader does (whatever the course of action) need to be involved, in order that the team can collectively reap the benefits of the training. The descriptive phase allows for a process of filtering the outcomes by collaboratively selecting the most relevant aspects.

This process of consolidation should be followed by a focused presentation of potential gains to the subject team as a whole. This dissemination and discussion is more than simply 'cascading' the content of a course. It involves a detailed reflection on the value of new ideas and the manageability of implementation. As the new 'expert', the teacher who has undergone training can be invited to adopt the role of trainer, which also serves the purpose of offering public respect to the teacher.

Implementation of new strategies should not be the sole responsibility of the individual teacher. Training is a means of improving team performance, and the establishment of a group working in collaboration enables the detailed evaluation and adaptation of new methods. Mutual observation, quality circle discussions, team teaching and project evaluation against agreed objectives and criteria all represent a planned and managed implementation.

Such an involved form of evaluation will, of course, generate data and information. Such evidence can be used to formulate a portfolio of INSET provision (Oldroyd and Hall 1991). The inclusion of action plans, targets, descriptive accounts, informed evaluation and personal assessments will only serve to provide the department/subject team with a resource for future continuous professional development.

10 Monitoring and evaluating to improve teaching, learning and motivation

INTRODUCTION

Kyriacou (1986) predicted that a focus on the translation of educational goals and aims into actual outcomes would lead schools to concentrate on the results of standardised tests and examinations as a means of evaluating performance. Indeed, strict government control through the Teacher Training Agency (TTA) which specifies teacher training standards and the monitoring of their implementation by OfSTED has resulted in considerable attention being paid to the measurable aspects of educational outcomes. Such a narrow view of evaluation methods can, indeed, have a detrimental effect, in that individual teachers can neglect the benefits of process-based issues in favour of examination results:

> By requiring schools to compete for pupils, and hence for funds, and by making schools more accountable to their local communities through publication of OfSTED reports and league tables of pupils' achievements, education policy has systematically encouraged ego orientation rather than mastery or task orientation, at least at the level of teacher motivation.
>
> (Galloway *et al.* 1998, p.143)

Teaching and learning are not easily measurable. Learning is, of course, dependent (at least in part) on good teaching and, as Brown (1995) points out, all teachers would agree that helping pupils to learn is central to their role. Traditional school practice does not, though, lend itself to qualitative evaluation. Becker *et al.* (1981) comment that 'closed door' teaching has promoted a classroom privacy and prevented universally accepted evaluation criteria from being developed. Indeed, they claim that individual success, reflected by promotion, is unlikely to be related to classroom performance and more often is an outcome of age, experience and attendance at relevant in-service courses.

Crucial to effective teaching and learning is, of course, the relationship between teacher and learner. Claxton (1988) goes as far as to claim that teaching and learning is, in fact, a contract between teachers and pupils. The pupil has to trust the teacher sufficiently to hand over responsibility in order to acquire knowledge, a quality or a skill that the teacher can pass over. Relationships, trust, knowledge, qualities and skills are all, particularly in combination, immeasurable and intangible, as each is dependent on a range of variables. Kyriacou lists variables for teaching:

- teacher characteristics (e.g. age, experience)
- pupil characteristics (e.g. age, ability, maturity)
- class characteristics (e.g. size, social dimension)
- subject characteristics (e.g. content, level of difficulty)
- school characteristics (e.g. ethos, facilities)
- community characteristics (e.g. affluence, population density)
- characteristics of the occasion (e.g. time of day, preceding lesson)

(Kyriacou 1986, p.9)

For the subject leader, such a range of variables poses problems in terms of assuring all pupils an equality of provision. Bennett (1976) presents four categories of variables when researching the effectiveness of teaching styles: presage, content, process and product. It is, of course, important that leaders allow for a range of individual teaching styles, which will depend on teachers' experience and cognitive and affective qualities (presage). However, the leader will want to assure a consistent approach offering the full range of learning opportunities to all pupils.

Planning, monitoring and evaluation must therefore take account of the variables and a range of data-gathering techniques should be employed. Bennett (1976), again, suggests three main methods: classroom observation, experimental studies and comparative studies. Kyriacou (1986) expands on these, including researching teachers' and pupils' descriptions and analyses of lessons.

The use of opinions of those involved in the teaching and learning process is valid for several reasons. First, as Brown (1995) points out, teachers are increasingly aware of the hidden curriculum, of the informal impact of activities on pupils' behaviour and attitudes. Armitage *et al.* explain that the values and beliefs of teachers are often 'caught' and not 'taught' (Armitage *et al.* 1998, p.91) and are not detectable to an outside researcher. Bennett's (1976) own research also showed that very often the outcomes tallied with teachers' own expectations. It is clearly essential to take teachers' viewpoints into account.

An understanding of learning as a combination of known and new knowledge (constructivist) validates the pupil perspective too. Driver and Bell (1986) note that learners are active participants in the learning process and that knowledge is personally constructed. Given that teaching and learning is not simply the transmission of knowledge, any evaluation must give due consideration to the learner.

Activity 10.1   Data-gathering methods

Consider the following means of gathering data. What are the advantages and disadvantages of each method?

	Advantages	Disadvantages
Observation		
One-to-one discussions with teachers		
Group discussions with teachers		
Discussions with pupils		
Evaluation forms to be completed by people		
Videos of pupils in lessons		
Examination of pupils' work		
Analysis of examination and test results		
Discussions with non-teaching staff		

Bearing in mind the advantages and disadvantages of each method, devise forms to facilitate the processes of data-gathering.

Although teaching and learning is indeed a process (and Activity 10.1 allows teachers to begin to assess its effectiveness), the product and content of teaching must not be ignored. The subject leader must be clear about the impact of process variables on the final outcomes. Again Kyriacou provides useful models for research. For Kyriacou (1986, p.11), process variables include teachers' enthusiasm, clarity of expression, use of questions, praise and criticism. The teacher's presentation skills involve both verbal and non-verbal communication skills (see Chapter 12). Effective classroom management and organisation are partially dependent on disciplinary techniques. Positive relationships with groups and individuals rely on a suitable atmosphere, quality feedback and interaction with pupils. Successful outcomes depend in part on the teaching of learning strategies, the provision of suitable tasks and the encouragement of pupil-initiated interaction (questions and discussions).

Product variables do include the outcomes of assessment and it is crucial that assessment allows for the identification of all positive aspects contained in Figure 10.1.

Activity 10.2   Assessing the full range of learning outcomes

Which assessment methods provide evidence of the outcomes of learning? Complete the table below.

	Knowledge	Interest	Intellectual motivation	Confidence and self-esteem	Pupil autonomy	Social skills
Written tests						
Self-assessment						
Oral assessment						
Peer assessment						
Observation of task						
Completion of profile						
Continuous assessment						

How should the outcomes of assessment be recorded?

Figure 10.1   Positive outcomes of learning

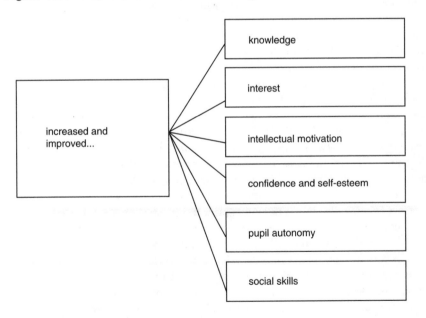

Quality assurance involves teacher quality, learner quality and a general ethos and ambience of motivation and stimulation. Subject leaders must focus their attention on each aspect to acquire as broad a picture as possible. It is through planning in advance, monitoring throughout the process and analysing the outcomes that as accurate a picture as possible can be acquired.

MONITORING PUPIL LEARNING

In order to monitor pupil learning, the subject leader and team member must share a collective understanding of what learning is in relation to the particular subject. A second key factor should be that class teachers are responsible for monitoring learning themselves. If the subject leader is to use the information provided by teachers for comparative analysis, there needs to be consensus on how the data is gathered.

Guidance on learning styles abounds. Historically, government reports (e.g. Hadow 1931, Plowden 1967) have encouraged discovery of learning, pupil activity and pupil creativity. Learning, also, certainly has many dimensions and Nicholls (1995) stresses cognitive, social and emotional factors. Learning is both individual and shared. The teacher provides learning opportunities for groups of pupils and individual pupils interpret the information in their own particular way. Minstrell and Stimpson (1996) distinguish between training and teaching in that the latter requires pupils to perform with understanding, rather than the teacher focusing on observable actions only. A behaviourist view (McClelland 1987) is that a learning outcome is determined jointly by learners' own efforts and their ability to perform a task. Evidently teachers must not neglect the personal input provided by the learner.

Claxton asserts that learning is 'a growth, not an accumulation' (Claxton 1988, p.27) and therefore the view that the pupil approaches a learning situation with existing ideas is essential to bear in mind (in addition to Claxton, see Bennett and Dunne 1994, Carré 1995, Minstrell and Stimpson 1996). It is the interaction of new knowledge with existing knowledge which represents learning. The teacher does, of course, have to take existing ideas and concepts into account, whether they be accurate or distorted. When planning learning, subject leaders can build into schemes of work activities which are designed to extract existing ideas and viewpoints prior to introducing new knowledge.

The constructivist view of learning, as that which takes place as a result of social interaction (Bruner 1986), is important to bear in mind. Pupils do need to talk, discuss and reflect in order to absorb knowledge. Vytgotsky (1978) goes one step further, suggesting that learners need to interact with others who are more knowledgeable in order to achieve real learning. Again, careful planning enables learners to profit from structured learning opportunities.

Such an approach to learning appears to be in direct conflict with a Piagetian stance. Bennett and Dunne explain that, for Piaget, intellectual competence is 'a manifestation of a child's largely *unassisted* activities'

(Bennett and Dunne 1994, p.52; our italics). There are, however, aspects of Piaget's work which assist an appraisal of learning. Kyriacou (1986) notes the concept of 'readiness', concluding that too simple a task demotivates learners and a too complicated one can foster inappropriate learning strategies, such as a total reliance on memory. Bennett and Dunne's (1994). assertion, however, that learners are intellectually active, stands true, and consequently teachers must relate new learning to contexts which are readily appreciated by learners.

Nicholls (1995) proposes concrete measures, which can be built into plans. She recommends that pupils are involved in and 'own' the purpose of a task; that they can propose and design learning activities, and that teachers should value and respect all pupils' interpretations.

Activity 10.3   Pupil ownership of learning objectives

1   Below are questions pupils may be asked to answer in order to provide a sense of ownership of learning objectives:

> How might this unit of work relate to your interests/hobbies outside school?
> In what ways will the content of this unit of work help you in the future?
> What do you already know about this topic?
> What do you think you need to learn about this topic?
> How will you use this new knowledge?

2   Can you devise activities to support pupils in answering these questions, which are directly related to a unit of work (e.g. brainstorming, role plays, group discussions)?

Planning and introducing a topic are essential phases of learning and the responsibility lies with the teacher. Claxton claims that:

> Learning is the search for an answer to a question that matters.
>
> (Claxton 1988, p.24)

It is therefore incumbent on teachers to present information which is appropriate in terms of difficulty and which is relevant in terms of content.

Atkinson and Shiffrin (1968) remind us that the initial presentation of new knowledge is received via the senses. Gardner's (1983) theory of multiple intelligences suggests that learners will respond differently to different types of input. Learners with developed musical intelligence will respond more positively to musical stimuli; pupils with a highly developed interpersonal intelligence will enjoy discussions, and so forth. The key to effective learning across a group of pupils is, of course, variety.

Activity 10.4   Presenting and introducing units of work

Take a unit of work and consider how any of the following might be used to introduce ideas, concepts or information to be covered.

Poetry	Pictures	Physical movement
Music	Discussions and debates	Anecdotes
Word salads	Television snippets	Songs
Puzzles	Jokes	Legends and myths
Cartoons		

Consult with colleagues. Can the same unit be presented to different pupils in different ways?

Learning also involves memory. Brown explains that memory is not a single process, but a series of interrelated ones. Only a limited amount of information can be stored in the short-term memory and learners need to devise strategies to transfer information to the long-term memory (LTM). Brown (1995, pp.30–1) suggests the following must be borne in mind if learners are to be able to process information effectively:

- rehearsal is a potent method of inputting into LTM
- permanent memory is more easily achieved if the input has links with existing memory (i.e. meaning)
- learners pay attention to information which has meaning
- meta-cognition provides an insight into how one's memory works and consequently improves the process

The lessons for teachers are clear. Built into the process of learning should be realistic and authentic tasks, and pupil evaluation of how the content has been learnt. Open discussion of learning techniques can serve to reinforce the content, as well as the method of learning.

Sequencing the learning experience requires subtle judgement by the teacher. Careful questioning, the deconstruction of tasks, the revision of key content are all essential elements. Reinforcement by the teacher must be related to individual pupil characteristics. Skinner (1968) recommends positive reinforcement in the form of rewards, and also negative reinforcement through sanctions to encourage learning. Claxton (1988) warns teachers not to make assumptions. For some pupils, he claims, the threat of a detention may not outweigh the wish to impress peers.

Teachers need to be aware of their role, but also of their influence on learners. Minstrell and Stimpson (1996) suggest the construction of understanding is personal, and the process of 'disassembling and reconstruction' of meaning requires the teacher to adopt a role of guide, not one of enforcer. Just as individuals need to come to terms with new information, so do groups of pupils. Rogers (1983) points out that groups have 'a life of their own' and teachers must nurture their relationship with a group. Group dynamics, ground-rules and clear expectations need to be articulated. Certain group activities are more effective with some groups than others.

Activity 10.5   Activity ground-rules

With a colleague, consider the following teaching and learning activities within your subject area. Devise ground-rules required for each, covering a range of groups differing in age, maturity, ability and motivation. Do the ground-rules differ according to these variables?

Teacher-led activities	Pair work	Group work
Practical work	Role plays	Writing
Individual work	Questions and answers	Quiet reading
Demonstrating	Individual work	

Can you provide classroom management guidance for colleagues?

In the early stages, pupils often need to be assigned specific roles, whereas later groups of pupils can organise themselves into effective learning groups. Teachers need to allocate appropriate tasks to particular groups.

Cockburn (1995) and Fisher (1990) have conducted studies into why learning 'goes wrong'. Very often pupils have 'too much to do' (Fisher 1990, p.89) and are unable to prioritise. Task ambiguity leads to stress, which supports Cockburn's view that clear objectives and instructions must be stated in simple terms by the teacher. Cockburn also notes that too often pupils focus on task-completion, rather than understanding. Pupil misbehaviour diverts the teacher's attention to discipline-related issues. Other causes of failure to learn are, Cockburn claims, attributable to the teacher: poorly designed tasks, tasks which do not challenge pupils, cases where the teacher has not diagnosed individual pupil needs, etc.

An academic discussion of learning needs to be related to particular subjects. Teachers should monitor learning. The DES (Conference N213, September 1988) produced a list of characteristics of effective learning. An adaptation of the list contained in Activity 10.6 provides a subject leader with a set of questions, answers to which will provide evidence of the quality of learning taking place.

Activity 10.6   Evaluating the quality of learning

1   Survey colleagues in your subject team in order to answer the questions below (drawn from the 1988 DES list of characteristics of effective teaching):

(a) Do pupils see the purpose of a topic to be learnt?
(b) Is there an obvious practical application of the new knowledge?
(c) Does the process of learning involve the solving of genuine prolems?
(d) Are the pupils active in the learning process?
(e) Do pupils have the opportunity to use their initiative and imagina tion?
(f) Do pupils acquire knowledge and skills?
(g) Does the topic encourage good work habits?
(h) Do pupils find the topic stimulating and enjoyable?
(i) Is teacher feedback constructive?
(j) Are pupils aware of progress they have made?
(k) Has coverage of the topic led to a change in the way pupils think about the content?
(l) Has completion of the topic led to a growth in confidence and self-esteem?

Follow up with a team discussion drawing out examples of good practice.

2   Ask teachers in your team from where they acquired the evidence (and how) in order to answer the above questions. Can you improve subject-team evaluation techniques?

Classroom observation, discussions with teachers and pupils, the analysis of outcomes and comparisons with parallel classes will generate evidence which contributes to the answering of such questions as those in Activity 10.6. The monitoring of learning is not an exact science, yet the lack of precision should not lead to inactivity. There is no doubt that interest in progress is motivating and stimulating to both teachers and pupils.

MOTIVATING LEARNERS

Like learning, it is difficult to define motivation, and it is therefore complicated to monitor it. From a behaviourist perspective, motivation can be measured by noting the time individuals spend 'on task' (Galloway *et al.* 1998).

Activity 10.7 Identify learners' levels of interest

Ask a learning support assistant or a teaching colleague to observe one or two pupils in a lesson. Ask them to time how long the pupils(s) remain attentive and on task. The timings should be related to particular activities and therefore you should provide the observer with a lesson plan.

Use the data to draw up a chart which will demonstrate how 'pupil types' (e.g. boys, girls, able, less able, quiet, boisterous, etc.) respond to different activities. The matrix below serves as an example.

	High achiever	Average achiever	Low achiever
Listening to the teacher	70%	30%	50%
Individual work	50%	20%	60%
Discussions (incl. Q & A)	80%	10%	50%
Role plays	40%	70%	80%
Experimenting	60%	80%	50%
Pair work	70%	40%	30%
Group work	60%	20%	20%
Demonstrating	90%	60%	80%
Reading	90%	50%	70%
Writing	100%	40%	60%
Creative individual work	100%	70%	80%
One-to-one with the teacher	100%	100%	100%

The percentages refer to the proportion of time on task in relation to the time allocated by the teacher. Can you and/or colleagues account for the results? Compare your own outcomes with those of a colleague. Are there reasons for the variations? What can be done to improve motivation?

Motivation, though, is not an outcome. It is, McClelland explains, to do with 'how behaviour gets started, is energised, sustained, directed and stopped' (McClelland 1987, p.14). Psychologists agree that there are essentially two types of motivation: intrinsic and extrinsic. Capel (1995) believes that intrinsic motivation has a more powerful impact, yet teachers have a greater control over extrinsic motivation.

It is important to acknowledge what actually motivates learners. Galloway *et al.* (1998) recognise three forms: task-oriented, ego-oriented and work avoidance. Maslow (1970) identifies a hierarchy of needs, and the suggestion is that successful learning can fulfil such needs, thereby leading to motivation.

For Maslow (1970) all people have physiological needs, which it can be argued are the responsibility of the family. Schools can provide security and a sense of safety. The need to belong and to be respected by others certainly can be met partially in school and self-actualisation, or the opportunity to fulfil one's potential, is certainly achievable in the classroom. Herzberg's 'two-factor theory' involves five aspects which serve to motivate (Herzberg *et al.* 1959).

Achievement brings the satisfaction of completing a task, recognition involves being appreciated and interest concerns the intrinsic appeal of a task. Being shown trust by those in authority contributes to a sense of motivation and, once tasks are completed, individuals can hope for advancement. Any two of these five factors in combination, Herzberg claims, motivate. Placing these in a school context is not a major challenge, and to do so enables teacher to plan to motivate children, rather than to simply hope that topics and tasks take their interest.

Activity 10.8   Planning to motivate pupils

Below are the five factors which make up Herzberg's 'two-factor theory'. How can these be encouraged within the processes of teaching and learning your subject?

- Achievement
- Recognition
- Interest
- Responsibility
- Advancement

Any teacher's aims must be to contribute to a pupil's self-confidence (Maslow 1970) and children, Maslow claims, enjoy a safe, orderly and predictable environment. By including pupils in the learning process, Kyriacou (1986) argues that pupils' self-esteem and sense of control increase.

To achieve such goals, teachers must consider pupils' needs when planning learning. Armitage *et al.* (1998) draw on the work of Morrison and Ridley (1989) when they argue that the presentation of new knowledge which is relevant to the individual as a member of a community and society as a whole is motivating. Learners are, in short, motivated by what is relevant and achievable. Turner notes that what pupils deem 'relevant' is ever-changing:

> Outside interests become increasingly important as the pupils get older. If the school task links with some future occupation, employment training or higher education, motivation is increased and engagement promoted.
>
> (Turner 1995, p.230)

Clearly the argument relates directly to secondary schooling, but the principle of relating content to context is applicable throughout the Key Stages (see Activity 10.3).

Galloway *et al.* (1998) provide a clear warning for teachers. Motivation must, they insist, be in the context of the classroom. Teachers cannot and must not exert an influence on personality. Teachers, though, can and do influence pupils' motivation. 'Artificial reinforcers such as prizes or tokens' (Brown 1995, p.18) reward good behaviour and positive learning outcomes. For rewards to have real meaning, there needs to be some consistency of use. Subject leaders are in a position to define good learning outcomes in consultation with colleagues. Intrinsic motivation is the satisfaction received from having mastered an activity. Teachers have a role to play here too. The quiet acknowledgement of effort and success can serve to reinforce pupils' own sense of achievement.

The use of praise and encouragement is an obvious means of motivating pupils. However, teachers' practice does not represent the enactment of good ideas. OfSTED (1993b) report that teachers' comments in classroom situations are predominantly negative.

Activity 10.9   Valuing rewards

Ask pupils to consider the following rewards. Which do they value the most? Can you add any rewards to the list?

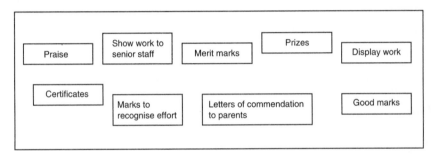

As a result of pupils' views, can you develop a meaningful rewards system within your subject area? Does such a system need to comply with a whole-school system?

Most agree (e.g. Maslow 1970, Kyriacou 1986, Capel 1995) that positive reinforcers are more effective than negative criticisms. Kyriacou comments that anxiety and stress can motivate, provided the goals are achievable. Constant reference to future examination performance must therefore be personalised. To those for whom a top grade is unachievable, mention of the highest grades serves only to reinforce a sense of helplessness and failure.

Maslow (1970) sees learning as a gateway to personal freedom. Learners need the opportunity to speak and act freely, to investigate what interests them, to uncover relevant information and to defend their own points of view. Learners want to be treated and assessed fairly and honestly. All these have implications for teaching and learning styles.

Capel (1995) suggests that teachers should recognise pupils' achievement.

Such a recognition may not be in relation to externally set assessment criteria, but by comparing current efforts with an individual's previous efforts. By being aware of pupils' interests and hobbies, the content of lessons can be related to meaningful and enjoyable contexts. The threat of sanctions, if tasks are not satisfactorily completed can, of course, be held over pupils, but once again the sanctions do need to be issued fairly and related to individual pupils' own ability and aptitude. The satisfaction of mastery is enhanced if learners are aware of progress made, whether that be in terms of effort or attainment. Lastly, the celebration of success, the achievement of personally set targets, is a must. Awards, prizes, the display of pupils' work can all serve as a public acknowledgement of success.

Systems and procedures, built into schemes or work- and lesson-plans, facilitate the motivation of pupils. Ultimate responsibility of application rests with class teachers, although the evaluation of teachers' application is made easier by the existence of standard procedures. The subject leader is therefore an enabler and also a key partner in the evaluative process.

IMPROVING TEACHING

The quality of learning and motivating pupils to learn are features of good teaching. There is plenty of literature available on effective teaching. Indeed, OfSTED (1993a, p.27) lists qualities of effective teaching which can form the basis of evaluation and appraisal:

- setting clear objectives
- pupils are made aware of objectives
- teachers have a secure command of the subject content
- the lesson content is suitable
- well-chosen activities promote learning
- activities are stimulating and engaging

The qualities listed can be seen to be detached from the reality and context of the classroom. Individual pupil differences impact upon the teacher's approach in particular. Galloway *et al.* see the teacher's role as directing 'the available energies of the pupil' (Galloway *et al.* 1998, p.22). Teachers are also faced with other tensions. The pressures of completing National Curriculum programmes of study, conducting Literacy Hours and addressing cross-curricular themes and dimensions compel the teacher to make a professional judgement of whether to 'go with the flow' or to 'get things done' (Woods and Jeffrey 1996, p.43). Mortimore *et al.* (1994) recognise many variables which influence teachers' approaches. Age, gender, social class, ethnicity, ability and behaviour all determine teaching styles. As a consequence, teachers have many decisions to make when planning and conducting lessons. Shulman (1994) explains that teachers have to consider what to teach, how to teach, when to teach and to plan to motivate, stimulate and pre-empt misunderstandings.

In monitoring teaching, subject leaders must therefore take into account the appropriateness of a particular teaching style to a particular teaching group. Mosston and Ashworth's (1986) continuum of teaching styles provides some assistance in the identification of the particular style (see Figure 10.2).

Figure 10.2   A continuum of teaching styles

Command style	(The teacher provides knowledge)
Practice style	(Pupils rehearse tasks repeatedly)
Reciprocal style	(Pupils question and the teacher answers)
Self-check style	(Pupils assess and relate to progress against teacher-provided criteria)
Inclusion style	(Teacher and pupil negotiate)
Guided discovery	(Teachers facilitate, pupils learn)
Divergent style	(Teachers differentiate according to individual needs)
Individual programme	(Teachers develop individualised learning programmes)
Learner-initiated style	(Learners determine their own programme of study, the teacher responds)
Self-teaching style	(Learners have no need for teachers)

When able to identify the particular style, its appropriateness can be gauged by relating the style to the impact on learning and motivation. Reference to Activity 10.7 ('Identify learners' levels of interest') will assist in such a task. Through observation of and discussion with colleagues, the effectiveness of styles and strategies can be ascertained, in the context of particular learning groups.

Cockburn (1995) argues that, in reality, teachers manage learning rather than attend to every individual's learning needs, due to the size of teaching groups. Consequently teachers require a full repertoire of strategies and techniques to cover the learning styles of the optimum number of pupils in any given group. Variety of methods is an essential quality and consequently no judgement on teaching quality should be made through a single observation. Observations and discussions allow teachers to justify their methods, to practise others and to expand their repertoire. Peer observation and collaborative teaching provide further opportunities for experimentation and self-evaluation. The subject leader as a manager has the responsibility to provide such opportunities and to record the outcomes of such innovative practice.

Teaching is more than the transmission of information. Bobbit Nolen (1995) argues that teachers should aim for learner autonomy. Consequently the process is as important as the product. Bobbit Nolen presents teacher qualities necessary for the encouragement of independent learning:

confidence in knowledge
responsive to individual needs
respect for pupils
willingness to discuss approaches to learning
acceptance of errors as learning opportunities

(Bobbit Nolen 1995, p.209)

In monitoring teaching of their subject, subject leaders can take into account these factors. In doing so, they can identify training needs and recognise a readiness for teachers to move pupils nearer to autonomy. In such a way, subject leaders can be sure that teaching is leading to learning in an incremental fashion.

Medium-term planning consists of more than the selection of activities which stimulate and motivate learners. Teachers must set conditions and targets for learning. Gagné (1977) insists that conditions should be set before the learning event takes place. By setting targets, and expressing these clearly to pupils, teachers are able to articulate their expectations for pupils in their charge (Capel 1995).

The attainment of high expectations must be rewarded. Expectations must not be too easily attained, however. Teachers agree, Capel (1995) claims, that high expectations lead to good behaviour and to pupils performing to the best of their ability. Failure to attain can be demotivating. Galloway *et al.* (1998) expect teachers, through sensitive feedback, to bridge the gap between attainment and aspiration. High expectations are not enough. Subject leaders need to set realistic challenging targets, but also to expect teachers to provide meaningful and helpful advice on how to achieve.

Activity 10.10   Articulating achievable targets

For a unit of work, relate performance descriptions to actual activities. Break the activities down into objectives which can be understood by the pupils. From this breakdown, devise a pupil profile, so that learners can identify targets and achievements as they progress through the unit.

Does this process of target-setting and self-assessment improve the learner's level of motivation?

Teaching how to learn, as well as what to learn, is important. An explanation of the purpose of resources and materials, carefully structured and sequenced questions, the provision of time for pupil–pupil interaction, the changing roles of a teacher (instructor, facilitator, assessor, etc.), all assist pupils in the development of meta-cognitive strategies. Gardner (1983) is critical of school-based learning, as it does not match up to learning which takes place outside school. Pupils need to make sense of the outside world through school-based work. Consequently, teachers need to draw on experiences of learners in their day-to-day life. Teachers can teach learners how to learn from experience, as well as by using inanimate media (such as books and diagrams) in order to convey information.

Activity 11.8 serves as a useful stimulus for the discussion of the purpose and value of resources used within a particular subject.

Minstrell and Stimpson (1996) distinguish between questions and tasks which generate knowledge and those which require the application of knowledge. Closed and open questions serve different purposes, and teachers need to be sure that questions are designed to encourage learning rather than simply to demonstrate the acquisition of verbatim knowledge.

Effective teaching is hard to define, but easy to recognise. Subject leaders can draw on central issues which apply to all teachers. Observation and scrutiny of plans does enable the appraisal of many aspects, as Shulman lists:

management of classrooms
organisation of activities
allocation of time to tasks
structure of tasks
praise and criticism
question formulation
lesson planning
judging pupil understanding
                    (Shulman 1994, p.127)

Discussions with teachers about teaching and learning are, however, equally constructive. The development of new ideas, the evaluation of practice and the consideration of techniques which are appropriate to particular learners, are all means by which quality teaching can be developed. The subject leader's role is to formalise procedures which facilitate such a process.

CONCLUSION

Schools are all about teaching and learning. Subject leaders need to motivate teachers and teachers need to motivate pupils. Teachers are professionals and consequently subject leaders need to show respect for practitioners' talents and skills, yet at the same time assure a quality of educational provision. There are lessons to be learnt from industry in terms of managing a service.

Holbeche (1998) notes how the rhetoric of the 1980s (involvement, empowerment, customer care and Total Quality Management) has been undermined by reality. A focus on short-term profit and a cost-oriented managerial approach does relate to schools' immediate need to achieve good examination results.

The ultimate threat posed by poor OfSTED reports may well have obstructed the move towards a democratic approach to management and the high value to be placed on interpersonal attitudes and reciprocal relationships. Subject leaders, though, are able to work against such short-termism. By motivating teachers to engage actively in the learning process through enquiry and research, they are promoting an ethos of learning. Pupils are valued and teachers highly respected as they shape their own practice to accommodate the outcomes of their own reflection. Holbeche concludes that career development is about personal satisfaction rather than promotion. Development is concerned with facing and overcoming challenges, and he suggests that employees need to grow within their role to do so. The role of the leader is to develop systems and approaches which enable challenges to be identified and subsequently faced with confidence. As Jones points out, a leader needs:

> to give verbal recognition and practical support to employees who enthusi-astically take part in team meetings, questioning, coming up with ideas, evaluating and being involved in the decision-making process.
>
> (Jones 1996, p.126)

Teaching and learning need to be managed. Teachers, as professionals, need to address pupils' needs and their own. In a dynamic school, where all learn from each other, teaching and learning must be of high quality.

11 Managing resources

INTRODUCTION

Following the Education Reform Act (DES 1988b), governing bodies of schools manage a budget of at least 80 per cent of all the resources available; normally the task of managing this allocation is delegated to the headteacher and thereafter to teachers in the school. The local management of schools and the subsequent 'Fair Funding' system has created a situation where schools resemble medium-sized businesses. There are, though, important differences between schools and commercial enterprises, as Knight (1993) points out. Schools are locked into a statutory function, staff and buildings are not easily altered, and there are few opportunities to raise capital. Consequently, the management of resources is effectively the distribution of funds for no obvious economic returns. It is, then, no surprise that common practice has been that the management of resources has been considered apart from curriculum management and educational leadership. Sayer (1989) notes that this division has been discernible through the scrutiny of role and job descriptions. Responsibility for the budget has often rested with non-teaching staff. Anthony and Herzlinger recognised a shift in emphasis since the ERA:

> The idea that the controller has a broader responsibility than merely 'keeping the books' is a fairly recent one in profit oriented organisations, and it is not well accepted in many non-profit organisations.
> (Anthony and Herzlinger 1989, p.30)

The delegation of funds has, of course, been instrumental in the creation of a new climate. The use of money for educational purposes differs, as Levacic (1989b) comments, according to the contingent factors which characterise each and every school. These 'contingent factors' are of great interest to subject leaders, in that it is they, collectively, who plan, oversee the delivery of and evaluate curriculum provision.

Indeed, subject leaders play a key role in negotiating the level of funding in terms of resourcing the 'department' and are therefore bound to be engaged in discussions which translate money into educational outcomes. The budget is, of course, expressed in quantitative, monetary terms, and agreement on the level of funding is dependent on a bilateral agreement between the budget holder (usually the head) and 'spenders' (among others, subject leaders).

Activity 11.1   Delegation of budgets

1   Who is involved in deciding the allocation of funds at your school?
2   Are decisions made through negotiation between the budget holder and the 'spender' on an individual basis?
3   Are decisions concerning the allocation of funds open and inclusive of all 'spenders'?

Anthony and Herzlinger state that the process of negotiation must assume a 'goal congruence' (Anthony and Herzlinger 1989, p.27), in that those involved in discussions must at least agree on the overall school aims. Arnold and Hope (1989) further the argument by asserting that the delegation of the budget by the head should reflect the areas of responsibility existing within the school. Individuals must therefore be charged with the task of planning and accounting for funds linked to their own areas of responsibility. It is not difficult to recognise a concept of accountability within such a structure.

Subject leaders must be active in the budget process and, in order to assure equity and fairness, must understand the process of allocating funds to the various cost centres in the school. There are many models for budget management, which is reminiscent of Levacic's earlier comments. Schools operate systems which suit their own needs and cultures, and indeed a presentation of different models will not provide an exact description of any one school's methods. However, aspects of several models may be deployed and consequently a full appreciation of one school's methods requires an understanding of the full range of alternatives.

An *incremental approach* to funding is one where previous funding arrangements for cost centres are regarded as fair. Overall increases are shared among cost centres, based on the percentage rate of increase. A *base budget approach* (recommended by the Audit Commission in *Management within Primary Schools*) involves the separation of maintenance and development. New developments must be justified in terms of their relevance to whole-school aims. Consequently innovation requires the estimation of intended outcomes. *Zero budgeting* assumes that all expenditure, whether maintenance or development, must be justified, and subject leaders are therefore required to bid into a central fund. *Programme budgeting* requires all costs to be linked to particular programmes, and plans must therefore be separated into the two categories of strategy and operations.

The adoption of any particular method, therefore, must account for a rational approach, when consideration must be taken of whole-school aims expressed through the school development plan. The allocation of funds will inevitably mirror, too, the power of different groups, which in turn may reflect historical trends.

Activity 11.2   Describing the method of budgeting

Using the terminology above, provide a short written description of how the budget is operated in your school.

In an attempt to avoid conflict, many schools have adopted *formula funding*, based on the number of pupils and lessons which are timetabled (see later). Formula funding is related to perceived needs. Schools calculate a 'weighting' which serves as a multiplier for the allocation of standard unit costs. LEAs use an age-weighting system for whole-school funding and the allocation of money to departments should reflect this overall level of funding:

Figure 11.1   Kent LEA age-weighting funding

Pre-reception	0.76
Y1 (non-statutory)	1.00
Y1 (statutory)	1.3
Y2	1.04
Y3–Y5	1.00
Y6	1.2
Y7–Y9	1.6
Y10–Y11	1.83
Y12–Y13	2.5

Some subjects are more expensive than others to resource. The establishment of a subject-based weighting is an in-school issue. Knight (1993, p.71) recommends the application of a simple formula in order to calculate a 'baseline' for discussion:

$$\frac{\text{existing allocation}}{\text{student periods (or proportion of pupil-contact time)}}$$

Formula funding is in many ways 'fair' (Easen 1985). There are, of course, certain anomalies: the system does not provide for non-teaching departments, such as the library, ICT and clerical support.

The curriculum is ever-changing, and schools must be fit and ready to adapt according to imposed or internally led processes of change. Budget arrangements must therefore be flexible, yet not so flexible that they can lead to (or positively encourage) inter-departmental conflict. With limited funding arrangements, subject leaders will inevitably be in competition with each other for funds. 'Programme budgeting' therefore has advantages in that bids for funds must be overtly linked to whole-school aims. It must, of course, be borne in mind that school aims may also change.

Activity 11.3 Fund allocation

Find out how colleagues perceive the method of allocating funds to the different subject areas in school. Is the system seen as 'fair' and does it account for maintenance of existing resources and future developments?

Part of assuring quality is careful planning. Subject leaders must represent their subject and develop plans which are both realistic in terms of money available and developmental in terms of improving the quality of provision in the future.

The notion of accountability does imply the measurement of educational outcomes in terms of financial input (Everard 1986). Educational outcomes, in their broadest sense, cannot be measured quantitatively. Fidler (1996, pp.26–30) dismisses the view that this difficulty removes the need for analysis. He recommends that a SWOT (Strengths, Weaknesses, Opportunities and Threats – see Chapter 6) Analysis must take into account the school environment, existing resources and organisational culture, but must also relate to the unit costs.

Activity 11.4 SWOT Analysis

Conduct a SWOT Analysis with reference to:

- the school environment
- existing resources
- organisational culture
- the availability of funds

Simkins (1989) also insists that micro-politics play a part in analysis, and West and Ainscow (1991) see direct links with budgeting and resourcing. Innovations and developments must be appropriately resourced if teachers are to be encouraged rather than deterred.

Levacic and Glover (1996) insist that this notion of relating spending to aims and objectives is only valid if those involved have confidence in the suitability of the processes of fund allocation. Subject leaders need, therefore, to develop a resource plan as an outcome of a budget plan. The practical procedures of: identifying resource needs, investigating available products, formulating requirements, assessing costs, ordering products, taking delivery and evaluating, only represent a fair and sensible way forward if the budget plan is similarly open and accessible. Such a plan should:

- respond equitably to needs of all subjects
- enable priorities to be accounted for
- promote organisational objectives
- encourage innovation
- facilitate long-term planning
- be understood easily
- be accepted throughout the school

(Adapted from West and Ainscow 1991, p.81)

PLANNING SPENDING

Everard and Morris place a subject leader's role *vis-à-vis* resource management in a single question:

The question is, or should be, how do we invest limited financial resources so as to maximise the benefit to the school ...

(Everard and Morris 1990, p.213)

One key word from this quotation is 'school'. Budgeting should begin with the 'corporate plan'. Subject leaders should be asking themselves what they want to achieve and, therefore, what resources are required to achieve the goals. The identification and prioritisation of objectives at the outset are necessary components of subject leaders' accountability.

Activity 11.5   Linking the budget to school priorities

Examine the school development plan. Which of the targets relate directly to your own subject? Could the purchase of new resources contribute to the meeting of targets expressed in the plan?

The second stage of planning is to consider the means by which resourcing can be funded. The negotiation of funds is not necessarily exclusively 'internal'. Harrison and Theaker (1989) draw our attention to other sources – local enterprises, Parent Teacher Association and LEA projects. An examination of potential external sources and agencies may even feature as a condition for funding from internal sources. School resources, particularly at primary level, are rarely regarded as the property of one subject department. Subject leaders should relate the future use of resources to other cost centres. There are many cases when initial costs may be shared by other subject areas and/or non-teaching departments.

Activity 11.6 Sharing resources

List the resources which are used in delivering your subject. Which of these 'belong' to your subject and which to others? Are you and your subject colleagues able to use resources without competing with other subject areas? Which resources should belong to your own subject area and which can you continue to 'borrow'?

OfSTED (1993a), in their guidance to inspectors on the appraisal of efficiency and value for money, provide useful guidance in the assessment of the viability of resources. Unit costs can be compared to those of other departments (or subjects in the case of primary schools) in the school, and indeed to those of other schools. The potential effectiveness is the relationship between financial outlay and intended learning outcomes. A viability study is, of course, medium- and long-term. Coopers and Lybrand state clearly:

> It will also be necessary to set targets against which performance can be measured.
>
> (Coopers and Lybrand 1988, pp.4–5)

Clearly Levacic's (1989b) assertion that the objectives of a programme or project need to be related to the evaluated outcomes stands firm.

Although the outcomes cannot necessarily be quantified, the input can in monetary terms. Subject leaders should plan their budgets at two levels, in order that the impact of implementation can at least be estimated (Jones 1989, p.122). Jones recommends a simple equation to calculate a unit cost (see Figure 11.2).

Figure 11.2 Unit costs

$$\text{Unit cost} = \frac{\text{Course length x hours taught per week}}{\text{Number of pupils meeting objectives}}$$

A second calculation is represented by Figure 11.3.

Figure 11.3 Optimum costs

$$\text{Optimum cost} = \frac{\text{Optimum course length x optimum hours per week}}{\text{Projected number of pupils meeting objective}}$$

Activity 11.7 Comparing unit and optimum costs to assess value for money

1 Using the formula above, calculate the unit costs for running the subject. Now calculate the optimum costs.
2 Is investment worthwhile in financial terms? Can the educational gains be related to the financial costs?

The relationship between unit costs, as they stand, and optimum costs, as projected, represents the potential 'value for money'. The resultant ratio can then represent the amount of money required to fund a particular project designed to raise pupils' levels of achievement.

Levacic (1989b) proposes a similar numerical analysis in order to establish a subject-weighting. The relationship between two subjects in terms of unit costs can represent a starting point for bilateral negotiation with the budget holder (head) for the subject leader. Discussions centred around funding will inevitably lead to a consideration of the relative merits of subjects in terms of their contribution to the school and curriculum as a whole. The maintenance of existing standards logically involves an incremental increase in funding to maintain the quality and quantity of resources in existence. More complicated is the section of the budget plan designed to account for development, which cannot be related to a specific programme or project.

Arnold and Hope recommend a process of planning which is less numerical. Figure 11.4 represents a system which allows subject leaders to justify bids for funding beyond simple maintenance. This model addresses concerns raised by many writers (e.g. Oldroyd and Hall 1991, Knight 1993) over the relationship between inputs and outputs, present performance and future performance.

Figure 11.4 Planning for improvement

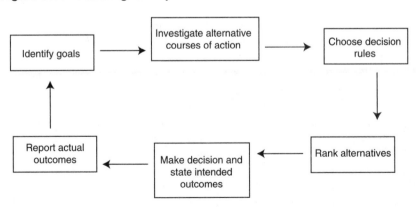

Source: Adapted from Arnold and Hope 1989, p.47

Budget planning must also take into account existing resources. Stock-taking must account for more than the simple identification of resources and teaching materials which already exist in the department. Subject leaders should account for resources which exist outside school and elsewhere in the school (see the earlier SWOT Analysis). The appropriateness of existing resources to the particular subject can be explained and, indeed, the regularity of use can be quantified. Inevitably the potential of resources must also be related to staff expertise in terms of their use, and lastly to implications of future change.

Knight (1993) recommends a resource audit as a means of identifying resource usage. He proceeds to suggest that a similar exercise can be conducted with a focus on desirable resources. Again, to relate the outcomes of the audit of 'existing resources' to the outcomes of a 'desirable resources' audit serves to highlight potential developments. National Curriculum documentation provides a useful basis for such an audit. The programmes of study represent learning opportunities which should be provided. Figure 11.5 represents, as an example, an audit instrument for modern foreign languages.

Each member of a subject team should rank the resource in terms of 'useful-ness' in relation to particular statutory requirements. A simple arithmetic calculation will reveal the value of existing resources and the potential of new resources.

Activity 11.8   Auditing your own resources

1   Conduct an audit along the lines of the one represented by Figure 11.5.
2   What do the outcomes tell you about:

- the relative usefulness of existing resources?
- the coverage of each part of the National Curriculum Programme of Study for your subject?

Investigations and plans need to be informed. Subject leaders and/or colleagues must be pragmatic, given the limited funds available. Harrison and Theaker (1989) suggest that teachers order inspection copies, scrutinise the use of particular resources in other schools, visit teacher centres and consult colleagues at subject conferences in order to gain an informed opinion. The Internet also offers support through the opportunity to network with colleagues and through reference to the BECTA website (http://www.becta.org.uk/projects/mmportables/software/evaluations/alltitles.html) for evaluations of educational CD-ROMs.

Throughout a school year, subject leaders face unexpected costs. Knight (1993) recommends the retention of a small proportion of the overall budget as a contingency fund. Clearly consideration of the amount to be retained must be given, and subject leaders can draw on experience and reference to budget

Figure 11.5   Auditing existing and desirable resources

Programme of study	Cassette players	OHP	Published course	CD-ROMs	Visual aids	Magazines	Posters	Paircards	Video player	Video camera	TV programmes	Satellite TV	TOTAL
Existing desirable resources													
1 Communicating													
(a)													
(b)													
(c)													
(d)													
(e)													
(f)													
(g)													
(h)													
(i)													
(j)													
(k)													
2 Language skills													
(a)													
(b)													
(c)													
(d)													
(e)													
(f)													
(g)													
(h)													
(i)													
(j)													
(k)													
(l)													
(m)													
(n)													
(o)													
3 Language Learning													
(a)													
(b)													
(c)													
(d)													
(e)													
(f)													
(g)													
(h)													
(i)													
4 Culture													
(a)													
(b)													
(c)													
(d)													
(e)													
TOTAL													

accounts for former years to establish a fund limit. This may well involve the management of the budget *vis-à-vis* colleagues. Subject leaders often wish to empower colleagues by allocating particular funds to account for their own responsibilities. It is therefore important to develop an agreed system to allow colleagues to bid into such a fund.

Activity 11.9   Delegating responsibility to subject colleagues

1   Should colleagues have personal responsibility for any part of the budget?
2   How can you monitor ongoing costs such as photocopying and consumables?
3   Who should oversee the monitoring process?

The budget is a plan. Monitoring of the plan by the establishment of a checklist is one way by which quality can be assured and whether or not actual expenditure has led to the objectives being achieved can be checked. Figure 11.6 contains such a checklist, which can also be applied to planning methods currently in use.

Figure 11.6   Budget-planning checklist

1   Is maintenance separated from development?
2   Is the monitoring process sound?
3   Does the subject funding allocation relate to last year?
4   Are budget needs prioritised?
5   By what criteria are needs prioritised?
6   Are others involved in the plan and in agreement with it?
7   How will the plans be evaluated?

Activity 11.10   Checking the budget plan

Apply the checklist in Figure 11.6 to your current practice. How can you improve your budget plans to improve resource management?

IMPLEMENTING A BUDGET PLAN

Having established procedures for the allocation of funds for educational purposes, the subject leader must organise the identification and purchase of suitable resources. Levacic (1989b) comments that any judgement on financial management involves, inevitably, an inspection of internal management procedures. The auditing process does not allow for the long-term implications of resourcing. A running theme throughout this chapter is the relating of purchases to educational outcomes. Everard and Morris (1990, p.201) provide a useful list of questions to help:

- What are the features of the item under consideration?
- What will it replace?
- What will the educational benefits be?
- How does the practical cost relate to existing resources?
- Do staff have experience of the new item?
- What will the problems of introducing the new resource be?
- Is the item reliable?
- What will the maintenance cost be?
- Is the item compatible with other existing resources?
- What support does the manufacturer/publisher provide?

Consultation with colleagues from inside and outside the subject area provides support in three areas which Everard and Morris (1990, p.200) identify as possible problems:

- distinguishing between the useful and the gimmick
- identifying the right moment to purchase
- using the equipment effectively

In addition to this short list, we can add:

- ensuring that use of the resource contributes to whole-school aims

The introduction of new ICT standards (TTA 1998a) raises many issues associated with resources. In essence, teachers and, in particular, subject leaders must be aware of the potential and the risks. Dean's (1991) recommendation pre-dates the ICT standards, but nevertheless remains relevant. Computers can teach some things better than teachers, due to their potential to be programmed to provide a one-to-one match for the stage of learning a pupil is at. Subject leaders do need to enquire into the potential of generic and subject-specific applications.

Once the final decision to purchase is made, simple procedures must be adhered to, in order to ensure successful implementation. Schools have usually developed pre-numbered, standardised order forms to facilitate future auditing. Such forms will inevitably require authorisation from the budget controller (head, deputy head, bursar). Subject leaders must be sure that the specification on order forms is clear (ISBN numbers, quantity, code specifications). Inevitably, communication with suppliers can be problematic and subject leaders are therefore advised to file copies of orders under 'awaiting delivery'. Ordering resources occurs throughout the year and consequently it is sensible to keep a running tally of expenditure and residue to avoid excessive over- or even under-spending. Careful monitoring is facilitated if one named person oversees delivery and, indeed, signs for receipt of an item (often the school secretary), yet it is helpful if a second person (the subject leader) checks the delivery against specifications contained on the order form. Order forms and delivery notes should therefore be filed together for future reference.

Payment is sanctioned by the school and therefore invoices (originals, not copies) should be checked against order forms and delivery notes. Payment must be recorded, usually in the form of a signature confirming that the set procedure has been followed.

Activity 11.11   Procedures for purchasing

Draw up a set of procedures for purchasing and for recording purchases, which fit in with whole-school practice.

The receipt of purchases is not, of course, the final act. Many resources incur additional maintenance costs, notably computer hardware (Evans *et al.* 1996). For this reason, other specialists (such as IT co-ordinators) should be involved in overseeing the purchase of equipment and, indeed, software. Implementation often requires further support and Evans *et al.* mention, in particular, support and training from IT specialists. With recent attention to literacy and numeracy, named specialists in school have a role to play overseeing the use of common textbooks, printed material and all types of educational applications.

EVALUATING RESOURCES

Everard and Morris (1990) recommend the close monitoring of the use of new resources. They note the need for a flexible approach in that benefits and disadvantages may emerge as resources are introduced. As a consequence, evaluation must not only relate to initial aspirations and intended outcomes, but also to actual use. Some simple questions can form the basis of such an analysis:

- are the resources being used regularly?
- does use of the resource require further investment?
- what would the learning outcomes be if the item(s) had not been purchased?

Detailed budgeting involves the linking of financial input to educational targets. Evaluation therefore consists partly of assessing whether the stated targets have been met. In addition, the process of evaluation includes the assessment of additional gains, unforeseen disadvantages and the identification of additional opportunities.

Target-setting is, of course, a skill in its own right. The quality of a target can be appraised through a SMART Analysis, shown in Figure 11.7.

Figure 11.7   SMART Analysis

S	Specific
M	Measurable
A	Attainable
R	Realistic
T	Time-linked

This analysis facilitates evaluation. First, the subject leader, in evaluating a resource, must generate data and information which relate directly to a carefully worded target. To measure the effectiveness means that statistics must be applied. Numerical data relating to success (examination results, pupils opting for a subject) will demonstrate if the target has been attained and if projected standards were actually realistic or not. Lastly, the accuracy of the time-limit originally stated can be assessed against the statistical evidence.

The outcomes of this evaluation of effectiveness present evidence against which external auditing and inspection bodies can pass judgement (Levacic 1989b).

Activity 11.12   Logging use of new resources

Devise a method and system of logging and reflecting on the use of new resources. Which aspects can be quantified? How can you arrange for colleagues to contribute to a qualitative evaluation?

Evaluation of resourcing is not only concerned with effectiveness (the relationship of outputs to objectives), however. Efficiency is the ratio of input to output and is of particular interest when funding is limited and defined (Anthony and Herzlinger 1989).

It is in the evaluation of efficiency that difficulties arise. Outputs are difficult to measure for not-for-profit organisations. Anthony and Herzlinger remind us, however, that all organisations do have outputs. Hulme (1989, p.192) lists such outputs:

*   results
*   achievements
*   career destinations
*   life opportunities

He also asserts that these outputs must be placed in the context of 'controlled inputs' and 'non-controlled' inputs (Hulme 1989, p.192). Consequently, the educational processes and other intangibles such as pupil enjoyment and motivation must be accounted for. Fitz-Gibbon (1989) also mentions attitudinal factors which cannot be evidenced, but may be related to issues such as participation in subject-linked extra-curricular activities. Cross-curricular benefits (e.g. improved study skills, attitudes and social skills) may also feature among possible educational gains. Performance indicators are therefore not objective, although the SMART Analysis does facilitate measurement. They are, as Hulme claims, 'sign-posts' which aid 'comparisons' (Hulme 1989, p.193).

Knight (1993) articulates the difficulty of accurate evaluation of budget plans and resource management. He states that certain factors may be identifiable: financial efficiency, resource efficiency and effectiveness, but also recognises the importance of the impact of resource use on pupil and teacher aims, values and methodology.

Teachers and learners can, through reflection, suggest educational gains. Subject leaders need to give due consideration to resource management when evaluating their use. However, as was intimated at the planning stage, it is wrong to separate resource and financial management from curriculum management. Evaluation is a process, not an event; and consequently subject leaders must enable ongoing discussion and reflection as a means of evaluating the curriculum.

Part IV

Leading and managing staff to raise achievement

INTRODUCTION

Schools are intensely human organisations where effective leadership will have a crucial, though often indirect, effect on pupil achievement. School and subject leadership will, however, have a direct and determining effect on staff performance. The 'culture' of a school can be defined using a set of broad criteria, but perhaps the key factor will be the nature and quality of relationships in the school. Subject leaders may well see the establishment and maintenance of constructive relationships between all the staff involved in the subject as a primary objective, as well as promoting effective relationships between staff and pupils, and between the pupils themselves. There are no formulæ to help subject leaders with these relationships, but a study of transformational leadership could offer some guidelines. The theory of transformational leadership has six underlying principles:

1 co-operation among teachers
2 ownership of tasks and changes by teachers
3 responsibility by teachers
4 accountability by teachers
5 relevance of tasks and changes as defined by teachers
6 delegation of authority based on the ability to make the necessary decisions
(Sergiovanni, cited in Day *et al.* 1998, p.67)

The effective subject leader will need the appropriate knowledge, understanding and skills to develop and sustain relationships, with 'affective' aspects (such as empathising, trusting, listening and being tactful) of paramount importance.

While these principles could underpin the leadership and management of a subject, they would need to be congruent with the overall school culture to ensure continuity and progression of tasks and changes. Subject leaders will want to galvanise the talents, energies and commitment of all those involved with the subject, and will want to ensure that leadership as well as management objectives focus directly on raising pupils' achievement in the subject. Chapter 9, on sustaining improvement, looks in detail at much of this. The OfSTED inspection handbook and the national standards developed by the TTA reinforce this explicit focus on pupil achievement (OfSTED 1993a, TTA 1998a). Indeed, the revised appraisal system has at least one teacher target related directly to pupils' achievement. However, a further and crucial aspect of this will be raising and sustaining the performance of staff.

The TTA's *National Standards for Subject Leaders* identify the tasks associated with leading and managing staff, and in this part the focus will be on:

- communication
- building, developing and sustaining teams

Before looking briefly at these aspects of the subject leader's work, some writers caution against focusing exclusively on tasks and remind us that teaching is an art as well as a craft. Leadership is too complex to be defined solely in terms of tasks. Previous chapters in the book have emphasised the importance of appropriate knowledge, understanding and skills, and their application and integration in performing tasks.

Some writers emphasise personal and emotional features as well so that leaders:

> must be able to create and sustain a climate in which there is room for planned personal, professional and institutional growth and development of rational and non-rational kinds – and this means being able to manage the reasoning and emotional selves of the individual and the team in order to succeed in the task.
>
> (Day *et al.* 1998, p.60)

COMMUNICATION

Communication is complex, but central to the efficient and effective operation of a subject. It is complex because any communication system cannot exist in isolation from the values, practices and prevailing culture of the school. You would expect a school culture that promotes and encourages openness, co-operation, delegation and risk-taking to be supported by a communication system that reflects and reinforces these values, and to have a compatible leadership and management approach. Differences in communication systems between school and subjects can co-exist, but extreme approaches are unlikely to be sustainable. Subject communications that encourage shared commitment and decision-making are unlikely to be successful if the school system is strongly hierarchical and controlling.

The *National Standards for Subject Leaders* summarise communication skills as 'the ability to make points clearly and understand the views of others' (TTA 1998a, p.8). Subject leaders must also be able to communicate effectively – orally and in writing – with the headteacher, other staff, pupils, parents, governors, external agencies and the wider community, including business and industry; negotiate and consult effectively; ensure good communication with, and between, staff who teach and support the subject; and chair meetings effectively (TTA 1998a, p.8).

The TTA's standards define communication skills with some clarity, but may need to be considered alongside Bell's definition of effective communication which focuses on attitudes to communication:

> as the link between thought and actions or behaviour. It is the process of conveying hopes, ideas, intentions or feelings from one person to others.
>
> (Bell 1992, p.86)

Successful communication is not necessarily judged in terms of the quality of the message or memo, but rather in the appropriateness of the resulting action or behaviour. Effective communication can be judged against several criteria, including clarity of purpose, clarity of message and appropriateness of style.

In Chapter 12 the following aspects of communication will be examined:

1   the purposes of communication
2   different types of communication
3   organising and managing meetings
4   chairing meetings
5   using information and communication technology

BUILDING, DEVELOPING AND SUSTAINING TEAMS

As pressures continue to grow on schools – whether in the form of government initiatives or from the media or parents in the form of raised expectations and accountability – the reliance on teams and teamwork to carry out tasks and meet subject objectives becomes even greater. Leading and managing subject teams can be defined using generic competencies, but contextual and situational factors are also crucial. While in the secondary school subject leadership will be defined in most cases by clear line and performance management of the team (in practice it may be more complex, depending on whether senior members of staff are in the team and whether some members belong to more than one team), in the primary school there are several constraints on the role. Webb and Vulliamy (1996) found contextual factors that constrain the subject leaders' role in primary schools, namely the subject and pedagogic experience of the leader/co-ordinator; lack of time to perform the role; and the nature of the power relationships within the school.

In most primary schools limited resources prevent subject leaders from performing their role, not least because of the shortage or absence of non-contact time. While job descriptions may include responsibility for strategic planning in the subject, monitoring and evaluating staff and pupil performance, and motivating and supporting colleagues, the extent to which subject leaders can fulfil these responsibilities is limited by the shortage of quality time and, in some cases, lack of suitable training.

In small primary schools the situation is even more difficult, with members of staff holding multiple portfolios of responsibility and headteachers assuming some of the responsibilities, including in many schools responsibility for the overall monitoring and evaluating of pupils' achievement.

Whether leading and managing a task or subject, teamwork is usually seen as the only practicable and manageable way of achieving the planned outcomes. Bell defined teamwork as a group of people working together on the basis of shared perceptions, a common purpose, agreed procedures, commitment, co-operation, and through resolving disagreements openly by discussion (Bell 1992, p.45).

In Chapter 13 the following aspects of teams and team-building will be discussed:

1   what is teamwork?
2   building the team
3   sustaining the team

12 Communication

INTRODUCTION

An open and supportive school and team culture promotes a communication system where staff are trusted, their views are sought and emphasis is placed on co-operation and involvement. In this culture communication is not used to control staff, either by suppressing information or distributing information selectively, but reflects and reinforces a team climate of openness and co-operation. It follows that in such a situation there will be congruence between the key features of communication and the leadership and management style of the subject leader. In the introduction to this section such a co-operative, empowering and delegating approach to leadership was defined by Sergiovanni as 'transformational' (Sergiovanni 1995).

Several typologies of leadership styles have been developed (Likert 1961, Nias 1980), with one of the most illuminative being that developed by Tannenbaum and Schmidt in 1973. Their model defines leadership styles and decision-making using four categories: telling (leader gives instruction and has a strong control instinct), selling (leader has clear views and values and attempts to convince others to follow), consulting (leader presents ideas, invites comments and suggestions, and reaches decisions by consensus) and sharing (leader develops other staff and delegates' actions and decisions within defined limits). Most effective subject leaders will operate using a hybrid of styles depending upon the particular incident or situation. A wide repertoire of styles permits the leader to make quick decisions when necessary, to consult as appropriate and generally to act according to the situation and conditions at the time.

As stated in the introduction to Part IV, communication is primarily about action (Adair 1986, Bell 1992), but there can be a tendency to communicate too much at one time or communicate in an unacceptable way – being too brusque or directive. The result can be inaction or limited action, as staff don't feel involved or may perceive the communication as too directive. Effective communication is when actions match the intentions of the message (which may include simply listing the contents). This is when the purposes of the communication are clear; there is sufficient information, but not too much; the style of communication is appropriate; and it is clear who is to take any action and by when.

Activity 12.1   Matching leadership and management styles to the team's communication practices

Select two of the above leadership and management styles and against each give an example of how the team's communication practices match and reinforce this style.

THE PURPOSES OF COMMUNICATION

Communication is transmitting information between people, either orally, in writing, through meetings, using the telephone or fax or e-mail. The purposes of communication will also include seeking information, instructing, motivating, consulting and persuading. The purpose of a communication will determine the most appropriate type or combination of types of communication to be used or the style of communication – it is difficult to motivate colleagues via letter or memos or to negotiate via e-mail (although not impossible).

In looking at the effectiveness of their communications, subject leaders may want to ask the following questions:

1   What are the purposes of any specific communication in the team?

Purposes can include informing colleagues about a particular event or development, getting a team member to perform a task, obtaining information from colleagues, seeking views as part of a consultation, trying to convince others of a particular idea or action, and praising achievements and performance.

2   Is the communication clear, unambiguous and concise?

The subject leader may want to check that the communication matches the purposes and objectives, and that any message is not open to misinterpretation. Most messages need to be brief and to the point – rambling prose is not usually welcomed.

3   What are the objectives of the communication?

Being clear about what needs to be achieved and spelling out exactly what has to be done is important. It might also be worth asking if the communication is necessary.

4   Is the communication addressed to the appropriate people?

Do others need to know? Is the communication for one member of the team or for all? If others in the team or school need to know, how will they be informed?

5   Is the style and type of communication appropriate?
    It is worth considering whether a brief chat might be more productive than a short note or memo, whether a meeting will be the most efficient means of achieving specific objectives. Balancing formal and informal communications, and ensuring that styles of communication are appropriate can contribute towards effective leadership.

6   Is the communication being sent at the most appropriate time?
    Putting off communications can result in missed opportunities and additional pressures if delayed too long. In most cases, messages are best delivered at the time decisions are made.

7   Is the communication being sent to the correct location?
    It may seem obvious, but it is worth checking which is the most appropriate location – home, pigeon hole in school, by hand, or by e-mail.

8   How will you know if the communication has been received?
    If the communication is written, are there ways of checking that it has been received?

9   How will you know if the necessary action has been taken?
    The subject leader may need to establish procedures to check if the communication has been acted upon and whether any feedback is required.

Activity 12.2   Purposes of communication

List the main purposes of communication in your team. Take one of the main purposes and use bullet points to indicate ways of making it more effective.

DIFFERENT TYPES OF COMMUNICATION

Effective communication is an essential skill for subject leaders and proficiency in all the different forms of communication is required. In this section, the three main forms of communication will be considered: namely, non-verbal, verbal and written.

Non-verbal communication

These are often difficult to control and open to misinterpretation. Body gestures and facial expressions are particularly difficult to control and in some situations can result in messages being distorted. In direct face-to-face communications we send out a variety of non-verbal cues. It may be helpful to be aware of these and to recognise their possible implications:

- Vocal cues – the tone and pitch of the voice can reinforce a particular meaning or emphasis, just as it can unintentionally modify a message.
- Body posture – the way in which you stand or sit can often influence a listener's reaction. Standing with feet apart and hands on hips may be an extreme example of defiance or authority, but it is still a practice adopted by some leaders.
- Body gestures – where to place hands and how to hold your head will depend to some extent on the nature of the communication and on the relationships/status of the communicator and listener.
- Eye contact – how often to make eye contact and for how long is often difficult to gauge. Not making eye contact at all could be interpreted as aloofness or perhaps insincerity.
- Body contact – how appropriate is it to touch an arm or a hand? Again, it depends on the situation and the relationship/status of communicator and listener.
- Orientation – most of us are familiar with the strategic placing of chairs in an interview or discussion. Should you face the listener or place the chair at an angle? The latter approach is normally perceived as being less threatening and more open.
- Personal space – gauging the distance between communicator and listener is important. Invasion of other people's space is not only threatening, but can be perceived as harassment.
- Appearance – modes of dress and general appearance can influence reactions to a communication.

(Headings are taken from Blandford 1997, p.58)

Recognising and being aware of the above non-verbal cues is as important for the listener as the communicator. In most situations a responsive and friendly approach by a leader would be accompanied by smiles, nods, open-handed gestures and eye contact. Unresponsive or aggressive approaches are often accompanied by stares, abrupt speech, looking above the listener and sometimes by a harsh tone in the voice. Leaders seeking to show control will often point, lean forward towards the listener, ignore responses and may speak quickly. A more nervous or submissive approach would involve nervous hand movements, avoiding eye contact, hesitating and speaking quietly.

Activity 12.3   Recognising non-verbal cues

This exercise should take place with a trusted colleague and be in confidence. Work with another subject leader and take it in turns to observe each other communicating with your teams (e.g. at a team meeting). List any non-verbal cues and share them with the other subject leader.

Verbal communication

Much of the communication in schools is verbal rather than written and ranges from brief informal contact in the corridor or staffroom, to discussions at team meetings, to presentations on parents' evenings. Before looking at the different forms of verbal communication, it is worth focusing on the vital skill of listening. Listening is not just hearing, but involves following a message or communication for understanding and trying to assess the feelings of the communicator. John Adair (cited in Thomas 1998, p.181) has identified five attributes as essential for effective listening: namely, being willing to listen, clearly hearing the message, interpreting the meaning (the speaker's meaning, not only your interpretation), evaluating carefully (suspending judgement at first, but then assessing value and usefulness), and responding appropriately – remembering communication is a two-way street.

Bell has taken these attributes further by listing some practical points:

- Do not interrupt. Let the other person finish speaking (unless they are straying too far from the point).
- Concentrate. Do not think about your next point, or you will miss what is being said.
- Hear what is said. It is a common mistake to 'half listen', hearing what you want to hear, rather than what is actually said.
- Note key points. Mentally summarise the most important points. It is often a good idea to start your reply by restating these key points.
- Be objective. Do not let your interpretation be distorted by your opinion or feelings about the other person, by their appearance or the way they speak.
- Evaluate. Weigh up what is being said.
- Decide the real meaning. Sometimes you have to look beyond the words themselves to get it. Points omitted, tone of voice, manner and facial expression can all provide added meaning.

(Bell 1992, p.91)

Activity 12.4   Being a good listener

Devise your own checklist of six items that will help you to be a good listener. Discuss these with a colleague and see if any vital ones are missing.

Face-to-face communication

This may involve the subject leader and one or more colleagues in the team or staff from outside the team (e.g. Special Educational Needs Co-ordinator) and is likely to be the commonest form of communication. On occasions these contacts will be unplanned and unexpected, but wherever possible it is worth considering some key questions and components for these types of communication as preparation:

1   What are the objectives of the communication?
2   What do I think are the objectives of the other participants?
3   Have I collected all the relevant information and data?
4   Have I rehearsed any possible objections from the participants?
5   It is useful to prepare a few questions in advance using closed, open and probing questions as appropriate. Remember, if you want to encourage participation in a discussion, questions that begin 'What do you think?' or 'How do you think we should … ?' are more productive than closed questions.
6   Prepare a short (and punchy) informal presentation of your case – it must be short, to the point and, if possible, should appear unrehearsed.
7   Know when to close down the discussion and summarise any agreement or conclusions.
8   Record any agreement and outcomes.

Such preparation and awareness can make communications more effective and, coupled with Bell's proposed structure for face-to-face communications, can make participants feel more involved and committed. Bell suggests the team leader should set the atmosphere, start the discussion, listen, clarify as appropriate, make proposals, discover feelings about proposals, look at solutions together with the team, agree actions and follow-up as necessary (Bell 1992, pp.92–3).

Speaking and presentations

Subject leaders will have to speak to a variety of audiences and will probably have to make presentations to pupils, staff, parents, governors and others in the local community. Adair has identified six principles of effective speaking: namely, be clear, be prepared, be simple, be vivid, be natural and be concise (cited in Thomas 1998, p.187). In making presentations West recommends brainstorming the key ideas as part of the preparation, selecting the most important and contemporary ideas and putting them in a logical order, and advises that it is neither possible nor desirable to attempt to cover everything on a topic or theme. A good introduction is vital and might consist of a brief outline of what is to be covered in the talk. It is worth summarising at regular intervals, keep to time, have a clear ending for the talk (this might involve summarising the key points or could involve a rhetorical and provocative question) and never patronise the audience (West 1995).

In making presentations to colleagues or to other audiences, the principles and recommendations from Adair and West will be helpful, but there are other considerations as well. It is always worth knowing your audience. Try to ascertain what their likely knowledge of the topic is – what do they expect from the presentation? Parental expectations may be very different from governors'. You will need to consider the use of visual aids, possibly including using computer support (e.g. PowerPoint). Always make contact with the audience, look at the audience, don't talk too fast, try to be relaxed and remember why you are making the presentation (i.e. what key messages am I trying to get across?).

Written communication

Subject leaders require well-developed verbal and writing skills that cater for a variety of audiences. The principles for effective writing are the same as for effective speaking – clarity, planning and preparation, simplicity, vividness, naturalness and conciseness, although written communications will tend to be more planned than verbal communications. These principles need to be applied in all formats (e.g. memos, notices and letters; development and action plans for the subject; targets for the subject; reports – progress reports to senior leaders/managers and governors, monitoring and evaluation reports, etc.; newsletters; articles – and updates of new initiatives and summaries of relevant research).

In preparing more complex documents, such as development plans and reports, subject leaders may want to work through stages:

1   Drafting

   - being clear about the planned outcomes
   - being clear about the audience
   - selecting the format
   - first attempt at the content

2   Revising

   - amendments resulting from responses to draft (members of the team or wider consultation)
   - check if planned outcomes are met
   - is the document coherent and fluent?
   - is the tone of the document as you want it?

3   Editing:

   - check for grammar, spelling and tone
   - check for repetition
   - remove any unnecessary content

4   Final version

Activity 12.5   Effective writing

Choose a recent letter or short report written by you and get the recipient to check it against John Adair's six principles of effectiveness – clarity, planned, simple, vivid, natural and concise. Make sure you receive full and frank feedback.

ORGANISING AND MANAGING MEETINGS

It may seem obvious but the first question for the subject leader is whether a particular meeting is necessary. If a meeting is necessary, then the second question should be about the reasons for the meeting. Clarity about the purposes of any meeting is vital, as is communicating the purposes to the participants prior to the meeting. Subject leaders will plan and play a prominent role in meetings, which may have one or more of the following purposes:

1   Giving and receiving information

 - updating in relation to the subject
 - administrative items
 - part of a consultation process about the subject (e.g. policy review)

2   Decision-making

 - reaching a conclusion together on a particular issue

3   Solving a problem

 - looking together at possible solutions to a problem

4   Persuading and influencing

 - negotiating with the team
 - discussion on changing a practice in relation to the subject – perhaps using evidence of pupil achievement or relevant research findings

5   Monitoring and evaluating

 - to check progress and share judgements on pupils' achievements, targets, or the subject development plan

6   Planning

 - looking at short-, medium- and long-term planning

7   Professional development

- to share good practices as part of continuing professional development
- to develop specific knowledge, understanding and skills
- to discuss a specific new initiative

8   Motivating

- to harness energies and commitment for a particular action
- to boost morale
- to celebrate achievement and successes

If meetings are to produce their planned outcomes, careful planning and preparation are vital. Once the purpose or purposes of a meeting are clear, the subject leader will need to check the arrangements and procedures before, during and after the meeting.

Before the meeting

In preparing and distributing the agenda, the subject leader will need to be aware of the most efficient and effective use of time – for the leader and for the team members. The agenda should, if possible, be distributed seven days in advance of the meeting, the planned outcomes for the meeting should be clear, and the starting and finishing time should be stated (and, if possible, timings for each item). A well-constructed agenda can save a lot of time and frustration, and should allow team members to contribute items. Below is a possible agenda format:

1   Apologies
2   Minutes/notes of last meeting
3   Matters arising
4   Items – designated as

- information only
- discussion only
- discussion and decision

5   Any other business
6   Date of next meeting

Minutes or notes of the meeting could be taken in turn by members of the team and then approved by the subject leader. All team members receive copies of the minutes and, for any formal meetings, copies are usually sent to the head-teacher and other senior managers, as well as those staff who share links with the subject.

Any information for the meeting would need to be distributed with the agenda (e.g. discussion papers) and the subject leader might check with any likely contributors that they are clear about the planned outcomes. The subject leader could also check the layout of the meeting room and should match this to the purpose of the meeting. For example, a semi-circle of chairs and a table are useful for briefings, and a circle of chairs and/or tables are useful for sharing.

During the meeting

The subject leader should state the purpose of the meeting and the planned outcomes at the beginning. They should encourage participation and check for contributions from non-participants, summarise at the end of each item, checking that the note- or minute-taker has a concise sentence or summary. They should decide when to close down any discussion when agreement or a decision is likely, re-state any action points, including who will be responsible and when action will be taken.

After the meeting

The subject leader checks the notes/minutes of the meeting and ensures distribution. In a small school, there may be a note- or minute-book for the staffroom. The subject leader will also confirm action points with the designated member of staff and any follow-up.

Informal meetings or working groups can be an effective means of consulting colleagues and brainstorming ideas. On occasions such groups can examine particular issues or ideas and bring them to a formal meeting. Some staff feel less inhibited in such working groups and feel freer to express their views and ideas.

Activity 12.6   Effective meetings

As subject leader you may wish to evaluate one of your meetings. Everard and Morris (1996, p.52) suggest you ask yourself the following questions:

1   Was the purpose of the meeting clear to all those who attended?
2   Was the attendance correct for the subject under discussion?
3   Were the participants adequately prepared for the meeting?
4   Was time well used?
5   How high was the commitment of the participants?
6   Did the meeting achieve its purpose?
7   What was the quality of the outcome?
8   Was there a clear definition of

- action to be taken following the meeting?
- responsibility for taking the action?
- a mechanism for review of the action?

Consider your last team meeting and answer the above questions. How will you improve your next meeting?

With the permission of the team, you might consider making a video of one of the team meetings and look at Everard and Morris's criteria with the team.

Chairing meetings

Much of the burden for making meetings effective rests with the person in the chair. Subject leaders do not have to chair all team meetings, but this section focuses on the subject leader when in that role. In chairing meetings the subject leader will need to take account of preparation and planning, managing time, guiding the meeting and ensuring action is taken.

In preparing and planning, the subject leader has to be clear about the purposes and planned outcomes for the meeting, and must be familiar with any background papers and issues. It is also helpful to be aware of any potential conflicts or disagreements. The chair will need to identify any key contributors and ensure that s/he is well briefed as necessary by colleagues. It is worth thinking ahead about each item and mentally rehearsing any likely action points.

In managing time, it is advisable to state the finishing time at the beginning of the meeting and if appropriate allocate time for each item, and then keep strictly to the agreed times.

Guiding the meeting will involve stating the purposes and planned outcomes at the beginning, allowing the discussion to flow whenever possible, and encouraging participation by all and preventing dominance by a few. Open questions to the team can often elicit responses from quieter members. It is helpful to summarise at regular intervals, give and seek clarification whenever necessary, and to decide when to draw discussions to a conclusion when agreement or consensus appears possible or to delay a decision to another meeting. Effective chairpersons repeat any conclusions reached for the team and the note-/minute-taker. The subject leader needs to ensure that any action points are clear, recorded and identify who is responsible for taking the action and by when.

The chairperson checks if the purposes and original outcomes for the meeting have been met and monitors any follow-up activities.

Chairing meetings effectively requires meticulous preparation and planning, an atmosphere that is conducive to free and open discussion and well-developed interpersonal skills. Effective chairing involves a judicious blend of confidence, control and sensitivity, and highly developed skills of listening, interpreting, analysing and synthesising.

Activity 12.7   Chairing meetings

Working with a fellow subject leader, take it in turns to observe each other chairing a team meeting and then give full and frank feedback.

You might find it helpful to look at:

1   Evidence of preparation and planning
2   Managing time
3   Guiding the meeting
4   Action points

USING INFORMATION AND COMMUNICATION TECHNOLOGY

ICT can be a great empowering force in schools, not least for subject leaders. Greater access to information in such areas as pupil records, finance, test scores and the curriculum (subject specific and across the school) should help subject leaders fulfil their leadership and management responsibilities. Access to data on pupils' achievements is part of the target-setting process and helps give a fuller picture of a pupil's overall achievements. Such advances are beginning to impact on the leadership and management aspects of the role, and will be enhanced when all schools are on the national grid for learning.

Poole reminds us, however, that teachers will need to rely not only on the computer or the latest digital satellite video links, but on our skills in communicating with each other. It will be through such communications that we will explore the issues of how and when to use information and communication technology effectively (Poole 1998).

The real challenge, however, remains how ICT will contribute directly to raising pupil achievement in subject areas. Part of the National Curriculum for Initial Teacher Training (DfEE 1998b) prepares students to use ICT in relation to subject-learning outcomes. The proposed government strategy to train all teachers in ICT will extend this focus across the profession. Subject leaders will be required to take a lead and help colleagues make use of, and maximise, the impact of ICT on pupils' subject achievements.

Subject leaders are increasingly using e-mail to network with colleagues in the same subject as a means of supporting each other, but also by raising issues and practices of concern with a view to sharing experiences. Electronic newsletters and e-mail are also being used to produce pre-meeting documentation, transmit information outside meetings (and thus save time), request information and celebrate successes in the subject. The potential impact of ICT is enormous, if still somewhat elusive, and probably cannot be fully realised until subject leaders and all teachers are fully trained and confident in using this technology to enhance learning outcomes and promote more efficient and effective internal and external communications.

13 Building, developing and sustaining teams

INTRODUCTION

Government pressures (such as formal external inspections by OfSTED, literacy and numeracy strategies, and target-setting and the accompanying raft of changes) have made schools modify the ways in which they work, in particular by placing a greater emphasis on the role and functions of teams – sets of teams from whole school to classroom. While secondary schools have traditionally operated with a hierarchical structure of subject and pastoral teams, primary schools generally work with a peer system where members of staff have responsibility for leading a subject (or subjects) and work with colleagues without necessarily line-managing them.

The term 'subject leader' is less common in primary schools than 'subject co-ordinator', but the roles and responsibilities are similar – with a greater emphasis on providing explicit leadership and management for the subject in the former. The OfSTED report *Primary Matters* (OfSTED 1994) considered the term 'co-ordinator' to be too limited and instead referred to 'subject managers'. Although there is no reference to leadership in the description of their roles, subject managers can be expected to:

(a) develop a clear view of the nature of their subject and its contribution to the wider curriculum of the school;

(b) to provide advice and documentation to help teachers to teach the subject and interrelate its constituent elements; and

(c) to play a major part in organising the teaching and the resources of the subject so that statutory requirements are covered.

(OfSTED 1994, para. 37)

It is interesting that by 1998 a greater emphasis was being placed on subject leadership.

In looking at teams and team-building, it is clear that when considering generic features it is also necessary to take account of the specific context – be it size of school, phase and type of school, or location of school.

WHAT IS TEAMWORK?

Members of the teaching and support staff can belong to more than one team, for specific subjects, cross-curricular areas or tasks, and in many schools are likely to belong to a pastoral as well as a subject team. This chapter focuses on subject teams and defines teamwork as individuals working together in such a way as to ensure that the planned objectives are greater than could be achieved by any member working alone. Bell believes that such objectives are achieved 'through shared perceptions; a common purpose; agreed procedures; commitment; co-operation; and resolving disagreements openly by discussion' (Bell 1992, p.45). According to Handy (1993), the purposes of teams in any organisation are to distribute and manage work, solve problems and make decisions, encourage members to contribute to decisions, to co-ordinate and liaise, to pass on information, to negotiate or resolve conflicts, to increase commitment and participation, and to monitor and evaluate work.

The shift in the focus from an individual teacher's expertise and responsibility to team and collective responsibilities for a subject can have enormous benefits for teachers and pupils, and can help to reduce individual stress. Teamworking, however, cannot happen by chance and requires positive leadership and management. Subject leadership may involve working with senior colleagues – a deputy head in a secondary subject team or the headteacher in the primary literacy team, for example. It is therefore important that the purposes and benefits of teamwork are clear and that the role of the subject leader is understood by all. Subject teams require a clear direction that involves all the members in agreeing the aims and objectives. The common purpose of any subject team is likely to focus on improving standards of learning and achievement for all pupils in the subject, and members will need to be committed to working together to achieve this. Chapters 6, 7, 9 and 10 look in detail at aspects of achieving this common purpose.

Bell (1992, p.46) has listed the benefits of teamwork as:

- Agreeing aims
- Clarifying roles
- Sharing expertise and skills
- Maximising use of resources
- Motivating, supporting and encouraging members of the team
- Improving relationships within the staff group
- Encouraging decision-making
- Increasing participation
- Realising individual potential
- Improving communication
- Increasing knowledge and understanding
- Reducing stress and anxiety

Teamwork is not about members conforming, but working together in a complementary way. The key to successful teamwork can often hinge on subject leaders
recognising and building on the different strengths of each team member and
on the quality of the working relationships.

It is clear from the above that leading and managing a subject team is
complex and is best supported when congruent with the prevailing leadership
and management culture in the school. Such congruence, however, is not a pre-
condition for effectiveness. Co-operation, sharing responsibilities and openness
are unlikely to be enhanced either by an authoritarian or by a *laissez-faire*
approach to leadership. Positive leadership and management of teams requires:
total clarity and commitment to the purpose and objectives of the team; high
levels of subject knowledge and understanding to support staff and plan ahead; a
commitment to the team as a learning organisation – to continuing professional
development, to lifelong learning and a willingness to learn from others; strong
and well-developed interpersonal skills; and confident relationships within the
team and with others in the school.

Specific leadership skills and approaches can be required according to the
nature of the task or activity – tight deadlines could warrant firm progress-
chasing, just as exploring ideas would warrant encouragement. In Chapter 12,
leadership styles were outlined from 'telling' to 'sharing'. These leadership
approaches do not operate in isolation, but are combined and integrated with
the subject leader's knowledge, understanding and skills (including interpersonal skills), according to the specific task or incident. A quick decision about a
resource or disciplinary issue might warrant a predominantly 'telling' style,
while planned changes to parts of a scheme of work would require a more
'consultative' and 'sharing' approach.

Activity 13.1   Benefits of teamwork

Take any three benefits of teamwork identified by Bell and for each write
down three ways in which you as subject leader have put these benefits into
practice (e.g. increasing participation).

Coleman and Bush (1994) identify the following features of effective teams:

Explicit and shared values

Agreeing and sharing the purposes, objectives and values of the team are of
vital importance. Sessions where teams discuss and agree the purposes, objectives and direction for the team are an important and valuable part of
team-building and sharing ownership. Constant reference to the purposes and
objectives – in monitoring, evaluation and reviewing, for example – is equally
important to reinforce and sustain strategic and operational aspects of the
team's work.

Situational leadership

The subject leader does not operate in a hierarchical way but delegates tasks and responsibilities according to the needs at the time, and the skills and expertise of the members of the team. Members of the team have clear and accountable responsibilities for aspects of the work, inducting new members or liaising with other staff or teams in the school, for example. This shared leadership harnesses the strengths of team members, can be used to develop members and is designed to be an effective way of meeting the team's purposes and objectives. Chapter 9 on sustaining improvement looked at some aspects of this.

Pride in the team

In this feature, members are confident in and committed to the team. High morale and a sense of loyalty are displayed. In part this will come from full involvement in the team, a culture of trust and honesty, achieving the team's objectives and celebrating successes in a genuine way.

Clear tasks

Objectives are shared and clear, and set within a realistic time-scale. Members of the team know what is expected of them and if asked to undertake a particular task are confident it can be achieved within a given period. At team meetings, for example, any resulting actions or tasks are clearly defined (what is to be done, by whom and by when) and recorded in the minutes.

Review

Reflection on practice and regular reviews of the work of the team are permanent factors.

Possible stages in a review   This is an internal process carried out by the subject leader and team members (others can also be involved if appropriate, including external consultants) and is designed to look at what is happening in a defined area of work in order to highlight strengths and plan for improvement.

Stage 1   Preparation

- Agree focus for the review
- What are the key questions to be asked?
- What evidence will be needed (and how will it be collected)?
- Who will collect the evidence and by when?

Stage 2   Collecting evidence

- Scrutinise any relevant documents (e.g. lesson plans, pupil records) in relation to agreed focus
- Other evidence in relation to focus – observation of lessons or meetings, pupil shadowing, etc.
- Discussions/meetings with parents, other staff, pupils, etc.

Stage 3   Reporting

- Write draft report (not necessarily by subject leader)
- Share draft and amend as necessary
- Final version of report
- Distribute report – focus will determine distribution list, but should include headteacher

Stage 4   Action

- Prepare an action plan

      (a) What is to be improved (clarity is vital)?
      (b) Identify planned objectives (clear and concise)
      (c) Activities to achieve objectives
      (d) Staff involved
      (e) Any training and development
      (f) Time-scale (including completion date)
      (g) Success criteria and evaluation (how will we know if successful? – evaluation is defined as making judgements against planned outcomes)
      (h) Resources needed
      (i) Review (check progress made and any re-targeting)

- Celebrate successes

Openness

Issues are discussed openly and frankly, and praise and criticism are integral to the work of the team. Any criticism is seen as constructive. Members are encouraged to reflect on the teaching and learning processes on a shared and regular basis in order to improve practice.

Lateral communication

Members are encouraged to communicate with each other and not always through the subject leader. Formal communications tend to be confined to team meetings.

Collaboration

Decisions are shared following full discussions and access to all the relevant information and data. This implies a 'consultative' and 'sharing' leadership style, but effective leaders will need the full repertoire of styles (i.e. including as necessary 'telling').

Action

Decisions and communications lead to action and each member of the team knows who is responsible, what has to be done and by when.

(Headings from Coleman and Bush 1994, pp.279–80)

BUILDING THE TEAM

Subject teams cannot operate in isolation in a school and will be driven not just by their own purposes and objectives, but by the aims and values of the school. These will underpin all the work of the school and are likely to have been formulated with contributions from subject leaders and their teams. It is, therefore, likely that team-building by subject leaders will be based on the prevailing school culture. Subject teams can have their own distinctive features, but total autonomy or independence is neither desirable, nor in the best interests of pupils or staff. Similarly, the subject leader may have to balance tensions between individual creativity by members and compliance with school and team rules.

Before beginning to build a subject team, leaders might usefully examine five key components of teamwork and relate them to their own school context:

1   Purposes and objectives of the team.
    Purposes might relate to securing high-quality teaching, effective use of resources and improved standards of learning and achievement for all pupils in the subject. The objectives will consist of specific statements related directly to the purposes (e.g. teaching and learning will be regularly and systematically monitored and evaluated).

2   How the team will work.
    This involves defining the procedures for areas such as communication, planning and decision-making (e.g. team meetings will be held on the first Monday of each month, etc.).

3   How the objectives will be achieved.
    What has to be done to meet the objectives, by which member or members of the team, and by when (e.g. responsibilities within the team).

4   How resources will be deployed.

   The subject leader will want to consider how to make the most efficient and effective use of resources based on the tasks to be performed rather than historical precedents (e.g. this might involve an audit of current resources against the team's objectives).

5   How tasks and the overall performance of the team will be monitored and reviewed.

   Team members will be encouraged to reflect on their own practices and pupils' achievements will be monitored.

Aspects of the work of the team will be reviewed on a regular basis, which will involve judgements being made with a view to action (this corresponds to one of the key features of effective teams that was mentioned earlier).

In examining the above components, the subject leader will want to think about ways of consulting and discussing them with members of the team. It is helpful to be aware of the possible strands of any discussion, but it can be counter-productive to have formed too many fixed ideas, just as it would be inadvisable to have no clear views about the purposes and objectives for the team.

Activity 13.2   Components of teamwork

As subject leader, take any two of the above components of teamwork and use bullet points to describe the features of your team. Share with the team and discuss any omissions.

In building a team, the subject leader might want to look at the following four stages in team development from Tuckman (1965):

1   Forming

   At this stage the team is composed of individuals who will want to contribute to discussions about the team's purposes and at the same time will begin to form opinions about other members of the team, and particularly about the team leader. Some members will want to establish themselves in the team, by the nature and style of contributions and by simple force of personality.

   The subject leader will be noting individual strengths, weaknesses and idiosyncrasies in readiness for the next stage of development.

2   Storming

   Although there is consensus on the purposes of the team, some members may have been having second thoughts and may want to challenge the original purposes. As a result there may be conflicts and hostilities between some members of the team. Such conflicts are quite common and a natural part of team development, and it will be for the subject leader to handle these conflicts and differences in a balanced and sensitive way. The result is usually a set of revised purposes and early discussions on the ways the team can work to achieve the planned objectives.

Any revisions usually involve prioritising the purposes. Discussions are likely to centre around the balance of securing high-quality teaching, effective use of resources and improved standards of learning and achievement for all pupils. Team members can then begin to look at communications (informal and formal), planning (short-, medium- and long-term) and decision-making (ways of contributing and influencing decisions).

3   Norming

The team begins to establish the ways it will work and how the objectives will be achieved. As these procedures and processes become established, a sense of team identity begins to crystallise and members of the team feel free to discuss issues openly, and begin to support each other. At this stage purposes, objectives, procedures, responsibilities, provisional resource allocations, and procedures for monitoring and reviewing are recorded in draft written form.

4   Performing

There is a sense of confidence and maturity in the team, such that problems and issues are raised and discussed openly. Subject leaders will encourage members to reflect on their practices and regular reviews of objectives and the work of the team are considered normal.

Throughout the forming, storming, norming and performing stages, the subject leader might note Adair's three elements of effective leadership: namely, achieving the task, building and maintaining the team, and developing the individual. The subject leader has to balance all three elements in order to achieve the team's purposes and objectives (Adair 1986). Meeting the professional development and career aspirations of individuals is an important aspect of this process and is considered in Chapters 9 and 14.

Activity 13.3   Team-building

1   List the main strengths of your team.
2   Take one area of work that you think could be improved. Using the four stages of review, write a draft plan to look in detail at it.

Activity 13.4   Team effectiveness

Below are criteria for team effectiveness. As subject leader, look at each of these and choose one that needs to be urgently addressed in your team. Prepare an outline action plan using the headings given earlier in the chapter (Stage 4 of the review process).

1   The purposes, objectives and values of the team are clear to all members, including new ones.
2   The strengths and weaknesses of the team are known, and members are encouraged to exercise initiative and be responsible for completing tasks.
3   Interventions by the leader are appropriate and according to the particular situation or task.
4   Members of the team feel motivated and identify with the team.
5   Tasks are completed and objectives achieved by individual and joint member efforts.
6   Team members reflect on their practices, individually and with colleagues.
7   The reviews of objectives and team performances are regular and open.
8   Members of the team celebrate successes and criticise in a constructive manner.
9   Communications in the team are two-way, open and effective.
10 Members feel involved in decision-making, but accept that on occasions some decisions have to be made by the team leader.
11 Team objectives are achieved, particularly those related to raising pupils' achievement in the subject.
12 Members feel valued and committed to continuing professional development.

Activity 13.5   Leadership of the team

What are your strengths and weaknesses in leading the team? You could ask team members and/or other subject leaders. Take one of your weaknesses and using bullet points list how you would tackle it.

SUSTAINING THE TEAM

Sustaining and developing a team requires a recognition and understanding of each member's strengths, weaknesses, idiosyncrasies and needs by others in the team, and more critically by the subject leader. Team members will, however, still want to be treated as individuals. On the other hand, if subject leaders are to motivate and sustain individuals and the team, full understanding of the needs of individuals will be necessary (some of which may be latent). Maslow identified five motivating factors in his hierarchy of needs. These were looked at in Chapter 10 in relation to motivating pupils and are just as relevant in respect of adults:

1 Physiological needs (including hunger, thirst, sleep)
2 Safety needs (security and protection from danger)
3 Social needs (belonging, acceptance, social life, friendship and love)
4 Self-esteem (self-respect, achievement, status, recognition)
5 Self-actualisation (growth, accomplishment, personal development)

(Maslow 1970)

Factors 3, 4 and 5 are classified as higher-order needs and could help subject leaders to relate individual needs to tasks and activities in the team. Higher-order needs can only be identified by regular dialogue between team members and the subject leader. Belonging to a team may be important to an individual, but the subject leader will want to talk about what this really means in practice to an individual member, and in particular how team membership can help self-image and contribute to other professional aspirations.

Individual team members may have their own picture of what they want to achieve in the team, what constitutes self-respect for them and what they consider to be appropriate recognition. Team members will want to continue to develop as professionals, some more rapidly than others. It will be for the subject leader to provide maximum opportunities to help team members develop personally and professionally. Some of this was considered in Chapter 9 on sustaining improvement. However, it is only through regular formal and informal dialogues that this can occur. The revised appraisal system proposed in the government's Green Paper *Teachers: Meeting the challenge of change* (DfEE 1998a) will focus on performance management and has the potential to help subject leaders and team members grow personally and professionally.

Successfully motivating oneself and others in the team is a key characteristic of effective leadership, even though at times it is difficult to get at some internally held forces, fears and needs.

Activity 13.6   Motivating team members

Listed below are ways in which you could motivate and meet the needs and aspirations of team members. Check each one against how you motivate members of your team. Choose one that you feel still needs to be addressed and list how you would tackle it.

1 Acting enthusiastically yourself and being seen to persevere with tasks and challenges.
2 Showing that you trust individuals and the team.

3   Leading and managing by example and not by manipulation.
4   Treating team members as individuals – by regular dialogues that focus on higher-order needs.
5   Treating everyone in a fair and equal way.
6   Taking responsibility for mistakes as well as successes.
7   Acknowledging and praising achievements and successes, and building on them.
8   Avoiding public criticisms of individuals.
9   Holding regular discussions about and working on the reinforcement of the purposes and outcomes for the team.
10   Setting realistic and challenging targets for all team members.
11   Encouraging individuals to develop their capacities to the full.
12   Involving all members of the team (teaching and support) in planning and decision-making.
13   Ensuring that communications are two-way, open and frank.
14   Contributing to and promoting the personal and professional development of all team members.
15   Delegating as much as possible to individuals and sub-groups.
16   Giving regular feedback on the performance of team members and on any discussions with others inside and outside the school.
17   Encouraging individuals to reflect on their practice, to share good practices and to learn from each other.
18   Providing opportunities for individuals to work together on a task and for colleagues to support each other in the team.

Finally in this chapter it is worth noting that, in order to build and sustain teams, subject leaders have to be motivated themselves. Lack of motivation in the subject leader is difficult to mask and it is therefore helpful on occasions to reflect on one's own position.

Activity 13.7   Motivating yourself

Answer each of the questions below. Put your answers in two columns – one headed 'positive' and the other 'issues'. If you have any issues, consider how you might remedy them – possibly by discussing them with a trusted colleague or friend.

1   Am I still committed to the purposes and objectives for the team?
2   Am I still committed to helping pupils realise their full potential in my subject or area of work?
3   How can I lead by example and show my undoubted strengths?
4   Do I need to check if Maslow's five main needs are being met by myself? For example, am I happy with my working conditions and environment?

5   Am I trying to do too much myself?
6   What difference have I made as a subject leader? It is worth making a note of instances when you have influenced colleagues, achieved a particularly difficult task, or helped a member of the team to gain promotion. Remember also that you may have made important contributions to whole-school policies and practices.

Part V
Looking ahead

14 Challenges and opportunities for the future

INTRODUCTION

The pace of educational change in the late 1990s has been frenetic. Teachers are faced with huge challenges as curricular change is imposed and as their own professional status is challenged. However, such challenges provide opportunities, which include the potential for enhanced subject provision and personal career development. In this short part of the book, we highlight key aspects of current developments which offer opportunities, yet which are seen by many as huge challenges to the profession. For subject leaders, we believe the initiatives fall into three overarching categories:

- curricular issues
- issues associated with the Green Paper *Teachers: Meeting the challenge of change* (DfEE 1998a)
- personal career development

We do not propose to present answers but to highlight issues and concerns which, if faced with a positive attitude, can be viewed as professional challenges and opportunities.

LITERACY

Subject leaders may not be excused for locating the responsibility for developing literacy in the English department, nor can secondary school leaders argue that literacy is the role of primary school educators. DfEE's *The Implementation of the National Literacy Strategy* (1997b) stresses the need for a continuous and cohesive approach, requiring all teachers to be respectful of a systematic way of working.

The delegation to the Standards and Effectiveness Unit (SEU) of the development of a clear operational blueprint has led to the introduction of a Literacy Hour, when the activities and teaching methods have been heavily prescribed. However, this single action is unlikely to ensure that the target of 80 per cent of

Key Stage 2 pupils reach the National Curriculum Level 4 in English. Secondary teachers will need to build on individual pupil attainments and indeed may well rely on pupils having the necessary literacy skills to tackle this subject.

All pupils need to read in all subjects. The definition of literacy is simple. Literacy is 'the ability to read and write' (DfEE 1997b, p.45). This view of literacy does not take account of the process of developing literacy. By unpacking the over-simplified definition, subject leaders from the full range of curricular subjects can recognise the particular contribution that the teaching and learning of their own subject can make. Literacy is also (adapted from DfEE 1997b) the ability to read and write with confidence, and to respect and be interested in books. School study will demand an awareness of the range of texts to which pupils are exposed, including a high proportion of non-fiction. Pupils therefore need to learn to orchestrate the full range of reading cues – to plan, draft, revise and edit their own writing. An interest in any particular subject requires an interest and development of subject-specific vocabulary and the spelling of appropriate words. Literacy is more than a pupil demonstrating fluency and legible handwriting: it is the accumulation of learning a process which is presented all day in all subjects. Subject leaders must be aware of the challenges and opportunities offered by the literacy project.

All subjects require different types of reading, and all teachers give advice and guidance on how to make best use of texts across the full range of subject areas. It is for these simple reasons that the DfEE does recommend consistency and cohesion with a systematic approach. Subject leaders are well placed within the school system to play a proactive role in implementing the recommended ten-point plan (DfEE 1997b, pp.29–30).

In knowing the demands of their own subject specialism, subject leaders can contribute to a whole-school action plan and be able to adapt subject provision as a response to the outcomes of an assessment of basic skills. The development of whole-school improvement targets must take account of expectations and performance of pupils across the curriculum. Through differentiation, schemes of work must account for all levels of ability, and ongoing assessment and monitoring of pupil performance (if formalised) will generate evidence of an improvement plan for under-achievers, and of course facilitate a cross-subject review of under-achievers' progress.

As all teachers share a responsibility for the development of literacy skills, then all teachers must themselves develop a sound understanding of the processes of learning to read and write. Any success depends on a commitment to improve staff skills in this area. All teachers must therefore receive appropriate support and guidance if they are to focus on key aspects beyond their own immediate subject specialism. A thorough examination of the appropriateness of teaching and learning styles will inevitably be necessary, as will the critical scrutiny and selection of appropriate teaching materials. As we point out in Part II, no action plan is complete unless a suitable method of monitoring the action plan is developed.

Subject leaders have the leadership and management skills to implement and monitor the National Literacy project, under the watchful eye of a specialist co-ordinator. A thorough examination of teaching approaches and strategies in relation to literacy offers the opportunity for improved performance and of compliance with a whole-school approach to a key aspect of the curriculum.

NUMERACY

The process for introducing the National Numeracy Strategy and aspiring to new targets (75 per cent of Key Stage 2 pupils to reach Level 4 of the National Curriculum) is very similar to that of the Literacy Project. The added complica-tion is, of course, a national shortage of specialised mathematics teachers. There is, therefore, a greater emphasis on the management of the implementation of the strategies through the deployment of local 'leading mathematics teachers', nominated by the LEA, teaching their own class in their school, or on occa-sions in another school. This clearly adds a dimension to the role of a mathematics subject leader in primary schools. Mathematics subject leaders may also be required to teach mathematics as a specialist to children in other teachers' classes. Other subject leaders may, in this case, be excused for believing that the new Numeracy Hour and other aspects of the numeracy strategy are the sole responsibility of the mathematics team.

A closer analysis of the official definition of numeracy will, however, suggest to all subject leaders that they have a contributory role to play in their own subjects.

> Numeracy at Key Stages 1 and 2 is a proficiency that involves a confidence and competence with numbers and measures. It requires an understanding of the number system, a repertoire of computational skills and an inclina-tion and ability to solve number problems in a *variety of contexts* [our emphasis]. Numeracy also demands practical understanding of the ways in which information is gathered by counting and measuring and is presented in graphs, diagrams, charts and tables ...
>
> (DfEE 1998a, p.19)

The DfEE's (1998c) own final report of the Numeracy Task Force claims that the recommended strategy has something to offer every teacher and every school. The strong recommendation of in-service training (INSET) will provide all teachers in primary, special and middle schools with an improved subject knowledge, thereby extending the potential range of teaching approaches. This cohesion and consistency should provide greater continuity between schools, and also develop a common language for reflecting on and discussing good prac-tice in mathematics teaching.

INSET opportunities therefore go beyond the recommendations for the Literacy Project. The DfEE (1998c) have responded positively to the request by teachers, during the consultation period, to have an opportunity to observe colleagues. Clearly the process of professional development through observation and reflection is at the heart of the implementation stage. Mathematics subject leaders in primary schools have a unique opportunity to build collaborative views on how mathematics should be taught and learnt.

The implementation of a numeracy strategy in Key Stages 1 and 2 will inevitably have an impact on secondary school teaching. The report recognises that numeracy skills are also important in other subject disciplines, such as science, geography and economics (DfEE 1998c, p.67). Subject leaders need to be fully aware of the impact that expected improved standards in literacy will have on the learning capabilities of pupils across the full range of subjects. Indeed the DfEE proceed to :

> recommend that secondary schools should start planning for this intake as soon as predictable.
>
> (DfEE 1998c, p.67)

It is not surprising, then, that the report suggests that teachers from different subject departments should be engaged in supporting the programme in the teaching of their own subjects.

The National Numeracy Strategy is not simply concerned with raising the standards in mathematics, in a way which many teachers fear is to the detriment of foundation subjects. Subject leaders must recognise the value such a focus will add to their own subject, through an integrated approach to curriculum planning. The opportunity is clearly that all teachers will be faced with more able, numerate children, thereby extending the potential for learning in other subjects. The challenge is to participate in and monitor the implementation of the National Numeracy Strategy through the full range of subject provisions.

INFORMATION AND COMMUNICATION TECHNOLOGY

Prime Minister Tony Blair's assertion that

> By 2002 all schools will be connected to the Superhighway, free of charge; half a million teachers will be trained [to teach with ICT]; and our children will be leaving school IT-literate, having been able to exploit the best that technology can offer
>
> (NGFL 1997, foreword)

is another short-term demand on teachers and subject leaders. A key feature of the government's drive to improve standards is the intended use of ICT in subject teaching. Newly qualified teachers have had to demonstrate appropriate standards, defined in Circular 4/98 (DfEE 1998b), and serving teachers will be required to operate at a similar level by 2002. In short, the use of computers is to be an essential element of all subject teaching and learning.

The first challenge for subject leaders is to recognise the potential functions of ICT and to discriminate between the use of technology for learning purposes, and the less useful function of occupying pupils.

The ICT standards contained in Circular 4/98 identify four major functions of ICT: speed and automatic functions, capacity and range, provisionality and interactivity. The terminology requires further explanation.

Speed and automatic functions This includes the capacity to accelerate the completion of key activities related to the subject. Producing graphical representations of statistics, editing texts and data-logging are all activities which teachers of all subjects might employ. The use of computers can enhance the presentation, accelerate the process and provide the learner with additional learning tools.

Capacity and range There is a mass of information available to learners electronically. CD-ROMs and on-line Internet resources provide learners with a greater range and scope of data and information than books can provide. The potential for research-based learning is evidently enhanced by use of ICT in the classroom.

Provisionality The potential to plan, draft, revise and edit texts is an obvious benefit of word-processing packages. For musicians, learners can compose; mathematicians can calculate problems step-by-step; artists can build pictures and images in stages. As a means of focusing on the processes of learning, computer technology undoubtedly adds to more traditional methods.

Interactivity The use of the Internet and e-mail are simple ways of encouraging communication with others. Video-conferencing offers a more sophisticated way of engaging learners with other learners and/or other sources of information in an interactive way. Computers provide the opportunity to gather information, but also to contribute to debates, discussions or simply to add data to existing databases.

ICT has the potential to bring the subject to life. Subject leaders must draw on the opportunities to enhance the provision of their own subject. The challenge is, of course, to provide all teachers with the wherewithal to exploit such opportunities. Working alongside the designated IT co-ordinator to raise awareness of opportunities, to plan implementation and technical support, and to monitor the extent to which ICT is enhancing both subject learning and the development of pupils' IT skills, is therefore a necessity.

Alongside the benefits for pupils, subject leaders will need to oversee teachers':

- knowledge and understanding of effective teaching methods using ICT
- ability to assess subject objectives when pupils use ICT

- understanding of which technologies are appropriate to aspects of teaching and learning
- technical skills
- understanding of the National Curriculum for IT
    (Adapted from Canterbury Christ Church University College 1998, p.13)

The government has plans to invest large sums of money in the training of all teachers. To gain full benefit for the subject, subject leaders need to be involved in the planning, delivery and evaluation of training initiatives designed to enhance subject learning through ICT.

CITIZENSHIP

Within the framework for personal, social and health education (PSHE) and citizenship at Key Stages 1 to 4 (QCA 1999a), the proposed statement of values, aims and purposes of the school curriculum recognises the need to promote the formation and maintenance of worthwhile and fulfilling relationships based on respect for themselves and others at home, school, work and in the community. The curriculum should develop pupils' abilities to work for the common good and to respond in a positive way to opportunities, challenges, responsibility, change and adversity.

In order to address such a range of issues, the PSHE provision has been expanded to include citizenship, partly through a statutory order for a foundation subject in the National Curriculum for citizenship, and partly through cross-curricular approaches. The statutory entitlement at Key Stages 3 and 4 is to enable pupils to learn about their duties, responsibilities and rights as citizens, the nature of democratic government and the skills required to participate in an active way in school, neighbourhood, community and social activities.

QCA (1999a) recommendations also include the view that schools should develop their own approaches through active learning, community involvement and the development of key skills (communication, working with others, the application of number, IT, improving one's own learning and performance, and problem-solving).

Subject leaders should take note of these recommendations, contained in the Crick Report (QCA and Crick 1998) and the QCA's *National Curriculum Review Consultation* (1999b). If teachers are to encourage pupils to develop the confidence to challenge the *status quo*, nurture independence of thought and exercise their rights as citizens, due thought must be given to the implications. Subject leaders must ensure that approaches to teaching and learning, and specific methodology, are in keeping with the philosophy of citizenship. Active learning, autonomous learning, participant evaluation and accountability to the learner all mirror the aims and objectives of the proposed citizenship programme.

The implications of citizenship as a cross-curricular dimension, as well as a foundation subject at Key Stages 3 and 4, is far-reaching. Curriculum planners need to examine the content of a syllabus for relevance, as well as the subject-related pedagogy. Liaison with a named co-ordinator will be essential, in order to establish when and how pupils can and should listen, argue, make a case, challenge and/or accept the greater wisdom or force of an alternative view.

Clearly there are risks. Teams of subject leaders need also to establish a sense of authority in order that pupils will learn to exercise responsibility and fulfil duties and responsibilities.

Citizenship is intended to foster, among other things, a respect for lifelong learning. The challenge for the subject leader is to establish an environment in which pupils can flourish and develop as active learners.

ISSUES ASSOCIATED WITH THE GREEN PAPER

The Green Paper *Teachers: Meeting the challenge of change* was published on 3 December 1998, with a consultation period that lasted until 31 March 1999. At the time of writing this book, the government is still considering responses to the Green Paper proposals and, although many teachers, headteachers and teachers' associations reacted angrily to some aspects of the Green Paper, few fundamental changes are expected from the government. The Green Paper outlines a system for the teaching profession that is designed to attract, retain and motivate good staff. Key proposals are:

a.   greater rewards and faster progress for the best teachers;
b.   progress through excellent classroom performance as well as management responsibilities;
c.   pay decisions informed by rigorous annual appraisal;
d.   more discretion on decision-making at school level within a national framework;
e.   transparent and fair school pay policies;
f.   no serving teacher to lose out on existing entitlements, but higher pay to be justified by performance and achievement.

(DfEE 1998a, p.5)

In essence the Green Paper is seeking to raise the status of the teaching profession through a fundamental reform of staffing structures, pay and conditions of service. It is intended that there will be a greater emphasis on the individual teacher who will be responsive to effective leadership, will have ambitions to lead, will be well-trained and, above all, will be committed to the government's goal of improving standards in education.

The main focus in the Green Paper is on performance management and a new system of pay. The headteacher's pay will be reviewed annually by the governors of the school against achievement targets. The headteacher will be responsible for an annual appraisal system for all staff which will determine their pay, professional development needs and, to a large extent, their career development. All teaching staff will be appraised on evidence of performance against agreed targets, including at least one for improved pupil performance.

The government proposes a new pay-scale which will extend beyond the current maximum for teachers. Teachers would have to apply for a performance assessment to proceed beyond the current maximum (now known as the 'threshold level').

All teachers will be assessed by the headteacher using national standards. External assessors will check these assessments and might also advise the governing body, who will take over responsibility for the new system from LEAs.

A new pay-scale will also be established for leadership posts in the school. Membership of this group is not fully defined in the Green Paper, but will include the headteacher, deputy, other senior managers, Advanced Skills Teachers and possibly some curriculum/subject leaders. Membership of the leadership group will no doubt be determined by the type and size of school, with greater scope for large secondary schools.

A National College for School Leadership will be established in late 2000 and will focus on policy, training, development and support, and on research. It will serve the needs of aspiring headteachers, deputies and middle managers and will 'set the pace and direction' of national debate on school leadership' (DfEE 1999b, p.7).

At the centre of the government's proposals to reform the teaching profession is the clear focus on performance. Salary and career progression will be determined largely by classroom performance and pupils' achievements. The annual appraisal of staff will involve meetings, direct observations and a file of evidence, and will be carried out by the line-manager, with the headteacher having overall responsibility. In secondary schools, subject leaders (as heads of department or faculty) will appraise members of their teams, but in primary and special schools it is unlikely that subject leaders will appraise colleagues, unless they do so in their role as headteacher, deputy or Key Stage co-ordinator.

There are several issues worth pursuing. The appraisal system is radically different from the current one, not least by placing greater emphasis on teacher performance than professional development needs. Two appraisal targets will relate to performance and one to professional development. A controversial aspect centres on the rubric that one of the performance targets must relate to pupils' achievement. To avoid this becoming a meaningless activity it will be necessary to relate performance targets to specific school and socio-economic conditions. There is the risk that a performance rather than developmental emphasis may relegate training and development in the minds of teachers, and make developing and sustaining the team more difficult for the subject leader. Indeed, the focus in the Green Paper on individual as opposed to team performance is a risky strategy and could damage efforts to raise standards. Earlier parts of the book have strongly advocated the need for effective teamwork and positive leadership – not least because of the growing demands on individual teachers.

In the Green Paper, little account is taken of team performance other than the whole-school team being able to compete for a school performance bonus. Some other aspects of the proposed appraisal system will also need to be addressed – for example, evidence for the appraisal interviews may involve additional work by the line-manager (and appraiser), including as necessary classroom observation.

An appraisal system based on performance management has the potential to raise staff and pupil achievements, particularly if some of the earlier reservations about targets being linked to pupils' achievements, time needed to collect evidence and balancing individual and team targets can be addressed. It may be more difficult to overcome the teaching profession's resistance to linking appraisal targets and pay. Whether true or not, many teachers believe that such an approach has been discredited outside education and that performance-related pay is less commonly used by industry and commerce. Line-managers may find that appraisal interviews could be dominated by discussions about pay (including ensuring that success criteria are not too challenging) rather than professional development needs and the setting of challenging targets. Performance targets set within a team leadership and management structure can reflect the culture of the team and be as open and challenging as the team can accommodate. Targets for individual teachers set within a payment system (including one related to pupils' achievement) run the risk of distorting the performance process towards meeting criteria related to payments.

The composition and line-management of teams could become more complicated for subject leaders in secondary schools where relations could be affected by the presence of an Advanced Skills Teacher who is part of the school leadership group (of which the subject leader may not be a member), and by the presence of a 'fast-track' teacher in the team who has passed the 'threshold' salary-scale and is on a similar salary to the subject leader. Such situations are unlikely to arise in primary or special schools and no doubt in time will be resolved in secondary schools.

To return briefly to the school leadership group. Membership of this group may become an issue for subject leaders in secondary schools. In primary schools, subject leaders are unlikely to be members unless they also have senior responsibilities (e.g. deputy headteacher or Key Stage co-ordinator). However, in secondary schools some curriculum/subject leaders may be members of the leadership group, playing a direct role in whole-school issues and being paid on the leadership pay-scale. Membership of the leadership group could reinforce a hierarchy of subjects (possibly increasing the gap between core and other subjects) and could affect the career prospects of those subject leaders who are not members of the leadership group.

It now looks as if the original timetable of implementing the new appraisal system in September 1999 will have to be relaxed, perhaps by a year. Primary schools are facing new initiatives in the Autumn term 1999 (e.g. numeracy strategy) and extensive training programmes will be necessary for governors, headteachers, line-managers, advisers and assessors, in relation to staff structures, pay and conditions of service. The additional time might result in a reconsideration of some of the potentially more damaging aspects of the Green Paper. It could also serve to highlight the many proposals in the Green Paper that could radically reform and raise the status of the teaching profession.

WHAT OF YOUR CAREER?

The word 'career' is often used to describe how people move onwards and upwards through one or more organisations, seeking more responsibility, more status and more remuneration. Advertisements for teachers still write of the attractions of a teaching career and the new General Teaching Council (GTC) has career development as one of its responsibilities (Sutcliffe 1999, p.15). It is assumed that people who read this book are interested in developing their careers – but is the idea of having a career an outmoded concept?

The 1990s produced a worldwide employment context dominated by turbulent international activity often leading to financial crisis and recession, particularly in the East. At the time of writing this book, NATO was bombing Yugoslavia, and China and Russia were once again making threatening noises towards the West. One certainty about this new millennium is that there is no certainty, particularly at corporate or government level.

Throughout the last century large companies and public organisations like the civil service engaged in succession planning that plotted out the likely career of young graduates and provided them with a succession of training and development opportunities to support their gradual promotion through the organisation. As we begin the twenty-first century, this kind of long-term, time-serving, following-in-the-footsteps type career progression for professionals has been replaced with short-term contracts and bonus-led target achievement. With this shift from corporate to personal responsibility for career development (symptomatic of the move away from the 'Nanny State'), it is now the individual not the corporate body that holds the key to the development and exploitation of potential. But is this true in schools? Who is accountable for developing teachers and leaders: the individual teacher, the school, LEA, GTC or the person themselves?

We are discriminating here between the provision of opportunity and the responsibility for taking advantage of it. Oldroyd and Hall (1991, p.15) describe four 'images' which they believe emerge from research into the context of school and teacher development:

The Enabling LEA – whose officers and advisers provide a superstructure of support.
The Self-Developing School – which has a senior management team that encourages interaction, communication and collaboration.

The Collaborative Team – who act as study groups, meet together to support and feedback about performance.

The Reflective Teacher – who is continuously concerned with promoting personal professional growth through reflection and education, training and collaboration with colleagues.

Together they suggest a continuum, from corporate provision of opportunity to personal access, of what is needed for professional growth.

Activity 14.1   Assessing responsibility for career development

Consider the implications of this shift of responsibility. Do you associate with the idea of taking responsibility for your own development? How does this impact on your role as a subject leader e.g. do you feel any responsibility for the development of your colleagues?

Does career development always mean seeking promotion?

Angela Thody does not think so. She believes that there are three aspects to what she describes as 'CAREER AWARENESS – a consciousness of job opportunities as choices available for career decisions':

Career development – for that stage in employment when upward advancement is being sought and relates to teachers seeking out activities which result in promotion, increased income, experience and power (e.g. management training).

Career enhancement – the stage which might also be called 'job enrichment'. This is not about moving upwards but rather growing sideways, and relates to activities which result in new directions and new activities (e.g. an M.A. in a new aspect of curriculum development, writing articles based on classroom research).

Career contentment – a stage where a leader or teacher recognises satisfaction with the position reached and that this is a good temporary or permanent place to stop. It relates to activities that support, improve and secure the *status quo* (e.g. collaborative in-school workshops focusing on improving classroom practice).

(Thody 1993, p.2)

The point here is that there is no value judgement being made of teachers who are in any of these positions, providing that they are aware of where they are. If leaders and staff are aware of their current mind-set they can make more informed choices about appropriate types of staff-development activity.

Activity 14.2   Analysing career awareness

1   Examine the three dimensions of career awareness. Reflect on your current position and the degree to which you are at the developing, enhancing or contentment stage of your career.
2   What types of staff-development activity are most appropriate for you at the moment?

Opportunities for career development

> Asking established deputies what motivated them to make their first application for a deputy's post elicits a wide and fascinating range of responses ... It would seem that the principal motivation came from a growing interest in either management, in a context wider than that of the classroom, or in a developing interest in one or more curriculum areas and a desire to be in a position to influence others across the whole school.
>
> (Thomas 1995, p.4)

Clearly, for those seeking career development, the next promotional step for subject leaders is to aspire to deputy headship or headship. At the time of writing the Teacher Training Agency has national responsibility for leading and supporting the development of those teachers seeking subject and school leadership. Although the Agency has committed itself to directly supporting subject leaders, it is not a top priority for the DfEE to pursue this to the extent that it might have wished. As a consequence, the publication of the TTA' s *National Standards for Subject Leaders* (1998a) was not accompanied by the introduction of any qualification (e.g. National Professional Qualification for Subject Leaders – NPQSL). However, the DfEE have given full backing to the TTA's initiatives for aspiring, new and experienced headteachers based upon the *National Standards for Headteachers* (1998c). Three programmes were introduced in the 1990s:

National Professional Qualification for Headship (NPQH) – a 100 per cent DfEE-funded programme (up to about £3,000) of training, development and assessment taking one to three years, leading to an award signed by the Secretary of State and entitling successful graduates to have NPQH after their name. At the time of writing, 6,000 candidates are engaged on the programme in England and Wales, with Northern Ireland beginning its first programme in 1999.

Headteachers' Leadership and Management Programme (HEADLAMP) – a 100 per cent DfEE-funded £2,500 entitlement for headteachers to gain support and continual professional development in their first two years of headship.

This is not a set programme, as headteachers are more or less free to access support and training from a large list of accredited providers. It does not lead to any qualification.

Leadership Programme for Serving Headteachers (LPSH) – a 50 per cent DfEE-funded/50 per cent LEA-funded programme for headteachers who have been in post for over five years. It is based on a four-day residential programme at which headteachers are given 360° feedback from their governors and staff about their leadership. There is no qualification for attending the programme.

The subject leader will be most interested in the NPQH. Currently, access to this programme is available to anyone who satisfactorily gains eligibility, no matter what their current role or status. Eligibility is determined by the analysis of the NPQH application, which is designed around the *National Standards for Headteachers*. Consequently, subject leaders who are interested in pursuing their careers via the NPQH are advised to take three actions:

Activity 14.3 Preparing to apply for NPQH

1   Gain a full understanding of the TTA's *National Standards for Headteachers*. These are obtainable from a variety of sources (see the TTA or DfEE websites). Subject leaders need to note the extra dimensions that are in the standards for headteachers that are not in the standards for subject leaders (e.g. the headteacher standards have a fifth key area, relating to accountability).

2   Discuss your aspirations with your headteacher and, using the standards for headteachers, describe the gap between your current experience and achievements and that of deputy headteachers or headteachers. Try to negotiate new areas of responsibility or a new task related to the school development plan that is beyond your subject area.

3   Start to collect and collate evidence of your strategic impact on the school, particularly anything which can be seen to have improved standards of pupil achievement. The best way to keep this information is to create a number of files in a filing cabinet labelled with the headings of the *National Standards for Headteachers*.

FINALLY

The writers hope that the theory, discussion and activities presented in this book contribute to all development aspects of subject leaders and the schools in which they serve.

Bibliography

Adair, J. (1983) *Effective Leadership*, 1st edition. London: Pan Books.

Adair, J. (1986) *Effective Teambuilding*. London: Pan Books.

Adair, J. (1988) *Effective Leadership*, 2nd edition. London: Pan Books.

Alexander, R., Rose, J. and Woodhead, C. (1992) *Curriculum Organisation and Classroom Practice in Primary Schools: A discussion paper*. London: DES.

Alexander, R., Rose, J. and Woodhead, C. (1993) *Curriculum Organisation and Classroom Practice in Primary Schools: A discussion paper*, London: DES.

Anderson, K., Cook, D. and Saunders, T. (1992) *School Governors*. London: Longman.

Ansoff, H.I. (1987) *Corporate Strategy*. London: Penguin.

Anthony, A.R. and Herzlinger, R.E. (1989) 'Management Control in Non-Profit Organisations'. In Levacic, R. (ed.), *Financial Management in Education*. Milton Keynes: Open University Press.

Armitage, A., Bryant, B., Dunnill, R., Hammersley, M., Hayes, D., Hudson, A. and Lawes, S. (1998) *Teaching and Training in Post Compulsory Education*. Buckingham: Open University Press.

Arnold, J. and Hope, T. (1989) 'The Budgeting Process'. In Levacic, R. (ed.), *Financial Management in Education*. Milton Keynes: Open University Press.

Ashcroft, K. and Palacio, D. (1995) 'Introduction to the New National Curriculum'. In Ashcroft, K. and Palacio, D. (eds), *The Primary Teacher's Guide to the New National Curriculum*. London: Falmer Press.

Atkinson, R.C. and Shiffrin, R.M. (1968) 'Human Memory: A proposed system and its control processes'. In Spence, K. and Spence, J. (eds), *Advances in the Psychology of Learning and Motivation*, vol. 2. New York: Academic Press.

Audit Commission (1991) *Management within Primary Schools*. London: HMSO.

Bailey, A.J. (1986) *Policy Making in Schools: Creating a sense of educational purpose*. Unpublished mimeo, University of Sussex.

Baker, K. (1990) Secretary of State for Education's letter to Chief Education Officers, 10 December.

Ball, D.L. (1991) 'Teaching Mathematics for Understanding: What do teachers need to know about subject matter?'. In Kennedy, M. (ed.), *Teaching Academic Subjects to Diverse Learners*. New York: Teachers College Press.

Ballinger, E. (1986) 'The Training and Development Needs of Managers'. In Day, C. and Moore, R. (eds), *Staff Development in the Secondary School: Management perspectives*. London: Croom Helm.

Balshaw, M. (1991) *Help in the Classroom*. London: David Fulton Publishers.

Barras, P. (1994) 'Getting a Secondary School Ready for OfSTED Inspection'. In Parsons, C. (ed.), *Quality Improvement in Education*. London: David Fulton Publishers.

Barthorpe, T. and Visser, J. (1992) *Differentiation: Your responsibility*. Stafford: NASEN.

Beare, H., Caldwell, B. and Millikan, R. (1997) 'Dimensions of Leadership'. In Crawford, M., Kydd, L. and Riches, C., *Leadership and Teams in Educational Management*. Buckingham: Open University Press.

Beattie, N. (1990) 'The Wider Context: Are curricula manageable?'. In Brighouse, T. and Moon, B. (eds), *Managing the National Curriculum: Some critical perspectives*. Harlow: Longman.

Becker, T., Erault, M. and Knight, J. (1981) *Policies for Educational Accountability*. London: Heinemann.

Bell, L. (1992) *Managing Teams in Secondary Schools*. London: Routledge.

Bell, L. and Day, C. (1991) *Managing the Professional Development of Teachers*. Milton Keynes: Open University Press.

Bennet, J. and Pumfrey, P.D. (1994) 'Health Education'. In Verma, G.K. and Pumfrey, P.D. (eds), *Cross-Curricular Contexts, Themes and Dimensions in Primary Schools*. London: Falmer Press.

Bennet, N. (1995) *Managing Professional Teachers: Middle management in primary and secondary schools*. London: Paul Chapman Publishing.

Bennet, N., Glatter, R. and Levacic, R. (1994) *Improving Educational Management through Research and Consultancy*. London: Paul Chapman Publishing.

Bennett, N. (1976) *Teaching Styles and Pupil Progress*. London: Open Books Publishing.

Bennett, N. (1995) *Managing Professional Teachers: Middle management in primary and secondary schools*. London: Paul Chapman Publishing.

Bennett, N. and Dunne, E. (1994) 'How Children Learn: Implications for practice'. In Moon, B. and Shelton Mayes, A. (eds), *Teaching and Learning in the Secondary School*. London: Routledge.

Bennett, N., Crawford, M. and Riches, C. (eds) (1992) *Managing Change in Education: Individual and organisational perspectives*. London: Paul Chapman Publishing.

Bennis, W. and Biederman, P.W. (1997) *Organizing Genius*. London: Nicholas Brearley Publishing.

Bennis, W. and Goldsmith, J. (1997) *Learning to Lead*. London: Nicholas Brearley Publishing.

Birch, D. (1989) 'Programme Budgeting for Colleges'. In Levacic, R. (ed.), *Financial Management in Education*, Milton Keynes: Open University Press.

Blandford, S. (1997) *Middle Management in Schools*. London: Pitman Publishing.

Bliss, T. and Timbrell, S. (1997) *Against the Odds: SENCo Survival – Planning and Reviewing the Individual Education Plans*. Bristol: Lucky Duck Publishing.

Bloom, B.S. (ed.) (1964) *Taxonomy of Educational Objectives*. London: Longman.

Bloom, S. (1978) *Peer and Cross Age Tutoring in the School*. Hawthorn: Australian Council for Educational Research.

Bobbit Nolen, S. (1995) 'Teaching for Autonomous Learning'. In Desforges, C. (ed.), *An Introduction to Teaching*. Oxford: Basil Blackwell.

Bollen, R. and Hopkins, D. (1987) *School Based Review: Towards a praxis*. Belgium: ACCO.

Bower, D. (1983) 'Managing for Efficiency, Managing for Equity', *Harvard Business Review* 61(4), pp.83–90.

Boyd, C. and Boyd, P. (1995) 'The School Context for Curriculum Change'. In Ashcroft, K. and Palacio, D. (eds), *The Primary Teacher's Guide to the New National Curriculum*. London: Falmer Press.

Bridges, D. (1981) 'Accountability, Communication and Control'. In Elliott, J., Bridger, D., Ebbutt, D., Gibson, R. and Nias, J. (eds), *School Accountability*. London: Grant McIntyre.

Brighouse, T. (1991) *What Makes a Good School?* Stratford: Network Educational Press.

Brighouse, T. and Moon, B. (eds) (1990) *Managing the National Curriculum: Some critical perspectives*. Harlow: Longman.

British Standards (1987) *Principal Concepts and Applications*, Part O. London: BSJ.

Broadbent, L. (1995) 'Making Sense of the Spiritual and Moral'. In Inman, S. and Buck, M. (eds), *Adding Value? Schools' responsibility for pupils' personal development*. Stoke-on-Trent: Trentham Brooks.

Broadfoot, P., Pollard, A., Croll, P., Osborn, M. and Abbott, D. (1994) *National Assessment: Who calls the shots?* Paper presented at AERA Conference, New Orleans.

Brochmann, F. (1989) 'Program Budgeting: Implications for secondary principals'. In Levacic, R. (ed.), *Financial Management in Education*. Milton Keynes: Open University Press.

Brown, G. (1995) 'What's Involved in Learning?'. In Desforges, C. (ed.), *An Introduction to Teaching*. Oxford: Basil Blackwell.

Brown, M. and Rutherford, D. (1996) *Leadership for School Improvement: The changing role of the head of department*. Paper presented at the British Educational Management and Administration Society Research Conference, 25–7 March, Robinson College, Cambridge.

Bruner, J. (1986) *Actual Minds, Possible Worlds*. Cambridge, MA: Harvard University Press.

Burke, H. (1995) 'Equal Opportunities and Personal Development'. In Inman, S. and Buck, M. (eds), *Adding Value? Schools' responsibility for pupils' personal development*. Stoke-on-Trent: Trentham Brooks.

Bush, T. and Middlewood, D. (eds) (1997) *Managing People in Education*. London: Paul Chapman Publishing.

Busher, H. and Hodgkinson, K. (1997) 'Managing the Curriculum and Assessment'. In Fidler, B., Russell, S. and Simkins, T. (eds), *Choices for Self Managing Schools*. London: Paul Chapman Publishing.

Calderhead, J. (1987) *Exploring Teachers' Thinking*. London: Cassell.

Calderhead, J. (1994) 'Teaching as a "Professional" Activity'. In Moon, B. and Shelton Mayes, A. (eds), *Teaching and Learning in the Secondary School*. London: Routledge.

Campbell, R.J. (1985) *Developing the Primary School Curriculum*. London: Holt, Rinehart & Winston.

Canterbury Christ Church University College (1998) *Information Communication Technology in Subject Teaching*. Canterbury: CCCUC.

Capel, S. (1995) 'Motivating Pupils'. In Capel, S., Leask, M. and Turner, T. (1995) *Learning to Teach in the Secondary School*. London: Routledge.

Capel, S., Leask, M. and Turner, T. (1995) *Learning to Teach in the Secondary School*. London: Routledge.

Cardno, C. (1998) 'Working Together: Managing strategy collaboratively'. In Middlewood, D. and Lumby, J. (eds), *Strategic Management in Schools and Colleges*. London: Paul Chapman Publishing.

Carlsen, W. (1991) 'Subject Matter Knowledge and Science Teaching: A pragmatic perspective'. In Brophy, J. (ed.), *Advances in Research on Teaching*, vol. 2. Greenwich, CT: JAI Press.

Carré, C. (1995) 'What is to be Learned in School?'. In Desforges, C. (ed.), *An Introduction to Teaching*. Oxford: Basil Blackwell.

Child, D. (1973) *Psychology and the Teacher*, 1st edition. London: Holt, Rinehart & Winston.

Child, D. (1986) *Psychology and the Teacher*, 4th edition. London: Cassell.

Citizens Charter (1999) www.servicefirst.gov.uk/index/inthouse.htm

Claxton, G. (1988) 'Teaching and Learning'. In Dale, R., Fergusson, R. and Robinson, A. (eds), *Frameworks for Teaching: Readings for the intending secondary teacher*. London: Hodder & Stoughton.

Clerkin, C. (1994) 'Preparing Job Descriptions: The head's role'. In Spear, C.E. (ed.), *Primary Management and Leadership Towards 2000*. London: Longman.

Cockburn, A. (1995) 'Learning in Classrooms'. In Desforges, C. (ed.), *An Introduction to Teaching*. Oxford: Basil Blackwell.

Cockcroft (1982) *Mathematics Count*. London: HMSO.

Coleman, M. and Bush, T. (1994) 'Managing with Teams'. In Bush, T. and West-Burnham, J. (eds), *The Principles of Educational Management*. Harlow: Longman.

Coopers and Lybrand (1988) *A Report to the Department of Education and Science*. London: DES.

Coulby, D. (1996) 'The Construction and Implementation of the Primary Core Curriculum'. In Coulby, D. and Ward, S., *The Primary Core National Curriculum: Policy into practice*, 2nd edition. London: Cassell.

Cowan, B. and Wright, N. (1990) 'Two Million Days Lost', *Education* 2(February).

Dale, R., Fergusson, R. and Robinson, A. (eds) (1988) *Frameworks for Teaching: Readings for the intending secondary teacher*. London: Hodder & Stoughton.

Davies, J. (ed.) (1995) *Developing a Leadership Role in Key Stage 1 Curriculum*. London: Falmer Press.

Day, C., Hall, C., Gammage, P. and Coles, M. (1993) *Leadership and Curriculum in the Primary School: Roles of senior and middle management*. London: Paul Chapman Publishing.

Day, C., Hall, C. and Whitaker, P. (1998) *Developing Leadership in Primary Schools*. London: Paul Chapman Publishing.

Day, C., Whitaker P. and Wren, J. (1987) *Appraisal and Professional Development in Primary Schools*. Milton Keynes: Open University Press.

Day, C., Whitaker, P. and Johnston, D. (1990) *Managing Primary Schools in the 1990s*. London: Paul Chapman Publishing.

Dean, J. (1991) *Professional Development in School*. Milton Keynes: Open University Press.

Dearing, R. (1994) *The National Curriculum and its Assessment*. London: SCAA.

Dennison, W.F. and Shenton, K. (1987) *Challenges in Educational Management: Principles into practice*. Beckenham: Croom Helm.

DES (1972) *Education: A framework for expansion*. London: HMSO.

DES (1978) *Primary Education in England*. London: HMSO.

DES (1979) *Aspects of Secondary Education in England: A survey by HM Inspectors of Schools*. London: HMSO.

DES (1982) *Education 5 to 9*. London: HMSO.

DES (1985a) *Swann Committee Report.* London: HMSO.

DES (1985b) *Better Schools.* London: HMSO.

DES (1988a) *National Curriculum Task Group on Assessment and Testing: A report (The TGAT Report).* London: HMSO.

DES (1988b) *Education Reform Act.* London: HMSO.

DES (1989a) *National Curriculum: From policy to practice.* London: HMSO.

DES (1989b) *Planning for School Development: Advice for governors, headteachers and teachers.* London: HMSO.

DES (1989c) *The Report of the Records of Achievement Steering Committee.* London: HMSO.

DES (1991) *Development Planning: A practical guide.* London: HMSO.

Desforges, C. (ed.) (1995) *An Introduction to Teaching.* Oxford: Basil Blackwell.

DFE (1994) *Code of Practice on the Identification and Assessment of Special Educational Needs.* London: HMSO.

DfEE (1997a) *Excellence for all Children: Meeting Special Educational Needs.* London: The Stationery Office.

DfEE (1997b) *The Implementation of the National Literacy Strategy.* London: The Stationery Office.

DfEE (1998a) *Teachers: Meeting the challenge of change,* Green Paper. London: The Stationery Office.

DfEE (1998b) *Teaching: High status, high standards,* Circular 4/98. London: HMSO.

DfEE (1998c) *The Implementation of the National Numeracy Strategy.* London: The Stationery Office.

DfEE (1999a) *All Our Futures: Creativity, culture and education.* London: The Stationery Office.

DfEE (1999b) *National College for School Leadership: A prospectus.* London: DfEE.

Driver, R. and Bell, B. (1986) 'Students' Thinking and Learning of Science: A constructivist view', *School Science Review* 67(240), pp.443–56.

Drucker, P.F. (1968) *The Practice of Management.* New York: Pan Books.

Duffy, M. (1990) 'A View from a Secondary School'. In Brighouse, T. and Moon, B. (eds), *Managing the National Curriculum: Some critical perspectives.* Harlow: Longman.

Earley, P. (1998) 'Middle Management: The key to organisational success?' In Middlewood, D. and Lumby, J. (eds), *Strategic Management in Schools and Colleges.* London: Paul Chapman Publishing.

Earley, P. and Fletcher-Campbell, F. (1992) 'How are Decisions made in Departments and Schools'. In Bennett, N., Crawford, M. and Riches, C. (eds), *Managing Change in Education: Individual and organisational perspectives.* London: Paul Chapman Publishing.

Easen, P. (1985) *Making School-Centred INSET Work: A school of education pack for teachers.* London: Croom Helm.

Edward, K.B. (1986) *Developing Management in Schools.* London: Blackwell.

Elliot, J. (1978) *Who Should Monitor Performance in Schools?* Unpublished mimeo, Cambridge Institute of Education.

Elliott, J. (1981) 'Teachers' Perspectives on School Accountability'. In Elliott, J., Bridger, D., Ebbutt, D., Gibson, R. and Nias, J. (eds), *School Accountability.* London: Grant McIntyre.

Elliott, J., Bridges, D., Ebbutt, D., Gibson, R. and Nias, J. (eds) (1981) *School Accountability.* London: Grant McIntyre.

Elmore, R. (1979) 'Backward Mapping: Implementation, research and policy decisions', *Political Science Quarterly*.

Emerson, C. and Goddard, T. (1989) *All About the National Curriculum: What you need to know, why you need to know it*. Oxford: Heinemann.

Evans, L., Humphries, T., Williams, G. and Williams, M. (1996) *Information Technology in the Primary School*. Cambridge: Pearson Publishing.

Everard, B. and Morris, G. (1990) *Effective School Management*, 2nd edition. London: Paul Chapman Publishing.

Everard, B. and Morris, G. (1996) *Effective School Management*, 3rd edition. London: Harper & Row.

Everard, K.B. (1986) *Developing Management in Schools*. London: Basil Blackwell.

Farrell, P. (1997) *Teaching Pupils with Learning Difficulties: Strategies and solutions*. London: Cassell.

Fidler, B. (1996) *Strategic Planning for School Improvement*. London: Financial Times Management.

Fidler, B., Russell, S. and Simkins, T. (eds) (1997) *Choices for Self Managing Schools*. London: Paul Chapman Publishing.

Fisher, R. (1990) *Teaching Children to Think*. Oxford: Blackwell.

Fitz-Gibbon, C. (1989) 'Using Performance Indicators: Educational considerations'. In Levacic, R. (ed.), *Financial Management in Education*. Milton Keynes: Open University Press.

Floyd, S. and Wooldridge, B. (1996) *The Strategic Middle Manager*. New York: Jossey Bass.

Foreman, K. (1998) 'Vision and Mission'. In Middlewood, D., and Lumby, J. (eds), *Strategic Management in Schools and Colleges*. London: Paul Chapman Publishing.

Foskett, N. (ed.) (1992) *Managing External Relations in Schools*. London: Routledge.

Fowler, W.S. (1990) *Implementing the National Curriculum: The policy and practice of the 1988 Education Reform Act*. London: Kogan Page.

Freeman, R. (1993) *Quality Assurance in Training and Education: How to apply BS5750 (ISO 9000) Standards*. London: Kogan Page.

Fullan, M. and Hargreaves, A. (1998) *What's Worth Fighting for in Your School?* Buckingham: Open University Press.

Gagné, R. (1977) *The Conditions of Learning*, 3rd edition. New York: Holt, Rinehart & Winston.

Galloway, D., Rogers, C., Armstrong, D. and Leo, E. (1998) *Motivating the Difficult to Teach*. London: Longman.

Galton, M. and Patrick, H. (eds) (1990) *Curriculum Provision in the Small Primary School*. London: Routledge.

Gardner, H. (1983) *Frames of Mind: The theory of multiple intelligences*. London: Harper Collins.

Gipps, C. (1993) 'The Structure for Assessment and Recording'. In O'Hear, P. and White, J. (eds), *Assessing the National Curriculum*. London: Paul Chapman Publishing.

Gipps, C. (1994) 'Quality in Teacher Assessment'. In Harlen, W. (ed.), *Enhancing Quality in Assessment*. BERA: Paul Chapman Publishing.

Goddard, D. and Leask, M. (1992) *The Search for Quality: Planning for improvement and managing change*. London: Paul Chapman Publishing.

Goleman, D. (1995) *Emotional Intelligence*. London: Bloomsbury.

Gorman, M. (1994) 'Education for Citizenship'. In Verma, G.K. and Pumfrey, P.D. (eds), *Cross-Curricular Contexts, Themes and Dimensions in Primary Schools*. London: Falmer Press.

Goulding, S., Bell, J., Bush, T., Fox, A. and Goodey, G. (eds) (1984) *Case Studies in Educational Management*. London: Harper & Row.

Grace, G. (1997) *School Leadership: Beyond education management*. London: Falmer Press.

Gray, H.L. (ed.) (1988) *Management Consultancy in Schools*. London: Cassell Educational.

Gross, J. (1993) *Special Educational Needs in the Primary School: A practical guide*. Buckingham: Open University Press.

Gulliford, R. (1985) 'The Teacher's Own Resources'. In Smith, C. (ed.), *New Directions in Remedial Education*. Brighton: Falmer Press

Guthrie, J. (1984) *Effective Educational Executives: An essay on the concept of strategic leadership*. In Goulding, S., Bell, J., Bush, T., Fox, A. and Goodey, G. (eds), *Case Studies in Educational Management*. London: Harper & Row.

Hadow, W.W. (1931) *Report on Primary Education*. London: HMSO.

Hall, D.T. (1996) *The Career is Dead – Long Live the Career*. New York: Jossey Bass.

Hall, G. (ed.) (1992) *Themes and Dimensions of the National Curriculum: Implications for policy and practice*. London: Kogan Page.

Hall, V. (1998) 'Strategic Leadership in Education: Becoming, being, doing'. In Middlewood, D. and Lumby, J. (eds), *Strategic Management in Schools and Colleges*. London: Paul Chapman Publishing.

Hallinger, P. and Heck, R. (1998) *Can Leadership Enhance School Effectiveness?* Paper presented to Third Annual ESRC Seminar on Redefining School Management. Milton Keynes.

Handy, C. (1984) *Understanding Organisations*, 1st edition. Harmondsworth: Penguin.

Handy, C. (1989) *Age of Unreason*. London: Hutchinson.

Handy, C. (1993) *Understanding Organisations*, 4th edition. Harmondsworth: Penguin.

Hanko, G. (1990) *Special Needs in Ordinary Classrooms: Supporting teachers*. Hemel Hempstead: Schuster Education.

Hardie, B. (1995) *Evaluating the Primary School*. Plymouth: Northcote House.

Hardie, B. (1998) 'Managing, Monitoring and Evaluation'. In Middlewood, D. and Lumby, J. (eds), *Strategic Management in Schools and Colleges*. London: Paul Chapman Publishing.

Hargreaves, D. (1992) *The New Professionalism: The synthesis of professional and institutional development*. Keynote paper presented at Fourth International Symposium: *Effective Teachers, Effective Schools*. University of New England, NSW, Australia.

Hargreaves, D. and Hopkins, D. (1991) *The Empowered School: The management and practice of development planning*. London: Cassell.

Harris, A., Jamieson, I. and Russ, J. (1996) *School Effectiveness and School Improvement: A practical guide*. London: Pitman.

Harris, A., Jamieson, I. and Russ, J. (1997) 'A Study of "Effective" Departments in Secondary Schools'. In Harris, A., Bennett, N. and Preedy, M. (eds), *Organizational Effectiveness and Improvement in Education*. Buckingham: Open University Press.

Harris, T.A. (1995) *I'm OK, You're OK*. London: Arrow Books.

Harrison, M. (ed.) (1995a) *Developing a Leadership Role in Key Stage 2 Curriculum*. London: Falmer Press.

Harrison, M. (1995b) 'Developing Skills to Become an Effective Key Stage 1 Subject Co-ordinator'. In Davies, J. (ed.), *Developing a Leadership Role in Key Stage 1 Curriculum*. London: Falmer Press.

Harrison, M. and Rainey, D. (1994) 'Economic and Industrial Understanding'. In Verma, G.K. and Pumfrey, P.D. (eds), *Cross-Curricular Contexts, Themes and Dimensions in Primary Schools*. London: Falmer Press.

Harrison, S. and Theaker, K. (1989) *Curriculum Leadership and Co-ordinators in the Primary School: A handbook for teachers*. Whalby: Guild House Press.

Hashweh, M. (1987) 'Effects of Subject Matter Knowledge in Teaching Biology and Physics', *Teacher and Teacher Education: An international journal of research and studies* 3(2), pp.109–20.

Herzberg, F.W., Mausner, B. and Snyderman, B. (1959) *The Motivation to Work*, 2nd edition. London: Chapman & Hall.

Hewley, M. (1990) 'Fitting the National Curriculum to One's Own Principles'. In Brighouse, T. and Moon, B. (eds), *Managing the National Curriculum: Some critical perspectives*. Harlow: Longman.

Hewton, E. (1988) *School Focused Staff Development*. Lewes: Lewes Press.

Hicks, D. (1995) *Future Education: Citizenship for today and tomorrow*. In Inman, S. and Buck, M. (eds), *Adding Value? Schools' responsibility for pupils' personal development*. Stoke-on-Trent: Trentham Brooks.

Hirst, P. (1993) 'The Foundations of the National Curriculum: Why subjects?'. In O'Hear, P. and White, J. (eds), *Assessing the National Curriculum*. London: Paul Chapman Publishing.

Hirst, P.H. (1974) *Knowledge and the Curriculum*. London: Routledge & Kegan Paul.

HM Treasury (1988) *The Government's Expenditure Plans 1988–89 to 1990–91*. London: HMSO.

HMI (1984) *Departmental Organisation in Secondary Schools*, HMI (Wales) Occasional Paper. Cardiff: Welsh Office.

HMI (1988) *The Annual Report of HM Senior Chief Inspector for Schools 1987/88*. London: HMI.

HMI (1991) *The Implementation of the Curricular Requirements of the ERA: An overview by HM Inspectorate in the first year 1989/90*. London: HMSO.

Hodgkinson, C. (1983) *The Philosophy of Leadership*. Oxford: Basil Blackwell.

Holbeche, L. (1998) *Motivating People in Learning Organisations*. Oxford: Butterworth/Heinemann.

Honey, P. and Mumford, A. (1983) *Manual of Learning Styles*. Maidenhead: Honey.

Hopkins, D. (1989) *Evaluation for School Improvement*. Milton Keynes: Open University Press.

Hopkins, D. (1995) *Unravelling the Complexities of School Improvement*. Unpublished paper presented to Secondary Heads Association (SHA) President's Inaugural Conference, University of Cambridge.

Hopkins, D., Ainscow, M. and West, M. (1994) *School Improvement in an Era of Change*. London: Cassell.

Hornby, G., Davis, G. and Taylor, G. (1995) *The Special Educational Needs Co-ordinator's Handbook: A guide for implementing the Code of Practice*. London: Routledge.

Howell, K.W., Fox, S.L. and Morehead, M.K. (1993) *Curriculum-Based Evaluation*. London: Brooks/Cole.

Hoyle, E. and Jones, K. (1995) *Professional Knowledge and Professional Practice*. London: Cassell.

Huberman, M. (1988) 'Teacher Careers and School Improvement', *Journal of Curriculum Studies* 20(2), pp.119–32.

Huberman, M. (1992) 'Teacher Development and Instruction in Schools'. In Hargreaves, A. and Fullan, M. (eds), *Understanding Teacher Development*. London: Cassell.

Huczynski, A. and Buchanan, D. (1991) *Organizational Behaviour: An introductory text*. New York: Prentice Hall.

Hughes, M., Ribbins, P. and Thomas, H. (eds) (1985) *Managing Education: The system and the institution*. Eastbourne: Holt, Rinehart & Winston.

Hull, J. (1994) *Assessment and Record Keeping for Special Educational Needs in Schools: Staff development package*. Stafford: NASEN.

Hulme, G. (1989) 'Performance Evaluation and Performance Indicators for Schools'. In Levacic, R. (ed.), *Financial Management in Education*. Milton Keynes: Open University Press.

Illich, I. (1972) *De-Schooling Society*. New York: Harper Books.

Inman, S. and Buck, M. (eds) (1995) *Adding Value? Schools' responsibility for pupils' personal development*. Stoke-on-Trent: Trentham Brooks.

Jackson, P. (1994) 'Life in Classrooms'. In Moon, B. and Shelton Mayes, A. (eds), *Teaching and Learning in the Secondary School*. London: Routledge.

Jayne, E. (1998) 'Effective School Development Planning'. In Middlewood, D. and Lumby, J. (eds), *Strategic Management in Schools and Colleges*. London: Paul Chapman Publishing.

Jones, D. (1989) 'A Practical Unit Cost Approach to Budgeting and Accountability in Colleges'. In Levacic, R. (ed.), *Financial Management in Education*. Milton Keynes: Open University Press.

Jones, S. (1996) *Developing a Learning Culture*. London: McGraw-Hill.

Joyce, B. and Showers, B. (1998) *Student Achievement through Staff Development: Fundamentals of school renewal*, 3rd edition. New York: Longman.

Kaufman, R. and Herman, J. (1991) *Strategic Planning in Education*. Pittsburg: Technomic Publishing.

Kelly, A.V. (1986) *Knowledge and Curriculum Planning*. London: Harper & Row.

Kent Curriculum Support Unit (1992) *Whole Curriculum Matters*. Sittingbourne: MSCST.

Knight, B. (1993) *Financial Management for School: The thinking manager's guide*. London: Heinemann.

Kohler, I. (1964) 'The Formation and Transformation of the Visual World', *Psychological Issues* 3, pp.121–47.

Kolb, D.A. (1983) *Experiential Learning: Experience as the source of learning and development*. New Jersey: Prentice Hall.

Kolb, D.A. (1985) *Experiential Learning: Experience as the source of learning and development*. New York: Prentice Hall.

Kyriacou, C. (1986) *Effective Teaching in Schools*. Hemel Hempstead: Simon & Schuster.

Lawton, D. (1983) *Curriculum Studies and Educational Planning*. Sevenoaks: Hodder & Stoughton.

Lawton, D. (1989) *Culture and the National Curriculum*. London: Hodder & Stoughton.

Leask, M. (1995a) 'Improving Your Teaching: An introduction to action research and reflective practice'. In Capel, S., Leask, M. and Turner, T., *Learning to Teach in the Secondary School*. London: Routledge.

Leask, M. (1995b) 'Teaching Styles'. In Capel, S., Leask, M. and Turner, T., *Learning to Teach in the Secondary School*. London: Routledge.

Lee, D. (1996) *TVEI and Curriculum Theory*. Bishops Norton: David Lee and Humberside Education Services.

Leigh, A. (1994) 'Change and Leadership'. In Bennet, N., Glatter, R. and Levacic, R., *Improving Educational Management through Research and Consultancy*. London: Paul Chapman Publishing.

Levacic, R. (1989a) 'Financial Management in Education: An emerging function'. In Levacic, R. (ed.), *Financial Management in Education*. Milton Keynes: Open University Press.

Levacic, R. (1989b) 'Managing a Delegated Budget: Three schools' experience'. In Levacic, R. (ed.), *Financial Management in Education*. Milton Keynes: Open University Press.

Levacic, R. (1989c) 'Formula Funding for Schools and Colleges'. In Levacic, R. (ed.), *Financial Management in Education*. Milton Keynes: Open University Press.

Levacic, R. (1989d) 'Financial Management in Education: An emerging function'. In Levacic, R. (ed.), *Financial Management in Education*. Milton Keynes: Open University Press.

Levacic, R. (ed.) (1989e) *Financial Management in Education*. Milton Keynes: Open University Press.

Levacic, R. and Glover, D. (1996) 'The Limits of Managerialism', *Managing Schools Today* February.

Lewis, A. (1991) *Primary Special Needs and the National Curriculum*. London: Routledge.

Likert, R. (1961) *New Patterns of Management*. New York: McGraw-Hill.

Lindsay, G. (1993) 'Baseline Assessment and Special Needs'. In Wolfendale, S. (ed.), *Assessing Special Educational Needs*. London: Cassell.

Lindsay, G. and Desforges, M. (1998) *Baseline Assessment Practice, Problems and Possibilities*. London: David Fulton Publishers.

Lynch, J. (1992) *Education for Citizenship in a Multi-cultural Society*. London: Cassell.

MacBeath, J. (1998) *Effective School Leadership*. London: Paul Chapman Publishing.

McClelland, D. (1987) *Human Motivation*. Cambridge: Cambridge University Press.

McCormick, R. and James, M. (1982) *Curriculum Evaluation in Schools*. London: Croom Helm.

MacGilchrist, B., Mortimore, P., Savage, J. and Beresford, C. (1995) *Planning Matters*. London: Paul Chapman Publishing.

McGregor, D. (1987) *The Human Side of Enterprise*. London: Penguin.

Mallick, K. (1994) 'Personal and Social Education'. In Verma, G.K. and Pumfrey, P.D. (eds), *Cross-Curricular Contexts, Themes and Dimensions in Primary Schools*. London: Falmer Press.

Manpower Services Commission (1985) *Arrangements for the TVEI Related In-Service Training Scheme (England and Wales)*. London: MSC.

Marland, M. (1976) *The Craft of the Classroom: A survival guide*. London: Heinemann Educational Press.

Maslow, A.H. (1943) 'A Theory of Human Motivation'. In Vroom, V. and Deci, E. (eds) (1970), *Management and Motivation*. Harmondsworth: Penguin.

Maslow, A.H. (1970) *Motivation and Personality*, 2nd edition. New York: Harper & Row.

Merttens, R. and Vaas, J. (1991) 'Assessing the Nation: Blueprints without tools', *Primary Teaching Studies* 5(3), pp.222–39.

Meyerson, D. and Martin, J. (1997) 'Cultural Change: In integration of three different views'. In Harris, A., Bennett, N. and Preedy, M. (eds), *Organizational Effectiveness and Improvement in Education*. Buckingham: Open University Press.

Middlewood, D. (1998) 'Strategic Management in Education in an Overview'. In Middlewood, D. and Lumby, J. (eds), *Strategic Management in Schools and Colleges*. London: Paul Chapman Publishing.

Middlewood, D. and Lumby, J. (eds) (1998) *Strategic Management in Schools and Colleges*. London: Paul Chapman Publishing.

Minstrell, J. and Stimpson, V. (1996) 'A Classroom Environment for Learning: Guiding students' reconstruction of understanding and reasoning'. In Schauble, L. and Glaser, R. (eds), *Innovations in Learning: New environments for learning*. New Jersey: Lawrence Erlbaum Associates.

Mintzberg, H. (1973) *The Nature of Managerial Work*. London: Harper & Row.

Mintzberg, H. and Quinn, J. (1991) *The Strategy Process: Concepts, contexts and cases*. London: Prentice Hall.

Moon, B. and Shelton Mayes, A. (eds) (1994) *Teaching and Learning in the Secondary School*. London: Routledge.

Morant, R. (1981) *In-Service Education within the School*. London: Unwin Education.

Morrison and Ridley (1989) in Preedy, M. (1989) *Approaches to Curriculum Management*. Milton Keynes: Open University Press.

Morrison, K. (1998) *Management Theories for Education and Change*. London: Paul Chapman Publishing.

Mortimore, P., Sammons, P., Stoll, L., Lewis, D. and Ecob, R. (1988) *School Matters: The junior years*. London: Open Books.

Mortimore, P., Sammons, P., Stoll, L., Lewis, D. and Ecob, R. (1994) 'Teacher Expectations'. In Moon, B. and Shelton Mayes, A. (eds), *Teaching and Learning in the Secondary School*. London: Routledge.

Mosston, M. and Ashworth, S. (1986) *Teaching Physical Education*, 3rd edition. Columbus: Merrill Publishing.

Mullins, L.J. (1996) *Management and Organisational Behaviour*. London: Pitman Publishing.

Murphy, P., Selinger, M., Bourne, J. and Briggs, M. (eds) (1995) *Subject Learning in the Primary Curriculum*. London: Routledge.

NARE (1990) *Curriculum Access for All: A SEN training pack for staff development*. Stafford: NARE.

Nasta, T. (1994) *How to Design a Vocational Curriculum*. London: Kogan Page.

National Commission on Education (1993) *Learning to Succeed*. London: Heinemann.

NCC (1989a) *A Framework for the National Curriculum*. York: NCC.

NCC (1989b) *A Curriculum for All*. York: NCC.

NCC (1989c) *Curriculum Guidance 1: A Framework for the Primary Curriculum*. York: NCC.

NCC (1990a) *Curriculum Guidance 3: The Whole Curriculum*. York: NCC.

NCC (1990b) *Education for Economic and Industrial Understanding*. York: NCC.

NCC (1990c) *Health Education*. York: NCC.

NCC (1990d) *Careers Education and Guidance*. York: NCC.

NCC (1990e) *Environmental Education*. York: NCC.

NCC (1990f) *Education for Citizenship*. York: NCC.

NCC (1991) *EIU Work Experience and the School Curriculum*. York: NCC.

NCC (1992a) *The National Curriculum and Pupils with Severe Learning Difficulties*. York: NCC.

NCC (1992b) *Starting Out with the National Curriculum*. York: NCC.

Newsom, J. (1963) *Half Our Future: Report of the Minister of Education's Central Advisory Council*. London: HMSO.

Newson, E. (1993) 'Play-based Assessment in the Special Needs Classroom'. In Harris, J. (ed.), *Innovations in Educating Children with Severe Learning Difficulties*. Chorley: Lisieux Hall Press.

NGFL (1997) *Connecting to the Learning Society*. London: NGFL.

Nias, J. (1980) 'Leadership Styles and Job Satisfaction in Primary Schools'. In Bush, T. (ed.), *Approaches to School Management*. London: Harper & Row.

Nias, J., Southworth, G. and Campbell, P. (1992) *Whole School Curriculum Development in the Primary School*. London: Falmer Press.

Nicholls, G. (1995) 'Ways Pupils Learn'. In Capel, S., Leask, M. and Turner, T., *Learning to Teach in the Secondary School*. London: Routledge.

Nixon, J. (1992) *Evaluating the Whole Curriculum*. Milton Keynes: Open University Press.

Nixon, J., Martin, J., McKeown, P. and Ranson, S. (1996) *Encouraging Learning: Towards a theory of the learning school*. Buckingham: Open University Press.

O'Hear, P. (1993) 'Coherence in Curriculum Planning'. In O'Hear, P. and White, J. (eds), *Assessing the National Curriculum*. London: Paul Chapman Publishing.

O'Neill, J. (1997) 'Managing through Teams'. In Bush, T. and Middlewood, D. (eds), *Managing People in Education*. London: Paul Chapman Publishing.

O'Neill, J. and Kitson, N. (eds) (1996) *Effective Curriculum Management: Co-ordinating learning in the primary school*. London: Routledge.

OfSTED (1993a) *The OfSTED Handbook: Guidance on the inspection of secondary schools*. London: OfSTED.

OfSTED (1993b) *Working Paper for the Inspection of Secondary Initial Teacher Training*. London: Office of HM's Chief Inspector.

OfSTED (1994) *Primary Matters: A discussion on teaching and learning in primary schools*. London: OfSTED.

OfSTED (1995a) *Guidance on the Inspection of Nursery and Primary Schools*. London: HMSO.

OfSTED (1995b) *Guidance on the Inspection of Secondary Schools*. London: HMSO.

OfSTED (1996) *The Implementation of the Code of Practice: A report by OfSTED*. London: HMSO.

OfSTED (1998) *The Annual Report of Her Majesty's Chief Inspector*. London: OfSTED.

Oldroyd, D. and Hall, V. (1988) *Managing Professional Development and INSET*. Bristol: NDCSMT.

Oldroyd, D. and Hall, V. (1991) *Managing Staff Development: A handbook for secondary schools*. London: Paul Chapman Publishing.

Orr, D. (1992) *Ecological Literacy: Education and the transition to a post-modern world*. New York: Albany State University NY Press.

Osborn, R.L. (1972) 'Paradox in the American Classroom', *Aspects of Education* 14, pp.12–17.

Øvretreit, J. (1992) *Health Service Quality*. Oxford: Blackwell.

Pachler, N. and Field, K. (1997) *Learning to Teach MFLS in the Secondary School*. London: Routledge.

Packwood, T. (1984) 'The Introduction of Staff Responsibility for Subject Development in a Junior School'. In Goulding, S., Bell, J., Bush, T., Fox, A. and Goodey, G. (eds), *Case Studies in Educational Management*. London: Harper & Row.

Paisey, A. (1984) *School Management: A case approach*. London: Paul Chapman Publishing.

Parsons, C. (1994a) 'The Politics and Practice of Quality'. In Parsons, C. (ed.), *Quality Improvement in Education*. London: David Fulton Publishers.

Parsons, C. (ed.) (1994b) *Quality Improvement in Education*, London: David Fulton Publishers.

Patterson, J., Purkey, S. and Parker, J. (1986) *Productive School Systems for a Non-Rational World*. Alexandria, VA: Association for Supervision and Curriculum Development.

Pedler, M., Burgoyne, J. and Boydell, T. (1978) *A Manager's Guide to Self-Development*. London: McGraw-Hill.

Peeke, G. (1994) *Mission and Change: Institutional mission and its application in the management of further and higher education*. Buckingham: SRHE/Open University Press.

Peters, T.J. and Waterman, R.H., Jnr (1982) *In Search of Excellence*. London: Harper & Row.

Plackett, E. (1995) 'Reading, Identity and Personal Development'. In Inman, S. and Buck, M. (eds), *Adding Value? Schools' responsibility for pupils' personal development*. Stoke-on-Trent: Trentham Brooks.

Plowden, A. (1967) *Report on Children and their Primary Schools*. London: HMSO.

Poole, P. (ed.) (1998) *Talking About Information Communication Technology in Subject Teaching*. Canterbury: CCCUC.

Pumphrey, P. (1994) 'Cross-Curricular Elements and the Curriculum: Contexts, challenges and responses'. In Verma, G.K. and Pumphrey, P.D. (eds), *Cultural Diversity and the Curriculum*, vol 4, *Cross-Curricular Contexts, Themes and Dimensions in Primary Schools*. London: Falmer Press.

QCA (1999a) *Framework for Personal Social and Health Education and Citizenship at Key Stages 1–4*. London: QCA.

QCA (1999b) *National Curriculum Review Consultation*. London: QCA.

QCA and Crick, B. (1998) *Education for Citizenship and the Teaching of Democracy in Schools: Final report of the Citizenship Advisory Group (The Crick Report)*. London: QCA.

Quinn, J.B. (1980) *Strategies for Change: Logical incrementalism*. Homewood, IL: Irwin.

Rainey, D. (1994) 'The European Dimension'. In Verma, G.K. and Pumfrey, P.D. (eds), *Cross-Curricular Contexts, Themes and Dimensions in Primary Schools*. London: Falmer Press.

Reason, R. (1993) 'Primary Special Needs and National Curriculum Assessment'. In Wolfendale, S. (ed.), *Assessing Special Educational Needs*. London: Cassell.

Ribbins, P. (1985) 'The Role of the Middle Manager in the Secondary School'. In Hughes, M., Ribbins, P. and Thomas, H. (eds), *Managing Education: The system and the institution*. Eastbourne: Holt, Rinehart & Winston.

Ribbins, P., Glatter, R., Simkins, T. and Watson, L. (1991) *Developing Educational Leaders*. London: Longman.

Richardson, R. (1992) 'Identities and Justice: Themes and concerns in education for citizenship', *Journal of Moral Education* 21(3).

Riches, C. (1997) 'Managing for People and Performance'. In Bush, T. and Middlewood, D. (eds), *Managing People in Education*. London: Paul Chapman Publishing.

Riley, K. (1994) *Quality and Equality*. London: Cassell.

Robinson, K. (1999) 'Creating Room for Creativity', *Times Educational Supplement*, 21 May.

Rogers, A. (1996) *Teaching Adults*. Buckingham: Open University Press.

Rogers, C. (1983) *Freedom to Learn for the 80s*. Columbus: Merrill Publishing.

Russell, S. and Reid, S. (1997) 'Managing Evaluation'. In Fidler, B., Russell, S. and Simkins, T. (eds), *Choices for Self Managing Schools*. London: Paul Chapman Publishing.

Sackman, S.A. (1992) 'Culture and Sub-cultures: An analysis of organisational knowledge', *Administrative Quarterly* 37, pp.140–61.

Sammons, P., Hillman, J. and Mortimore, P. (1995) *Key Characteristics of Effective Schools: A review of school-effectiveness research*. London: OfSTED.

Sayer, J. (1987) *Special Needs in Ordinary Secondary Schools for All? Strategies for Special Needs*. London: Cassell.

Sayer, J. (1988) 'Identifying the Issues'. In Gray, H.L. (ed.), *Management Consultancy in Schools*. London: Cassell Educational.

Sayer, J. (1989) *Managing Schools*. London: Hodder & Stoughton.

SCAA (1995) *Planning the Curriculum at Key Stages 1 and 2*. London: HMSO.

SCAA (1996) *Supporting Pupils with Special Educational Needs: Key Stage 3*. London: SCAA.

SCDC (1987) *Curriculum at the Crossroads*. London: SCDC.

Schauble, L. and Glaser, R. (eds) (1996) *Innovations in Learning: New environments for learning*. New Jersey: Lawrence Erlbaum Associates.

Schein, E.H. (1985) *Organisational Culture and Leadership: A dynamic view*. San Francisco: Jossey Bass.

Scott, C. and Jaffe, D. (1989) *Managing Organisational Change*. London: Kogan Page.

Senge, P. (1990) *The Fifth Discipline*. New York: Doubleday.

Sergiovanni, T.J. (1995) *The Principalship: A reflective practice perspective*. London: Allyn & Bacon.

Shipman, M. (1979) *In-School Evaluation*. London: Heinemann.

Shorrocks, D. (1993) 'National Curriculum Assessment in England and Wales'. In Shorrocks, D., Frobisher, L., Nelson, N., Turner, L. and Waterson, A., *National Curriculum Assessment: The primary school*. London: Hodder & Stoughton.

Shorrocks, D., Frobisher, L., Nelson, N., Turner, L. and Waterson, A. (1993) *National Curriculum Assessment: The primary school*. London: Hodder & Stoughton.

Shulman, L.S. (1994) 'Those Who Understand: Knowledge and growth in teaching'. In Moon, B. and Shelton Mayes, A. (eds), *Teaching and Learning in the Secondary School*. London: Routledge.

Simkins, T. (1989) 'Budgeting as a Political and Organisational Process in Educational Institutions'. In Levacic, R. (ed.), *Financial Management in Education*. Milton Keynes: Open University Press.

Skinner, B.F. (1968) *The Technology of Teaching*. New York: Appleton Century Crofts.

Smith, I. (1994) 'Environmental Education'. In Verma, G.K. and Pumfrey, P.D. (eds), *Cross-Curricular Contexts, Themes and Dimensions in Primary Schools*. London: Falmer Press.

Smyth (ed.) (1989) *Critical Perspectives on Educational Leadership*. Boston: Allyn & Bacon.

Southworth, G. (1998) *Leading Improving Primary Schools*. London: Falmer Press.

Stakes, R. and Hornby, G. (1997) *Change in Special Education: What brings it about?* London: Cassell.

Stoll, L. and Fink, L. (1996) *Changing our Schools*. Buckingham: Open University Press.

Stones, E. (1979) *Psychopedagogy: Psychological theory and the practice of teaching*. London: Methuen.

Sutcliffe, J. (1999) 'Put a Tiger in your GTC', *Times Educational Supplement* 21 May.

Tann, S. (1995) 'Organising Learning Experience'. In Desforges, C. (ed.), *An Introduction to Teaching*. Oxford: Basil Blackwell.

Tannenbaum, R. and Schmidt, W.H. (1973) 'How to Choose a Leadership Pattern', *Harvard Business Review* 36(2), pp.95–101.

Taylor, W. (1994) 'Classroom Variables'. In Moon, B. and Shelton Mayes, A. (eds), *Teaching and Learning in the Secondary School*. London: Routledge.

TES 13 September 1991.

Thody, A. (1993) *Developing Your Career in Educational Management*. London: Longman.

Thomas, G. (1995) *Primary School Deputies' Handbook*. London: Pitman Publishing.

Thomas, N. (1998) *The John Adair Handbook of Management and Leadership*. London: Thorogood.

Tizard, B. and Hughes, M. (1984) *Young Children Learning*. London: Fontana.

Tod, J., Castle, F. and Blamires, M. (1998) *Implementing Effective Practice*. London: David Fulton Publishers.

Tofte, B. (1996) 'A Theoretical Model for Implementation of Total Quality Leadership in Education', *Total Quality Management* 6, pp.469–86.

Troman, G. (1996) 'Models of the 'Good' Teacher: Defining and redefining teacher quality'. In Woods, P. (ed.), *Contemporary Issues in Teaching and Learning*. London: Routledge.

TTA (1998a) *National Standards for Subject Leaders*. London: TTA.

TTA (1998b) *Leadership Programme for Serving Headteachers* (application pack). London: TTA.

TTA (1998c) *National Standards for Headteachers*. London: TTA.

TTA (1998d) *Career Entry Profile*. London: TTA.

TTA (1998e) *National Standards for Special Educational Needs Co-ordinators*. London: TTA.

Tuckman, D.W. (1965) 'Development Sequence in Small Groups', *Psychological Bulletin* 63(6), pp.384–99.

Turner, T. (1995) 'Active Learning'. In Capel, S., Leask, M. and Turner, T., *Learning to Teach in the Secondary School*. London: Routledge.

Verma, G.K. and Pumfrey, P.D. (eds) (1994) *Cultural Diversity and the Curriculum*, vol. 4, *Cross-Curricular Contexts, Themes and Dimensions in Primary Schools*. London: Falmer Press.

Vroom, V. and Deci, E. (eds) (1970) *Management and Motivation*. Harmondsworth: Penguin.

Vytgotsky, L.S. (1978) *Mind and Society: The development of higher psychological processes.* Cambridge, MA: Harvard University Press.

Waddington, J. (1985) 'The School Curriculum in Contention: Content and control'. In Hughes, M., Ribbins, P. and Thomas, H. (eds), *Managing Education: The system and the institution.* Eastbourne: Holt, Rinehart & Winston.

Wallace, M. (1991) *School-Centred Management Training.* London: Paul Chapman Publishing.

Wallace, M. (1991) 'Flexible Planning: A key to the management of multiple innovations', *Educational Management and Administration* 19(3), pp.180–92.

Walsh, K. (1988) 'Appraising the Teachers: Professionalism and control'. In Dale, R., Fergusson, R. and Robinson, A. (eds), *Frameworks for Teaching: Readings for the intending secondary teacher.* London: Hodder & Stoughton.

Ware, J. (ed.) (1994) *Educating Children with Profound and Multiple Learning Difficulties.* London: David Fulton Publishers.

Warnock, M. (Chair) (1978) *Special Educational Needs: Report of the enquiry into the education of handicapped children and young people.* London: HMSO.

Waters, D. (1979) *Management and Headship in the Primary School.* London: Ward Lock.

Webb, R. (1994) *After the Deluge: Changing roles and responsibilities in the primary school.* York: ATL Publications.

Webb, R. and Vulliamy, G. (1996) *Roles and Responsibilities in the Primary School.* Buckingham: Open University Press.

Weindling, D. (1997) 'Strategic Planning for Schools: Some practical techniques'. In Preedy, M., Glatter, R. and Levacic, R. (eds), *Educational Management: Strategy, quality and resources.* Buckingham: Open University Press.

Wertheimer, M. (1945) *Productive Thinking.* New York: Harper Books.

West, M. and Ainscow, M. (1991) *Managing School Development: A practical guide.* London: David Fulton Publishers.

West, N. (1995) *Middle Management in the Primary School: A development guide for curriculum leaders, subject managers and senior staff.* London: David Fulton Publishers.

West, N. and Ainscow, M. (1991) *Managing School Development: A practical guide.* London: David Fulton Publishers.

West-Burnham, J. (1997) *Managing Quality in Schools,* 2nd edition. London: Pitman Publishing.

Westwood, P. (1987) *Commonsense Methods for Children with Special Needs.* London: Cassell.

Whitaker, P. (1981) *The Primary Head.* London: Heinemann Educational.

Winkley, D. (1990) 'A View from a Primary School'. In Brighouse, T. and Moon, B. (eds), *Managing the National Curriculum: Some critical perspectives.* Harlow: Longman.

Wolfendale, S. (1992) *Primary Schools and Special Needs: Policy planning, provision,* 2nd edition. London: Cassell.

Wood, D. (1988) *How Children Think and Learn.* Oxford: Blackwell.

Wood, J. (1984) *Adapting Instruction for the Mainstream.* Columbus, OH: Charles E. Merrill.

Woodhead, C. (1993) 'Do We Need a New National Curriculum?'. In O'Hear, P. and White, J. (eds), *Assessing the National Curriculum.* London: Paul Chapman Publishing.

Woods, P. (ed.) (1996) *Contemporary Issues in Teaching and Learning.* London: Routledge.

Woods, P. and Jeffrey, R. (1996) 'A New Professional Discourse? Adjusting to managerialism'. In Woods, P. (ed.), *Contemporary Issues in Teaching and Learning*. London:
Routledge.

Wyllyams, C. (1993) 'Assessing for Special Needs in the Secondary School'. In
Wolfendale, S. (ed.), *Assessing Special Educational Needs*. London: Cassell.

Young, M. (1995) 'The Future Basis for a 14–19 Entitlement'. In Inman, S. and Buck, M.
(eds), *Adding Value? Schools' responsibility for pupils' personal development*. Stoke-on-
Trent: Trentham Brooks.

Index